THE LAST BEST HOPE

THE LAST BEST HOPE

A Democracy Reader

Stephen John Goodlad

Editor

JOSSEY-BASS
A Wiley Company
San Francisco

Jossey-Bass books and products are available through most bookstores. To contact Jossey-Bass directly, call (888) 378-2537, fax to (800) 605-2665, or visit our website at www.josseybass.com.

Substantial discounts on bulk quantities of Jossey-Bass books are available to corporations, professional associations, and other organizations. For details and discount information, contact the special sales department at Jossey-Bass.

TCF Manufactured in the United States of America on Lyons Falls Turin Book. This paper is acid-free and 100 percent totally chlorine-free.

Library of Congress Cataloging-in-Publication Data

The last best hope: a democracy reader / Stephen John Goodlad, editor.—1st ed.
    p. cm.—(The Jossey-Bass education series)
Includes bibliographical references and index.
  ISBN 0-7879-5681-3
  1. Democracy. I. Goodlad, Stephen John. II. Series.
JC423.L363 2001
321.8—dc21   00-013124

FIRST EDITION
PB Printing   10 9 8 7 6 5 4 3 2 1

The Jossey-Bass Education Series

CONTENTS

PART ONE
Why Democracy?

PART TWO
Concepts and Complexities

PART THREE
Citizenship and Character

PART FOUR
Democracy and Its Troubles

PART FIVE
The Public and the Personal

PART SIX
Education in a Democratic Society

PART SEVEN
Human Potential and Democracy's Future

SOURCE TEXTS

CHAPTER ONE
"Democracy," from *Building a Bridge to the Eighteenth Century: How the Past Can Improve Our Future,* by Neil Postman (New York: Knopf, 1999), pp. 136–144, 152–154. Copyright © 1999 by Neil Postman. Reprinted by permission of Alfred A. Knopf, a Division of Random House Inc.

CHAPTER TWO
From "Prologue," in *An Aristocracy of Everyone: The Politics of Education and the Future of America,* by Benjamin R. Barber (New York: Ballantine Books, 1992), pp. 3–15. Copyright © 1991 by Benjamin R. Barber. Reprinted by permission of Ballantine Books, a Division of Random House Inc.

CHAPTER THREE
"What Makes Democracy Work?" by Robert D. Putnam, from *National Civic Review 82* (Spring 1993), pp. 101–107. Reprinted by permission of Jossey-Bass, Inc., a subsidiary of John Wiley & Sons, Inc.

CHAPTER FOUR
"The Democratic Virtues," from *Radical Democracy,* by C. Douglas Lummis (Ithaca: Cornell University Press, 1996), pp. 143–157. Reprinted by permission of Cornell University Press.

CHAPTER FIVE
"Was Democracy Just a Moment?" by Robert D. Kaplan, from *The Atlantic Monthly 280* (December 1997), pp. 55–80. Reprinted by permission of *The Atlantic Monthly.*

CHAPTER SIX
"The Masses in Representative Democracy," from *Rationalism in Politics and Other Essays,* new and expanded edition, by Michael Oakeshott

(Indianapolis, Ind.: Liberty Fund, 1991), pp. 363–383. Originally published in *Freedom and Serfdom: An Anthology of Western Thought,* edited by Albert Hunold (Dordrecht, Holland: D. Reidel Publishing Co., 1961), pp. 151–170. Copyright © 1961 by D. Reidel Publishing Co. Reprinted with kind permission from Kluwer Academic Publishers.

CHAPTER SEVEN

"Reorientation in Education," from *Democracy as a Way of Life,* by Boyd H. Bode (New York: Macmillan, 1937), pp. 75–95.

CHAPTER EIGHT

"The Education of Character," from *Between Man and Man,* by Martin Buber, trans. by Ronald Gregor Smith (New York: Collier Books, 1965), pp. 104–116. (Originally an address to the National Conference of Palestinian Teachers, Tel-Aviv, 1939.)

CHAPTER NINE

"Market Democracy in a Neoliberal Order," from *Profit Over People: Neoliberalism and Global Order,* by Noam Chomsky (New York: Seven Stories Press, 1999), pp. 91–102, 109–118. Excerpted from the annual Davie Memorial Lecture at the University of Cape Town, South Africa, May 1997. Reprinted by permission of Seven Stories Press.

CHAPTER TEN

"Law and Justice," from *Declarations of Independence: Cross-Examining American Ideology,* by Howard Zinn (New York: HarperPerennial, 1990), pp. 110–118, 145–146. Copyright © 1990 by Howard Zinn. Reprinted by permission of HarperCollins Publishers, Inc.

CHAPTER ELEVEN

"Jefferson, Morrill, and the Upper Crust," from *The Unsettling of America: Culture and Agriculture,* by Wendell Berry (San Francisco: Sierra Club Books, 1977), pp. 146–160, 168–169. Reprinted by permission of Sierra Club Books.

CHAPTER TWELVE

"Democracy and Human Nature," in *The Collected Works of John Dewey, Later Works: Volume 13, 1938–1939,* edited by Jo Ann Boydston (Carbondale, Ill.: Southern Illinois University Press, 1988). Copyright © 1988 by the Board of Trustees, Southern Illinois University; reprinted by permission.

CHAPTER THIRTEEN
From "Conclusion: Egalitarian Solidarity," in *Equality and Democracy: A New Press Back-to-Basics Book,* by Philip Green (New York: New Press, 1998), pp. 185–206. Reprinted by permission of The New Press.

CHAPTER FOURTEEN
From "What Difference Does Moral Imagination Make?" in *Moral Imagination: Implications of Cognitive Science for Ethics,* by Mark Johnson (Chicago: University of Chicago Press, 1993), pp. 198–207. Reprinted by permission of the University of Chicago Press and Mark Johnson.

CHAPTER FIFTEEN
"How Colleges of Education Package the Myth of Modernity," from "Universities and the Culture of Denial," in *The Culture of Denial: Why the Environmental Movement Needs a Strategy for Reforming Universities and Public Schools,* by C. A. Bowers (New York: State University of New York Press, 1997), pp. 84–93. Reprinted by permission of the State University of New York Press. Copyright © 1997 by State University of New York. All rights reserved.

CHAPTER SIXTEEN
"Democratic Education in Difficult Times," by Amy Gutmann, from *Teachers College Record* 92 (Fall 1990), pp. 7–20. Reprinted by permission of *Teachers College Record,* Blackwell Publishers.

CHAPTER SEVENTEEN
"What Is Education For?" from *Earth in Mind: On Education, Environment, and the Human Prospect,* by David W. Orr (Washington, D.C.: Island Press, 1994), pp. 7–15. Copyright © 1994 by David W. Orr. Reprinted by permission of Island Press.

CHAPTER EIGHTEEN
From "The Domain of the Future," in *Creativity: Flow and the Psychology of Discovery and Invention,* by Mihaly Csikszentmihalyi (New York: HarperCollins, 1996), pp. 291–305, 314–316. Copyright © 1996 by Mihaly Csikszentmihalyi. Reprinted by permission of HarperCollins Publishers, Inc.

CHAPTER NINETEEN
"Practical Utopianism," from *Utopias, Dolphins and Computers: Problems of Philosophical Plumbing,* by Mary Midgley (London: Routledge, 1996), pp. 15–26. Reprinted by permission of Routledge.

INTRODUCTION

THE LAST BEST HOPE: A DEMOCRACY READER is designed to serve two purposes. First, it presents the basic themes and ideas essential to a critical understanding of the relationship between democracy and education. Second, it develops and elaborates on some of those themes and ideas in a manner that we hope will generate ongoing study and discussion.

This is not a "debate" book. That is, it does not attempt to present the pros and cons of every issue raised. Although the text does contain opposing views, it also represents a particular take on its subjects. That said, if any single, guiding principle has informed the selection of works for inclusion in this collection, it has been that the readings should serve to stimulate discussion and debate among the book's readers.

Many of the ideas introduced in *The Last Best Hope* center on the tensions among what might be described as oppositional forces. For instance, we look at the relationship between democracy and the "uncontrolled market" (as one author describes it), between education and the environment, between law and justice, and between democratic character and what Michael Oakeshott calls the "mass man." The themes developed include the concept of humans as social animals engaged in the project of learning to live together on a finite planet, the place of democracy within this project, and democracy as not just a political concept but as a concept that embodies a unique social structure, a unique set of behaviors, a moral and ethical framework, and a citizenry that is distinguished by particular qualities or characteristics.

In addition to elaborating on certain ideas and developing particular themes more fully, *The Last Best Hope* also examines a number of important questions such as What conditions are necessary for democracy to exist and flourish? Is democracy a sustainable ideal? What does individual freedom mean in a democratic society? What are democratic virtues? What does it mean to live democratically? What is the relationship between democracy and morality? Why are imagination and creativity vital to promoting and sustaining democratic societies? What role does or should education play in a democracy? And what makes a democratic society (as opposed to merely a political system) different from other societies?

Why a Democracy Reader?

The chapters in *The Last Best Hope* were selected in large part because they correspond to major themes, concerns, and ideas that emerged in a series of discussions sponsored by the Institute for Educational Inquiry in Seattle, Washington, on the subject of developing democratic character in the young. These discussions began in fall 1997 and continued into spring 1999. Workgroup members were Mary Catherine Bateson, Benő Csapó, John I. Goodlad, Robert Hoffert, Stanley Katz, Nel Noddings, Roger Soder, Kathleen Staudt, Paul Theobald, and Julie Underwood. The group's work resulted in a book, edited by Roger Soder, John I. Goodlad, and Timothy J. McMannon, entitled *Developing Democratic Character in the Young*. As that book neared completion, it became evident to the authors that they were drawing from—and building on—ideas, information, and arguments that could not be adequately explored in the context of that volume. It was felt that this subject matter deserved a book of its own. Thus emerged the idea for *The Last Best Hope*.

About the Book

The Last Best Hope is organized into seven parts. Each part contains two or three chapters. In Part One, the first chapter, by Neil Postman, asks what we mean when we use the word *democracy* and why democracy might be an especially suitable and desirable form of government for human societies. The second chapter, by Benjamin R. Barber, explains why one cannot talk about democracy without also talking about education.

Part Two begins with a chapter by Robert D. Putnam that asks, What makes democracy work? We then examine the democratic virtues in a chapter by C. Douglas Lummis. Part Two concludes with Robert D. Kaplan's consideration of the question, Was democracy just a moment?

Part Three explores the concept of democratic character. We begin with Michael Oakeshott's essay on the masses in representative democracy. We then look at a chapter from Boyd H. Bode's *Democracy as a Way of Life*. Part Three concludes with Martin Buber's thoughts on the education of character.

Part Four raises several important issues that affect democracy and its citizens. Noam Chomsky provides a brief but important glimpse of some of the major issues of our time. Howard Zinn then explores some of the differences between law and justice in a democratic society. We conclude with Wendell Berry's thoughts on the goals and purposes of American education—what they are and what they were intended to be.

Part Five explores approaches that might help us to address some of the issues raised in the preceding chapters. It begins with John Dewey's look at democracy and human nature. Philip Green then explores the notion of egalitarian solidarity. The section concludes with Mark Johnson's discussion of the moral imagination.

Part Six focuses on democracy, the environment, and the schools, beginning with Chet Bowers's explanation of how colleges of education package the myth of modernity. Amy Gutmann follows with a chapter on democratic education in difficult times. Our consideration of education as a public good concludes with David W. Orr asking the not-so-simple question, What is education for?

The two chapters in Part Seven look ahead by offering a glimpse of both the possible and the necessary. The first chapter, by Mihaly Csikszentmihalyi, presents examples of two people who are translating their principles and ideas into action in an effort to make a better world for all of us. The book concludes with Mary Midgley's chapter on practical utopianism—what it is and why we need it.

Footnotes and citations have been reproduced as they appeared in the original versions of these selections. This has been done to help those interested in pursuing particular topics in greater depth as well as to assist educators who want to develop curricula focusing on either education and democracy in general or any of the subtopics introduced. In a few cases, notes have been added for clarity.

Democracy demands of its citizens the ability to discuss, to debate, and to learn from one another. To the extent to which this book encourages and contributes to such discourse, it can be measured a success.

Seattle, Washington STEPHEN JOHN GOODLAD
December 2000

ACKNOWLEDGMENTS

FOR THEIR TIME, FAITH, IDEAS, ENCOURAGEMENT, and many other contributions, the following people deserve special recognition: Paula McMannon, whose patience, perseverance, and good humor have been invaluable; Tim McMannon, an impeccable editor, a fine intellect, and a good friend; Roger Soder, who oversaw this project and sighted landfall where I saw only fog; and the members of the Working Group on Developing Democratic Character in the Young, in whose presence it was an honor and a privilege to be.

That writers and editors are a strange and reclusive breed, living and working in isolation from the rest of the world, is at least partly a misconception. A very special thanks belongs to Lynne Nakamura for cultivating the kind of healthy, loving environment that all creative endeavors demand.

Last, though certainly not least, there are no words that can adequately convey my heartfelt gratitude for the generous support, encouragement, and love of my parents.

S.J.G.

THE EDITOR

Stephen John Goodlad is a writer and philosopher whose interests in recent years have centered on the relationships among environmentalism, ecology, and democracy and, in turn, the implications of these relationships for education and schooling. One important facet of this research has been a focus on the connection between what is termed democratic character and the notion of ecological identity: their similarities, differences, and potentialities. He lives in Seattle, Washington, and divides his time among a variety of teaching, writing, and research projects.

PART ONE

WHY DEMOCRACY?

BEFORE WE CAN BEGIN to examine the particulars of democracy as a concept, and before we can begin to think about the many complexities that such a concept entails, we first need to get a sense of just what we mean when we use the word *democracy*. What may appear at first blush to be a rather unambiguous term reveals itself upon further consideration to be anything but.

It is a formidable undertaking to try to unravel democracy's meaning. But social critic and communications theorist Neil Postman rises to the occasion admirably in Chapter One, "Democracy." From a consideration of the contributions to democratic thought made by such notable intellects as Aristotle, Hobbes, Jefferson, Kant, Locke, Mill, Montesquieu, Rousseau, and Tocqueville emerges the notion of a special kind of community rich in the nuance and directness of the human voice, of "face-to-face confrontations and negotiations with differing points of view," and always "the possibilities of immediate action." Although our conception of democracy may forever remain a myth, a kind of fantasy, it is nevertheless an important and perhaps even a necessary myth—one deeply rooted in the fertile soil of our humanity.

In "An Aristocracy of Everyone," the second chapter in this book, Benjamin R. Barber, a professor of political science, makes explicit the connection between democracy and education ("the enabler of democracy") when he argues that there is "only one road to democracy," and that road is education. In a democracy, he writes, "there is only one essential task for the educator: teaching liberty."

These two chapters lay the groundwork for much of what follows in the subsequent chapters. They present important ideas that, as we begin to unpack them, lead us on a journey directly into the very heart of the human condition. But if we believe in and value our autonomy and our dignity as a people and as individuals, and if we agree that each of us is entitled to certain inalienable rights and liberties, then we must heed the words of Neil Postman, Benjamin Barber, and others: we must take democracy and its responsibilities seriously.

I

DEMOCRACY

Neil Postman

IN ORDER TO AVOID AN ERROR some political scientists make, I am bound to begin this chapter by noting the obvious: Democracy is not a thing, a process, or an idea. It is a word, and a word that has had a checkered career at that. Its origin can be traced to the Greek city-states, and in its rough-and-tumble road it has been used to mean a multitude of things, not all of them pleasant. Plato, of course, would have none of it, since it implied giving power to those who had neither the intellectual resources nor the moral rigor to govern wisely. If he needed empirical proof of his political philosophy—which he didn't—he could find it in the judgment rendered against Socrates (by a vote of 280 to 220) which condemned the wisest man of Athens to death.

Aristotle was hardly less contemptuous of "democracy." He posited three kinds of government that are good and three that are bad. The good include monarchy, aristocracy, and constitutional government; the bad are tyranny, oligarchy, and democracy. Although he did not believe in equality any more than Plato, Aristotle introduced the curious qualification that when the worst—democracy—is corrupt, it is better than the best when the *best* is corrupt. Of course, what the Greeks meant by "democracy" was quite different from meanings more common today. Aristotle, for example, tells us that to elect magistrates is oligarchic, while to choose them by lot is democratic. We also know that the "demos"—the citizens of Athens who were eligible to participate in public affairs—consisted mostly of an elite class, excluding women, slaves, farmers, and, in general, those who earned their bread by the sweat of their brows. Of the

3

350,000 souls who lived in or close to Athens, only 20,000 qualified as citizens.

The Romans did not much favor "democracy," especially its implications of direct participation by "the people." They used the term "republic" to describe their system of consuls elected by a senate which was not indifferent to "vox populi." The word "democracy" barely stayed alive in Western civilization throughout the medieval period and the Renaissance but was retrieved with considerable energy in the seventeenth century, when political philosophy reawakened and the question of the nature and foundations of the state, and of political authority, assumed renewed importance.

With the exception perhaps of Machiavelli, Thomas Hobbes, no friend of "democracy," may be regarded as the first modern political theorist. His *Leviathan*, published in 1651, was exceedingly influential, largely as a justification of absolute monarchy. For Hobbes, the fundamental concern in governance was the maintenance of public order and so the avoidance of the mortal danger of anarchy. He was against the sharing of power and was not excessively troubled by despotism. Democracy in any form, he believed, would inevitably lead to anarchy. Hobbes's most influential opponent was John Locke, who, in 1689 and 1690, wrote his *Two Treatises On Government*. The first is a condemnation of the idea of hereditary power. In the second he put forward an idea that has attached itself to the word "democracy" to this day, even when the word is used by those who detest its referent. "The beginning of politic society," he wrote, "depends upon the consent of the individuals to join into and make one society." He introduced the idea of a "contract," borrowed, of course, although set in a different context, from the biblical covenant of the Jews with God. Rousseau used the same term later in his famous work *The Social Contract*, published in 1762. (It must be noted that Rousseau's argument for a social contract comes closer to Hobbes than to Locke, since Rousseau emphasized the obligation of the state to protect the individual; that is, protection from anarchy.)

Throughout the Enlightenment, the question of the source of legitimate authority and power was thoroughly explored, although Locke's idea of what might be called a "democratic polity" was not exactly what we have in mind today. Voltaire favored an "enlightened monarchy." Diderot wanted a "constitutional monarchy" (and tried to convert Catherine the Great to that view). Both Locke and Montesquieu favored a division of powers, but Rousseau clearly did not. Locke emphasized the importance of private property in any contract an individual makes with society. But not all Enlightenment philosophers, and not Rousseau in particular, were impressed with that idea.

As you can infer from these highly selective, fragmentary examples, I am not interested here in providing a history of the word "democracy." I am interested in making the point that any sentence that begins with "Democracy is . . . ," as if there is some essential, God-given meaning to the word, misleads us. Its meanings have varied widely, and its use in an unqualified positive sense is fairly recent. Indeed, as the word moved from Europe to America, it was certainly not greeted with the respect it is given today. American philosophers were mostly of a mixed mind as to what the word suggested. The word does not appear in the Declaration of Independence or the federal Constitution. Jefferson did call his party the Democrat-Republican to distinguish it from the Federalists. But in his first inaugural address, he said, "We are all Republicans, we are all Federalists"; he did not say, "We are all democrats." Many of America's founders—Alexander Hamilton and John Adams, for example—used the word in a pejorative sense. Adams considered democracy an ignoble and unjust form of government but was opposed to aristocracy largely on the grounds that aristocrats, being superior, were dangerous. We must keep in mind that the Founders (Gore Vidal refers to them as the Inventors) were men of wide learning and refined intellect, and were not without what we would call "elitist" tendencies. Jefferson was, on one occasion, denounced by Patrick Henry for "abjuring his native victuals"; that is to say, Jefferson liked French cooking. It should also be remembered that in America's beginnings, citizens did not directly vote for the president, vice-president, or members of the Senate; and . . . the Founders favored a Roman conception of republicanism more than the Greek "democracy." The word's recent positive meanings have not always protected it from being used in ways that Plato, Aristotle, Hobbes, Locke, and all the rest would call despotism. In the 1930s, for example, the world's greatest dictators—Benito Mussolini, Adolf Hitler, and Joseph Stalin—used the word to praise the tyrannies they headed. In a speech in Berlin in 1937, Mussolini proclaimed that "the greatest and soundest democracies which exist in the world today are Italy and Germany." Stalin claimed that the Soviet Union was the most democratic regime in all history. And, of course, even today despots use the word to describe their regimes—indeed, are almost compelled to use it.

As we approach a new century, we can say that for most of us, the word has taken on a more or less settled meaning, and one that is wholly favorable. Its key part is the implication of the freely given consent of the governed to abide by the laws and policies of those agencies whose activities control the life of a community. Exactly how that consent is given expression and by whom and when is usually defined by some sort of constitution, which is subject to amendment. And to insure that those who have given their consent have done so without duress and as mature and thoughtful citizens, freedom of thought and speech must be allowed the widest possible latitude. When we add to this Kant's idea that persons are to be respected as an absolute end in themselves, and must not be used as a mere means for some external purpose, we have a fair description of what the word is presently taken to mean. In this description, I am saying nothing that any reader will find new or, I should think, disputable. What is missing from it is a point that is desperately important to those living now, and which Enlightenment thinkers addressed, even as they gifted us with the modern ideas we include under the heading of "democracy." The point can, in fact, be found as far back as Aristotle in his contention that democracy is best for small city-states, oligarchy for medium-sized states, and monarchy for large states; that is to say, that there is a relationship between the kind of government that is desirable and the means of communication that are available. Aristotle thought that, ideally, democracy implied that a person standing in the center of a city could, when giving an oration, be heard by all the citizens. Considering the fact that there were no amplification devices, one might think this unrealistic. However, Benjamin Franklin actually tested the idea (although for different reasons) in trying to determine exactly how far and by how many people the voice of the great orator Reverend Whitefield could be heard. His conclusion: from Market Street to a particular part of Front Street in Philadelphia, and by 30,000 people.

Putting Franklin's experiment aside, we may say that Enlightenment philosophers were not unaware of the connections between political life and communication. Indeed, Montesquieu gave considerable attention to the question of how an environment controls the forms of social life including the laws, the economy, and what he called the national character. In his *On the Spirit of Laws,* he is mostly concerned with the physical environment rather than the symbolic environment—that is to say, the natural ecology rather then the media ecology. He argued that the terrain—mountains or plateaus, jungles or desert, inland or coastal—is the basic determinant of social life. That there is some truth in this cannot be denied. But there may be greater truth in the idea that the means by which people communicate with each other, including their government, are the keys to how workable any system is. John Stuart Mill dwelt on this point, arguing that the active participation of the governed in the processes of government is an essential component of a democratic system. "The food of feeling," he wrote, "is action. . . . Let a person have nothing to do for his country, and he will not care for it." That, I assume, is what John F. Kennedy meant in saying, "Ask not what your country can do for you but what you can do for your country." Political indifference is the death of democracy. This is a point well understood by Tocqueville, who stressed the role played by political associations in giving health and vitality to the American system. He wrote:

> The inhabitant of the United States learns from birth that he must rely on himself to combat the ills and trials of life; he is restless and defiant in his outlook toward the authority of society and appeals to its power only when he cannot do without it. . . . If some obstacle blocks the public road halting the circulation of traffic, the neighbors at once form a deliberative body; this improvised assembly produces an executive authority which remedies the trouble before anyone has thought of the possibility of some previously constituted authority beyond those concerned.[1]

Tocqueville, more than any other student of democracy, also focused his attention on the role of media in giving American form to democracy. By media (a word he did not, of course, use) he meant the printed word. He wrote about the style of literary expression in a democracy, and, in particular, how a democratic polity produces a different literature than does an aristocracy.

> Here, then, is a motley multitude with intellectual wants to be supplied. These new votaries of the pleasure of the mind have not all had the same education; they are not guided by the same lights, do not resemble their own fathers; and they themselves are changing every moment with changing place of residence, feelings, and fortune. So there are no traditions, or common habits, to forge links between their minds, and they have neither the power nor the wish nor the time to come to a common understanding. But it is from this heterogeneous, stirring crowd that authors spring, and from it they must win profit and renown.[2]

The only thing odd about this quotation is that it appears to be a description when it is, in fact, a prophecy. For at the time it was written American literature had not yet broken free of its English roots, which Tocqueville regarded as reflecting an aristocratic tradition. One might say (as did Hemingway) that American literature begins with Mark Twain. Or, as I would prefer, Edgar Allan Poe. In any case, early American literature is distinguished more by pamphlets and newspapers than by books. In 1786, Benjamin Franklin observed that Americans were so busy reading newspapers and pamphlets that they scarcely had time for books. (One book they apparently always had time for was Noah Webster's *American Spelling Book,* for it sold more than twenty-four million copies between 1783 and 1834.) Franklin's reference to pamphlets ought not to go unnoticed. The proliferation of newspapers in all the Colonies was accompanied by the rapid diffusion of pamphlets and broadsides. Tocqueville took note of this fact. "In America," he wrote, "parties do not write books to combat each other's opinions, but pamphlets, which are circulated for a day with incredible rapidity and then expire."[3] And he referred to both newspapers and pamphlets when he observed, "The invention of firearms equalized the vassal and the noble on the field of battle; the art of printing opened the same resources to the minds of all classes; the post brought knowledge alike to the door of the cottage and to the gate of the palace."[4] At the time Tocqueville was making his observations of America, printing had already spread to all the regions of the country. The South had lagged behind the North not only in the formation of schools but in its uses of the printing press. Virginia, for example, did not get its first regularly published newspaper, the *Virginia Gazette,* until 1736. But toward the end of the eighteenth century, the movement of ideas via the printed word was relatively rapid, and something approximating a national conversation emerged. For example, the *Federalist Papers,* an outpouring of eighty-five essays in defense of the proposed new Constitution, written by Alexander Hamilton, James Madison, and John Jay (all under the name of Publius), originally appeared in a New York newspaper during 1787 and 1788 but were read almost as widely in the South as in the North.

The influence of the printed word in every arena of public discourse was insistent and powerful not merely because of the quality of printed matter but because of its *monopoly.* This point cannot be stressed enough, especially for those who are reluctant to acknowledge profound differences in the media environments of then and now. One sometimes hears it said, for example, that there is more printed matter available today than ever before, which is undoubtedly true. But from the seventeenth century to the late nineteenth century, printed matter was virtually *all* that was available. There were no movies to see, radio to hear, photographic displays to look at, CDs to play. There was no television or Internet. Public business was channeled into and expressed through print, which became the model, the metaphor, and the measure of all discourse. The resonances of the linear, analytical structure of print, and in particular, of expository prose, could be felt everywhere—for example, in how people talked. Tocqueville remarks on this in *Democracy in America*. "An American," he wrote, "cannot converse, but he can discuss, and his talk falls into a dissertation. He speaks to you as if he were addressing a meeting; and if he should chance to become warm in the discussion, he will say 'Gentlemen' to the person with whom he is conversing."[5] This odd practice is less a reflection of an American's obstinacy than of his modeling his conversational style on the structure of the printed word. Since the printed word is impersonal and is addressed to an invisible audience, what Tocqueville is describing here is a kind of printed orality, which was observable in diverse forms of oral discourse. On the pulpit, for example, sermons were usually written speeches, delivered in a stately, impersonal tone, consisting, as Tocqueville remarked, "largely of an impassioned, coldly analytical cataloguing of the attributes of the Deity as revealed to man through Nature and Nature's Laws."

What I am driving at is that the modern conception of democracy was tied inseparably to the printed word. . . .

It is [also] necessary to keep in mind here—especially for those who believe e-mail and the Internet provide new opportunities for community—that we too easily confuse simulations with reality; that is to say, electronic community is only a simulation of community. A real, functional political community requires the nuance and directness of the human voice, face-to-face confrontations and negotiations with differing points of view, the possibilities of immediate action.

Which leads to a final consideration. . . . In the context of the future of "democracy," it needs to be noted that our conception of the word's meaning is, itself, a myth, a kind of fantasy about what ought to be. But such fantasies, when shared by all, connect individuals to each other, providing a common language, a set of ideals, and a program for the future. The Declaration of Independence, the Constitution, the Gettysburg Address, Martin Luther King Jr.'s "I Have a Dream" speech are all fantasies, in the sense I am using the word. These fantasies, these dreams, are the legacy of the Enlightenment and have served as the foundation of how we define "democracy." The question, therefore, must arise, Do the new media of communication help or hinder in the development of shared dreams of democracy? Do our movies, TV shows, and songs bind us or loosen us?

There are, of course, other factors that can threaten the maintenance of a common political and national narrative—a "global economy" is one. But a discussion of that would require a whole book of its own. Here I raise the point that the fantasies and dreams of what we have come to call "democracy" were created by masters of the printed word. What new dreams will be created by masters of digital communication? And whose definition of "democracy" will it include? I have no ready or even nearly ready answers to these questions. It is better to disappoint one's readers than to mislead them. What I am asking for is a serious conversation about the relationship between our new media and our old democracy. Grossman, in *The Electronic Republic,* begins such a conversation. I have intended in this chapter to add to it. And I am hoping it will be continued—even if only on television.

NOTES

1. Alexis de Tocqueville, *Democracy in America,* trans. George Lawrence (New York: Doubleday, 1969), p. 189.

2. Tocqueville, *Democracy in America,* p. 473.

3. Tocqueville, *Democracy in America,* p. 58.

4. Tocqueville, *Democracy in America,* pp. 5–6.

5. Tocqueville, *Democracy in America,* p. 260.

2

AN ARISTOCRACY OF EVERYONE

Benjamin R. Barber

AROUND THE WORLD the cry "Democracy!" has shattered tyranny's silence and caused the most stubborn of dictators to lose their confidence in the politics of fear. Walls are coming down and iron curtains are being drawn for the last time. The Statue of Liberty is an icon for young men and women who have never known freedom in lands that have never been democratic. Even in these hard and cynical times, America remains for many abroad what Lincoln called the "last best hope." But is it still that for Americans? Can it be? That is our paradox.

Millions of immigrants vote annually with their feet to come to a land where nearly half of us don't bother to vote at all. A paragon of democracy abroad, America often seems to be ruled by apathy and privatism at home. People die around the world in the struggle to acquire freedoms we sometimes don't seem to notice we have. They struggle to establish free political parties while we abandon ours in the search for candidates untainted by party or politics.

Because we regard ourselves as born free, we take our liberty for granted. We assume that our freedom can be enjoyed without responsibility and that, like some great perpetual motion machine, our democracy can run forever without the fuel of civic activity by engaged citizens. The most sympathetic overseas critic America has known, Alexis de Tocqueville, once issued a warning to all would-be democrats: There is nothing so arduous as the apprenticeship of liberty. Are we Americans willing to be journeymen citizens? Are there institutions where we can learn liberty? Can our schools be nurseries of citizenship?

There is endless talk today about education, but between the hysteria and the cynicism there seems to be little room for civic learning, hardly any for democracy. Yet the fundamental task of education in a democracy is the apprenticeship of liberty—learning to be free. While we root our fragile freedom in the myth that we are born free, we are in truth born dependent. For we are born fragile, born needy, born ignorant, born unformed, born weak, born foolish, born unimaginative—born in chains. To cast them off as angels might is our unrealizable fantasy. The best we can do is rationalize or legitimize them. Our dependency is both physical—we need each other and cannot survive alone—and psychological; our identity is forged through a dialectical relationship with others. We are inescapably embedded in families, tribes, and communities. As a consequence, we must *learn* to be free. That is to say, we must be taught liberty. We are born small, defenseless, unthinking children. We must be taught to be thinking, competent, legal persons and citizens. We are born belonging to others; we have to learn how to sculpt our individuality from common clay.

The literacy required to live in civil society, the competence to participate in democratic communities, the ability to think critically and act deliberately in a pluralistic world, the empathy that permits us to hear and thus accommodate others, all involve skills that must be acquired. Excellence is the product of teaching and is liberty's measure. There is no excellence without freedom. From Plato to Mill, philosophers have understood that only the free and self-sufficient can be virtuous. For them, so few were virtuous because so few were free. They understood virtue as the excellence (they called it *areté*) of cognitive, affective, and associational practices: living well and living justly in the human world.

Human association depends on imagination: the capacity to see in others beings like ourselves. It is thus through imagination that we render others sufficiently like ourselves for them to become subjects of tolerance and respect, sometimes even affection. Democracy is not a natural form of association; it is an extraordinary and rare contrivance of cultivated imagination. Empower the merely ignorant and endow the uneducated with a right to make collective decisions and what results is not democracy but, at best, mob rule: the government of private prejudice and the tyranny of opinion—all those perversions that liberty's enemies like to pretend (and its friends fear) constitute democracy. For true democracy to flourish, however, there must be citizens. Citizens are women and men educated for excellence—by which term I mean the knowledge and competence to govern in common their own lives. The democratic faith is rooted in the belief that all humans are capable of such excellence and have not just the right but the capacity to become citizens. Democratic education mediates the ancient quarrel between the rule of opinion and the rule of excellence by informing opinion and, through universal education in excellence, creating an aristocracy of everyone.

Is this phrase no more than a provocative oxymoron? An impossible contradiction, as advocates of classical aristocracy may say? To certain critics of democracy, the *aristoi* must be more than merely excellent or virtuous, for to them the superiority of some depends on the inferiority of the rest. What can it mean to excel in a world where everyone is regarded as possessing a potential for the best? In their eyes, excellence cannot be entirely self-referential but, like vanity, must exist in terms of the relative merit of others. Without the *hoi polloi,* that mindless rabble who go under the name *plebes* or *demes,* the *aristoi* cannot conceive of their own superior worth. Who wants virtues anyone can have? It is not enough for me to win, goes the old half-serious jest, others must lose.

The democratic educator seeks a different sort of excellence, an inherent virtue that does not depend on comparative standing. To grade on a curve is a popular strategy in highly competitive, elite institutions where some must fail for others to succeed; but in classrooms devoted to cultivating the intrinsic excellence of each student, there may be more A's than C's (or more D's than B's). Democracy insists on leveling—that is the price of equality—but it aims always at leveling up, never at leveling down.

When democratic citizenship insists on leveling, then: it demands that slaves be emancipated not that masters be enslaved; that suffrage be granted to the dispossessed not taken from the powerful; that I win the exercise of my rights not that you lose the exercise of yours. Aristocrats condemn democracy because they believe it subjects the wise to the rule of the foolish; but the aim of democratic education is in fact to subject the foolish to wisdom in order that they may both govern themselves *and* govern wisely. Jefferson knew something about the aristocratic distrust of popular sovereignty. If you deem ordinary people insufficiently discrete to govern, he advised, don't take away their power, educate their discretion. Perhaps this is how he managed to be an aristocratic Southern gentleman farmer *and* the founding generation's most persuasive democrat. It is certainly why he considered his founding of the University of Virginia to be among the most decisive political acts of his career on behalf of democracy; for, if his tombstone is to be believed, along with his authorship of the Declaration of Independence and the Virginia Bill of Rights, he prized his dedication to education more highly than his two terms in the presidency.

Lincoln, too, tempered realism with hope, believing always that even the darkest human natures were counseled by "better angels" with whom a teacher or statesman or preacher (he was all three) might yet collaborate in making small men larger. He knew that freedom was not natural to men and women. He also learned in the course of the Civil War that unless all possessed it, none could securely enjoy it and that the teaching of liberty was the greatest political challenge of all.

If, as Rousseau sometimes seemed to think, we were really born free and only subsequently made dependent by adverse conditions, teaching would be little more than a matter of preservation. "Build a wall round your child's soul," he implored in *Émile*. If, as Plato argued in *The Meno*, we were born with traces of an ancient knowledge, then teaching would be a question of recovery. Plumb the soul's memory for clues to deeply ingrained knowledge, then restore to consciousness memory's secrets. But born dependent, we require an education in liberty. Born selfish, we must be taught mutuality. Born hungry, we need to learn moderation. Born distinctive and differentiated, we have to acquire tolerance, civility, and mutual respect. Born in a variety of shapes and sizes and colors, we are anything but peers and our equality is a precious acquisition: something to be slowly, often painfully, learned in spite of the evidence of our senses.

Rousseau wanted to persuade us that equality was natural, and there is little harm in regarding it as a disposition of all humans if that helps us think of it as deeply rooted and thus reinforces our commitment to it. But for all practical purposes, equality is not the condition of learning and experience but is produced by them. If education must create both liberty and equality, it becomes the foundation of all individual growth and of all collective civilization. Nothing is more important. The great country, the great society, the great community is, first of all, the well-educated country, the learned society, the community of excellence. This nation knows it, proclaims it, even rhapsodizes about it. Then it busies itself with other matters. It talks pedagogy but spends its resources elsewhere. It denigrates teachers as unprofessional but refuses them professional wages. Compare the starting salaries of lawyers, doctors, engineers, and teachers, and it becomes obvious why it is the schools that are in crisis.[1] In his final Harvard commencement address before retiring in 1991, President Derek Bok could only sigh at the "eerie indifference" that hangs over a land perpetually in crisis over its bankrupt educational establishment which seems to produce only poverty, crime, and illiteracy among its young people.

Crisis—and Again, Crisis

It seems histrionic, even alarmist, once again to proclaim a crisis in education, for crisis has been the norm for decades. Over twenty years ago, Vintage Books published a two-volume *University Crisis Reader* chockful of materials on the then-current controversy in the liberal university.[2]

The tocsin was first sounded when the Soviets sent *Sputnik* aloft at the end of the Eisenhower era, seeming to threaten this country's technological leadership. When toward the end of the sixties all authority, pedagogical as well as political, seemed in jeopardy, there was again a "crisis." When educational scores began to tumble and reading ability to deteriorate in the seventies, there was another "crisis." In the early eighties, when the National Commission on Excellence discovered a growing illiteracy that put the future of the nation "at risk," crisis loomed anew.[3] When, during President Reagan's second term, Secretary of Education William Bennett and philosopher Allan Bloom brought to the notice of the American public the disintegration of the traditional canon and the erosion of academic standards at every level of the educational establishment and blamed liberals and pedagogical Progressives, there was a still more profound "crisis." And today, as the nation grows less and less competitive with its economic rivals in Europe and Asia; as its corporations are forced increasingly to institute their own programs to develop a marginally literate work force;[4] as more young black men are ending up in jail than in college and a whole generation of inner-city youth is being ravaged by a tripartite plague of drugs, gangs, and AIDS; as more than 20 percent of the nation's children (45 percent of black children) are growing up in poverty and more than 30 percent are dropping out of school before receiving a high school diploma; as a million teenage girls are having babies before they graduate and 2.5 million adolescents are contracting sexually transmitted diseases; as media-manufactured hysteria over "political correctness" and compulsory multiculturalism turns every pedagogical debate into a terminal ideological struggle, a yet more desperate "crisis" arises.

But crisis by definition cannot be chronic. On tenth hearing, the alarm bells inspire despair rather than action. Tired out by our repeated crises, we roll over in bed. A long sleep becomes more and more like death, and a radical awakening is called for. At risk are not only our children, but our future; not only our schools, but our democratic institutions.

Most of the books published on the newest episode of our chronic educational crisis have preferred to sunder democracy and education. In their conservative, antidemocratic thrust, Allan Bloom's *The Closing of the American Mind*, Roger Kimball's *Tenured Radicals*, John Silber's *Straight Shooting*, Charles J. Sykes's *Profscam*, and Dinesh D'Souza's *Illiberal Education* all associate educational crisis with progressivism, radical professors, and a concern for equality (among students, cultures, and pedagogical paradigms).[5] [But my argument is based upon the premise] . . . that education and democracy are inextricably linked and that in a free society the link is severed only at our peril. Education must be both public and democratic if we wish to preserve our democracy's public spaces. Thus, my argument is less an argument for education than a cry for democracy; less a plea for the rehabilitation of the classroom than an appeal for the restoration of the community; less a defense of the present than a challenge for the future; less a call for reform from within our schools than a manifesto for a revolution in how we understand them. We need in education a transformation as far-reaching as the one that has seized Eastern Europe and what was once the Soviet Union, as radical as the abrupt ending of the cold war, as profound as the metamorphosis of America's vanquished enemies in World War II into its most dependable allies and most formidable rivals.

Yet, astonishingly, in the great American polity dedicated to the future, to prosperity, to tolerance, and to democracy, education is the orphan of the Enlightenment—much wailed over, little nourished, the subject of endless editorials but of pitifully small-minded spending and painfully constricted ideological debate. In 1991, Minnesota's teacher of the year, Cathy Nelson, was laid off (for the fourth time). Although she had thirteen years of service to Fridley High School, others had more. In this same year, the Richmond, California, Unified School District, praised for its innovative approaches by the Bush administration, went bankrupt for lack of funding.[6] Dollars alone won't buy education, any more than dollars alone provide national defense. But just as dollars will buy the tanks, planes, and military training requisite for defense, so dollars can buy the facilities, teacher-to-student ratios, equipment, and quality instruction requisite for education—if they are put in the right place.[7] Dollars at least move us a step beyond talk, but in fiscally tight times, the cheapness of talk is precisely its virtue.

So there is rhetoric aplenty but no revolution. In this "Decade of the Child," America's infant mortality and school dropout rates look positively third world. In New Haven, Connecticut, home of Yale University, the infant mortality rate is the highest in the nation. The Europeans still send their children to school 240 days a year; with only a few brave exceptions, we remain satisfied with 180.[8] There is talk of reform, but little change: For all the experimentation of the eighties, according to the Carnegie Foundation Report Card on School Reform, teachers themselves remain "dispirited, confronted with working conditions that have left them more responsible, but less empowered." Even more frustrating than "loss of status, bureaucratic pressures, negative public image, and the lack of recognition and rewards," teachers tell of a devastating decline in morale. "During this period of unprecedented activity on behalf of education," concludes the report, "49% of teachers say morale has gone down, less than one-fourth say it has gotten better."[9] One can find a spirited classroom with a relatively independent teacher, but it's often in a neighborhood so poor as to have little effect. One can discover empowered parents, but in Chicago, school districts are so implicated in politics that parental corruption is inevitable. Yes, there is an innovative district in California with real successes to report, but one which has been allowed to go bankrupt. There are model classrooms in New York City, but in schools rife with drugs and crime and stripped of teaching resources.[10]

Teachers remain among the least respected and least remunerated of American professionals. Every year, I ask an introductory political science class of three to four hundred students how many plan to make a career in primary or secondary education. In the past five years, I have never counted more than five hands. When asked how many plan to go to law or business school, over half the hands routinely go up. Teach for America, a brave new organization devoted to bringing graduates of some of the nation's most elite colleges and universities into some of its most wretched classrooms, has had to assure candidates that they need not necessarily commit themselves to a career in education. The group's first year of operation saw a large minority of its teachers leave their posts. Why? Because these and other young people find themselves in classrooms where they enjoy neither the authority to pursue their own pedagogical strategies nor the respect of their own students, let alone their country.

Conservative critics continue to blame radical teachers and their (consequently) incorrigible pupils, as if in an otherwise literate, civilized society a bunch of lazy young anarchists and their unprincipled wards had somehow gotten loose inside the schoolyard and were wreaking havoc on an unsuspecting and undeserving nation. To such critics, there is something oxymoronic about the very idea of democratic education. Democracy implies a lowering of standards to suit the masses, a lowest common denominator appropriate to ignorant majorities; education implies a raising of standards and a pedagogy for the best and brightest. For them, democracy means substituting rap for Bach and subway graffiti for Rembrandt, whereas education means reminding people of the culture of excellence to which they ought to be aspiring. That may be why at least some of these conservative critics have expressed a reluctant (or not so reluctant) willingness to toss democracy overboard in an attempt to rescue a ship they call excellence, by which they mean not civic competence but high culture and the canon. One simple way to improve educational standards defined this way is to educate only "the best." You cannot fail if you exclude those most likely to fail.

In a recent book, John E. Chubb and Terry M. Moe reconfirmed earlier research showing that students' abilities, along with the social and economic status of their parents and peers, are decisive in determining how effectively schools educate their charges.[11] The "best schools" and the "best colleges" are best, not because they offer the "best education," but because in large part they draw the best students—best prepared and best equipped, and possessing the best social and educational backgrounds. Like the good theater director who knows that his most important task is to hire fine actors who require little direction to shine, the conservative knows that the good educator is the one who seeks out fine students who require little effort to shine. But the object of public schools is not to credential the educated but to educate the uncredentialed; that is, to change and transform pupils, not merely to exploit their strengths. The challenge in a democracy is to transform every child into an apt pupil, and give every pupil the chance to become an autonomous, thinking person and a deliberative, self-governing citizen: that is to say, to achieve excellence.

Advocates of democratic education too often rise to elitist criticism by insisting that, if the choice is between educating some well and everyone badly, let's hold our breath and educate everyone badly. They often seem as anxious to jettison excellence (or just plain competence) in the name of educational equality as elitists are to jettison equality (or just plain fairness) in the name of educational excellence. Many public school teachers and administrators are exhausted and burned out. For them, excellence is as remote as suburban schools, where every student has a computer and 90 percent of the class goes to college.

[There is] . . . no dichotomy between democracy and excellence, for the true democratic premise encompasses excellence: the acquired virtues and skills necessary to living freely, living democratically, and living well. . . . Every human being, given half a chance, is capable of the self-government that is his or her natural right, and thus capable of acquiring the judgment, foresight, and knowledge that self-government demands. Not everyone can master string physics or string quartets, but everyone can master the conduct of his or her own life. Everyone can become a free and self-governing adult. Everyone can have a stab at happiness.

Education need not begin with equally adept students, because education is itself the equalizer. Equality is achieved not by handicapping the swiftest, but by assuring the less advantaged a comparable opportunity. "Comparable" here does not mean identical. Math whizzes may get high school calculus, while the less mathematically inclined get special tutoring. Who knows, the math whizzes may even be invited to become the math washouts' tutors. Schooling is what allows math washouts to appreciate the contributions of math whizzes—and may one day help persuade them to allocate tax revenues for basic scientific research, which math illiterates would reject. Schooling allows those born poor to compete with those born rich; allows immigrants to feel as American as the self-proclaimed daughters and sons of the American Revolution; allows African-Americans, whose ancestors were brought here in bondage, to fight for the substance (rather than just the legal forms) of their freedom.

The fundamental assumption of democratic life is not that we are all automatically capable of living both freely and responsibly, but that we are all potentially susceptible to education for freedom and responsibility. Democracy is less the enabler of education than education is the enabler of democracy. Americans need to reexamine the relationship between their schools and their political institutions, between the classroom and civil society, between education and democracy. There was a time when the relationship was taken for granted. Public, private, and religious schools in America's earlier days expressed a common commitment to education as a concomitant of democracy. Historically, the meaning of *public* education was precisely education into what it meant to belong to a public: education in the *res publica*—in commonality, in community, in the common constitution that made plurality and difference possible.

So many modern reforms, radical as well as conservative, seem to have lost sight of the public meaning of public education. Multicultural curricula achieve a needed broadening of perspectives and permit many Americans who have felt excluded to achieve a sense of group worth, yet this often is achieved at the cost of what groups share with one another. Voucher schemes enhance parental choice and increase competition among different kinds of schools, yet they thwart common schooling and subordinate education's public ends to private market choices. In the search for choice, for difference, for pluralism, for participation—all worthy aims in a society too often limited in choices, insensitive to difference, and attached to a bogus unity rooted in one dominant group's hegemony—the fundamental linkage between schooling and community and between education and democracy is simply lost.

Learning begins at birth, and much of it takes place at home or in the marketplace, in the streets or in front of the television. Yet what happens in these venues is largely a private matter. While society can cajole and hint and guide and suggest, the greater part of what transpires in the minds and hearts of the young is beyond it. This makes formal schooling, however inadequate, our sole *public* resource: the only place where, as a collective, self-conscious public pursuing common goods, we try to shape our children to live in a democratic world. Can we afford to privatize the only public institutions we possess? Must we choose between excellence and equality?

I do not think so. In the tradition of Jefferson and Dewey, I believe it is possible to understand all public education as liberal education—teaching liberty—and thus to understand liberal education as democratic education. Education in vocationalism, preprofessional training, what were once called the "servile arts" (*artes serviles*), may be private. But public education is general, common, and thus in the original sense "liberal." This means that public education is education for citizenship. In aristocratic nations, in elitist regimes, in technocratic societies, it may appear as a luxury. In such places, education is the private apprenticeship in the professions, the credentialing of elites, and perhaps the scholarly training of a few for lives of solitary intellect. But in democracies, education is the indispensable concomitant of citizenship. Where women and men would acquire the skills of freedom, it is a necessity.

The autonomy and the dignity no less than the rights and freedoms of all Americans depend on the survival of democracy: not just democratic government, but a democratic civil society and a democratic civic culture. There is only one road to democracy: education. And in a democracy, there is only one essential task for the educator: teaching liberty.

NOTES

1. Since 1972, teachers' salaries have increased sixty-eight postinflation dollars a year. Average salary in 1990 was $31,000; under $23,000 in North and South Dakota, Arkansas, and West Virginia; between $35,000 and $40,000 in Connecticut, Washington, D.C., New York, California, Maryland, and New Jersey. Lawyers' salaries averaged $60,000, chemists $47,000, and accountants $36,000. (*The Berkshire Eagle,* July 1990).

2. Immanuel Wallerstein and Paul Starr, *The University Crisis Reader* (New York: Vintage Books, 1971). Readers anxious to learn how the views of

some key players have changed (or not) over the years are urged to consult this anthology. . . .

3. In *A Nation at Risk: The Imperative of Educational Reform* (Washington, D.C.: Carnegie Foundation, 1983), the National Commission on Excellence wrote with more than a little melodrama of a nation threatened by "a rising tide of mediocrity" that imperiled "our very future as a Nation and a people." It made an ominous comparison between what is happening to American education and "an act of war."

4. A few examples: Nabisco has spent tens of millions of dollars on a "Next Century's Schools" program. Aside from donations to schools (e.g., Coca-Cola promised $50 million over the course of the nineties), many corporations are being forced to open their own educational centers for remedial work with poorly educated employees. Boston University took over Boston's Chelsea school district, but despite an infusion of cash, has achieved mixed results. . . .

5. Allan Bloom, *The Closing of the American Mind* (New York: Simon & Schuster, 1987); Roger Kimball, *Tenured Radicals: How Politics Has Corrupted Higher Education* (New York: Harper & Row, 1990); John Silber, *Shooting Straight: What's Wrong with America* (New York: Harper & Row, 1990); Charles Sykes, *Profscam: Professors and the Demise of Higher Education* (New York: St. Martin's, 1990); Dinesh D'Souza, *Illiberal Education* (New York: Free Press, 1991).

6. This district, comprising a forty-seven-campus, 31,000-student area, is the fifteenth largest in California. The district filed for bankruptcy on April 19, 1991, and is currently being reorganized.

7. Conservatives and progressives alike agree that American education is top-heavy with layers of expensive administration smothering the classrooms where learning goes on. See the collection of articles in *Academe* (November–December 1991) for a sampling of the debate about bloated administration in higher education. Per capita spending on public education in America is high compared to some other advanced societies, but the status and comparative wages of teachers, and the money set aside for actual educational programs, remains low.

8. In New Orleans, two months have been added to the school year, but "experts" seeking instant results (the American disease) are already calling the experiment a failure.

9. The Carnegie Foundation for the Advancement of Teaching, *Report Card on School Reform: The Teachers Speak* (Washington, D.C.: Carnegie Foundation, 1988), 11. For accounts from the perspective of teachers, in marked contrast to all the lugubrious conservative tomes, see Tracy Kidder's,

Among Schoolchildren (Boston: Houghton Mifflin, 1989) and Samuel G. Freedman's *Small Victories: The Real World of a Teacher, Her Students and Their High School* (New York: Harper & Row, 1990), as well as Jonathan Kozol's striking school portrait, *Savage Inequalities* (New York: Crown, 1991).

10. Inequalities in school district financing are stunning: In New Jersey, the fifty-four richest districts spend over $4,000 per pupil in their schools, while the twenty-eight poorest spend less than $2,900. Princeton schools (which spent a whopping $8,344 per pupil in 1990) offer a computer for every eight children; Camden has one for every fifty-eight children. Montclair's kids can learn foreign languages in preschool; Patterson's have to wait until they reach tenth grade. (Figures are [for] the 1984–1985 school year. *New York Times,* June 1990, sec. E). A similar story can be told in Maryland where Montgomery County's wealthy districts take in $6,000 per elementary school pupil, while rural Caroline County's districts take in $4,000. For twenty-nine students in Caroline's Preston School, this amounts to $57,000 their class doesn't have. (*Washington Post,* national weekly edition, 21–27 January 1991.)

11. John E. Chubb and Terry M. Moe, *Politics, Markets and America's Schools* (Washington, D.C.: Brookings Institution, 1990). Chubb and Moe go on to argue that "school organization" (related to teacher "morale") is the other critical factor.

PART TWO

CONCEPTS AND COMPLEXITIES

IN THIS SECTION we move from the general to the more specific in our consideration of democracy as a concept and of its many related complexities. We begin in Chapter Three with Robert D. Putnam's "What Makes Democracy Work?" To further our understanding of democracy and of the conditions necessary for it to flourish, Putnam, a political science professor whose research has for many years focused on democratic theory, develops the idea of social capital, which, he explains, centers on social trust and in turn is rooted in civic engagement. The stability and effectiveness of democracy as a form of government, Putnam argues, are directly correlated with the degree to which a society has developed its social capital.

Putnam's emphasis on social capital corresponds in significant ways to the consideration of "democratic virtues" presented in Chapter Four by C. Douglas Lummis, a professor of cultural studies living in Tokyo, Japan. Democracy, Lummis observes, "is an order based on trust." But not just any trust or any faith will do. "The only faith that can make us 'better, braver, and more active,'" Lummis explains, "without the danger of also making us stupid and intolerant, is faith in real human beings: democratic faith." Democratic faith, he argues, "is the true faith of which all other faiths are evasions; it is the faith of which all other faiths are imitations or indirect expressions or distorted forms; it is *radical* faith, at once the most natural and the most difficult." Taken together, these notions of social capital and democratic faith help form the theoretical foundations for democratic character, a concept explored in Part Three of this book.

That democratic faith is indeed radical may be more true than many of us would care to admit. In Chapter Five, "Was Democracy Just a Moment?" writer and social critic Robert D. Kaplan takes a hard look at the pressures and complexities of the modern world and at what those forces might mean for democracy's future. It is a blunt and sobering assessment that leaves us wondering if—despite what governments and the mass media tell us—democracy even has a future. One thing remains abundantly clear: democracy can never be taken for granted. Those who want to live in a democratic society will have to learn to shoulder its many responsibilities.

3

WHAT MAKES DEMOCRACY WORK?

Robert D. Putnam

WHY DO SOME DEMOCRATIC GOVERNMENTS succeed and others fail? This is a burning question today in all parts of the world—from Moscow and Mogadishu to South Central Los Angeles. Just when America's democratic ideals are held in highest global esteem, growing numbers of Americans fear that democratic government is faltering here at home. Revitalizing our democracy will require an answer to this question: What makes democracy work? I want to suggest one possible reply, by recounting two stories and a parable. Each seems distant from our immediate concerns, but all three are thought-provoking for those of us concerned with civic life in our communities.

A botanist who wants to study plant growth might plant genetically identical seeds in different pots of soil, water them differently, and watch to see which flourish and which wither. A political scientist wishing to similarly study the development of political institutions would need somehow to implant the same organization—as conceived on paper—in different political, economic and cultural contexts, and watch the results.

That sort of research is ordinarily impossible, but in 1970 Italians laid the groundwork for precisely this experiment by creating a new set of regional governments all along the Italian peninsula. All had the same formal structural organization, and all had important powers and much money to spend—nearly one-tenth of the entire GNP of Italy, or roughly the same fiscal resources of American state governments. But the soils in which these identical organizations were implanted were very different.

Some regions in Italy were economically backward, while others were as economically advanced as anywhere in the world. Some regions were traditionally Catholic, some deeply Communist, some essentially feudal, and so on. For nearly a quarter century my colleagues and I have closely observed this experiment in democratic regional governance.

It soon became clear that despite their identical form, these various regional governments worked very differently. As we had expected, some of them proved to be utter failures—inefficient, slothful, corrupt. Others, however, were very effective—creating innovative day care centers, industrial parks, jobs programs, family clinics, environmental programs, and the like. Citizens in these latter regions enjoyed better government than many Americans.

My colleagues and I measured the effectiveness of the regional governments in many ways. For example, in each region a local confederate wrote to the education agency, "My younger brother has just graduated from high school and would like to attend a vocational educational program. Please send the application." Then we counted how long it took for a reply to arrive. If the letter remained unanswered, we telephoned the ministry and counted how many calls were necessary. And if that failed, we visited the ministry personally and counted the number of visits that were necessary to obtain the application.

We used this and many other objective measures of government performance, from cabinet stability to budgetary promptness to legislative innovation. We also asked thousands of Italians about their regional governments, and we discovered that their evaluations were highly correlated with ours. We and Italian voters agreed on which governments were working well and which were failures. This is the starting point for my first story: Some of the new governments flourished while others withered. Why? What explains why some governments work and others do not?

We considered many possible answers: wealth, education, party politics, urbanization, social stability, and so on. None of these answers fits the facts; none was directly correlated with government performance. The right answer surprised us, though it likely would not have surprised Alexis de Tocqueville, that astute 19th-century French observer of democracy in America: What best predicted good government in the Italian regions was choral societies, soccer clubs and cooperatives. In other words, some regions were characterized by a dense network of civic associations and an active culture of civic engagement, whereas others were characterized by vertical patron-client relations of exploitation and dependence, not horizontal collaboration among equals.

Some regions of Italy have a rich network of community associations. Their citizens are engaged by public issues and take an active role in politics. They trust one another to act fairly and obey the law. Social and political networks here are organized horizontally, not hierarchically. In these "civic" communities, democracy works. At the other pole are the "uncivic" regions, where the very concept of citizenship is stunted. Engagement in social and cultural associations is meager, and the social structure is hierarchical. Public affairs is someone else's business, not mine. Laws are made to be broken, and people live in fear. Trapped by these vicious circles, nearly everyone feels exploited and unhappy—and democracy fails.

So that is the first story: Why are some communities governed well?— choral societies. The correlation between civic engagement and effective government is virtually perfect. Before we consider the implications of that discovery, however, let me ask a second question and tell a second story. The question is obvious: If the civic fabric is so important, why are some communities civic and others not? To answer that question, we need to enter a time machine and return to Italy around 1000 A.D.

Early medieval Italy, and indeed all of Europe in those years, was a very unpleasant place to live, because social life was anarchic. The risk that a peasant's grain might be stolen was so great that he grew only what he could eat himself. The risk that one would be robbed on the way to market was so high that no one went to market. Life, as Hobbes would later put it, was "nasty, brutish and short," because civic order was absent. That is why these came to be known as the Dark Ages.

Then, in two different parts of Italy, two very different solutions to this problem of social order were invented almost simultaneously. In southern Italy, a roving band of Norman mercenaries settled down and created the first feudal monarchy in Europe. It was a clever system. The peasants were protected by the knights, who took their cut of their agricultural production in return for maintaining order. The knights were kept in line by the barons, who took their cut. And the barons huddled under the king at the top.

This simple vertical system turned out to be very effective in imposing and maintaining social order. It was now safer to get grain to the market. The economy began to grow, and soon the Norman kingdom of southern Italy was the wealthiest, most advanced realm in Europe, with the first public university, the first civil service, and a rich flowering of art. King Frederick II was called *Stupor Mundi*—"the wonder of the world"— because he and his predecessors had created order out of chaos. His rule was authoritarian, but it was much better than no rule at all.

Meanwhile, in a band of cities stretching across north central Italy, from Venice to Bologna to Florence to Genoa, a very different solution was invented to address the same problem of social order. Instead of the vertically structured system of king, barons, knights and peasants, however, small groups of neighbors in the north began to form mutual self-protection pacts. Each member agreed that if any of them were attacked, the others would defend him. These groups came to be called "tower societies," named for the towers they built for refuge during times of trouble. Members of these tower societies even wrote contracts describing their mutual obligations, which was in some sense odd, since no courts existed to enforce the agreements. This very point—how were tower societies formed in the first place?—turns out to be the most crucial mystery of my story.

Whatever its provenance, the new system worked well. Neighboring tower societies formed alliances, and soon towns began to grow up. Town governments were actually formed out of these horizontally organized mutual aid associations. So successful was this idea of horizontal collaboration that the principle began to spread to other spheres of social activity. In economic life, guilds were invented—associations among equals for mutual professional benefit. In religion the same pattern evolved: Whereas in the hierarchically organized South, the Pope appointed the bishops, who in turn appointed the priests, in the communal North, local parishes elected their own leaders. Soon, a dense interlocking web of horizontal associations evolved—tower societies, guilds, neighborhood associations, religious fraternities, and even choral societies. These communal republics soon created remarkably advanced systems of government, with the medieval equivalent of professional city managers, modern laws, marketable public securities, and so on.

And then, the third most important economic invention in history appeared. (Of the first two, no one knows when the market was invented, but money was invented in Mesopotamia several thousand years earlier.) Ancient Egypt and Rome had markets and money, but even they had failed to develop this third innovation—*impersonal credit*. Impersonal credit exists when I loan you money, even though I do not know you personally. You use it to build a factory or to buy a ship to sail to distant markets, and then you return the money to me, with a bit extra for my troubles. Impersonal credit was invented in these city-states of medieval northern Italy.

Impersonal credit is astonishingly valuable, because it allows those with money to lend to others who can use it more effectively, so that everyone is better off—more jobs, more production, more goods, more wealth. Large-scale commerce and industry could not exist without impersonal credit, because without it, capital could not be accumulated and invested efficiently. The invention of impersonal credit enabled northern Italians to create by far the most advanced economy in the world. Italian bankers provided credit throughout Christendom, and virtually all the largest cities in Europe were to be found in Italy.

Impersonal credit requires trust—etymologically, the word "credit" comes from the Italian verb, "to believe." Trust among northern Italians rested on that uniquely close-knit fabric of civic life described above. When a resident of a communal republic obtained a loan, he in effect "mortgaged" his connections to all other citizens. Civic connections formed a kind of collateral, enabling northern Italians to trust one another. The communal republics were built to a surprising degree on trust—not perfect and unconditional trust, of course, which is why lawyers and courts were needed. To any unprecedented degree, however, this society was based on impersonal trust and generalized reciprocity. The root of social trust was civic engagement.

This horizontal social organization was fantastically efficient, not merely at bringing public order, but also in enabling northern Italy to become by far the wealthiest, best governed place of its era. By comparison to the rest of early medieval Europe, southern Italy, with its feudal monarchy, seemed advanced, but by comparison to the rest of the world, including southern Italy, the communal republics of the North soon gained a kind of dominance that Victorian England or post-war America never dreamed of. With their new wealth, northern Italians began to invest in art and high culture. The Renaissance was a direct consequence of the economic boom, which was a direct consequence of credit, which was in turn a direct consequence of the trust expressed in tower societies and choral societies. Civic engagement paid handsome dividends.

Sadly, because these cities were so attractive, they also became very crowded, and thus were tragically vulnerable to disease. In the summer of 1348, for example, half of all Italian townspeople died from the Black Death. And such deadly plagues recurred for several centuries. Moreover, rising foreign dynasties in France and Spain began raiding prosperous Italy. Italian dominance over Europe began to fade.

But for a period of about 300 years, Italy dominated the known world, because of these two political inventions—the feudal monarchy in the South and the even more efficient communal republics of the North. And if we draw a map of Italy tracing the incidence of civic engagement in 1300, and then draw a map of Italy reflecting the incidence of choral societies and effective democratic governance in 1993, the two maps are identical.

Now, if we draw a map of Italy in 1993 according to wealth, we will find that communities with many choral societies are also more advanced economically. I originally thought that these fortunate communities had more choral societies because they were wealthy. After all, I thought, poor peasants don't have time or energy to spend singing. But if we look closely at the historical record, it becomes clear that I had it exactly backwards. Communities don't have choral societies because they are wealthy; they are wealthy because they have choral societies—or more precisely, the traditions of engagement, trust and reciprocity that choral societies symbolize.

Of two equally poor Italian regions a century ago, both very backward, but one with more civic engagement, and the other with a hierarchical structure, the one with more choral societies and soccer clubs has grown steadily wealthier. The more civic region has prospered because trust and reciprocity were woven into its social fabric ages ago. None of this would appear in standard economics textbooks, of course, but our evidence suggests that wealth is the consequence, not the cause, of a healthy civics.

An important moral emerges from these two stories. Economists often refer to physical capital. A screwdriver is a form of physical capital: By investing in a screwdriver, one becomes more productive. About 25 years ago, the economist Gary Becker used the term "human capital" to refer to the fact that education can have the same effect. Investing in training—human capital—enables one to become more productive.

Some social scientists are beginning to speak of "social capital"—networks and norms of civic engagement. Conversely, in some modern countries—in our own urban ghettoes and in our suburbs, for example—the last several decades have witnessed a silent erosion of social capital. There are more empty seats at PTA meetings and church masses, for example, and fewer of us spend time on public affairs—particularly political activities. Compared with earlier generations, we are less engaged with one another outside the marketplace and thus less prepared to cooperate for shared goals. This decline in social capital helps explain the economic and political troubles of our own democracy.

These first two stories also frame a final important question: If we lack social capital, how can we create more? This tough dilemma was once posed to me by the reform-minded president of one of the backward regions of southern Italy. After dinner one evening he complained, "What you seem to be telling me is that nothing I can do will improve my region. Our fate was sealed hundreds of years ago." This is a central conundrum of our time: How can we invest in social capital?

There is no simple reply, but the question must be addressed by every serious public official or community activist in America today. Investments in our nation's portfolio of social capital must occur at the local level. A concluding parable—this time not from Italy but from Central America—dramatizes this point.

In many neighborhoods around San Jose, Costa Rica, recent immigrants from the countryside live amid social disorganization and crime. In the last few years, however, one such neighborhood has earned a reputation for being safer and more pleasant, even though its residents are no more affluent. This fortunate area somehow has achieved a strong sense of neighborhood solidarity. For example, nearly every resident has bought a football referee's whistle, and if a thief is spotted, everyone blows his whistle to alert his neighbors. The neighborhood has also taken up a collection to buy a local siren and set up a telephone network. If a local widow, for example, becomes distressed at night, one phone call suffices to set off the siren and summon help. This neighborhood-alert system has cut robberies dramatically—from roughly two a week to roughly one a year.

What makes this neighborhood different? The founder of the neighborhood association has a simple answer: *El Ley del Saludo*—"The Law of the Greeting." When the association was formed a few years ago, its members agreed that everyone would leave for work five minutes early every morning to have the time to say "hello" to each of his neighbors. This informal norm soon built ties of friendship and mutual solidarity among the previously anonymous residents of the neighborhood. Once those ties were established, it was relatively easy to agree on practical crime-fighting steps.

As the relative tranquillity of this neighborhood has become more widely known in San Jose, people from other neighborhoods have visited to inquire into the secret of their success. "When we tell them about 'The Law of the Greeting,'" reports the association's founder, "they smile dismissively and ask us where we got the whistles, or how we got a government grant for the siren." These inquirers are, of course, missing the point: The key to collective action is not physical capital, but social capital. "The Law of the Greeting" represents investment in social capital at its very simplest.

Solving America's social problems requires much more than a national "Law of the Greeting," but that is not a bad metaphor for the actions, public and private, that are needed. To revitalize our democracy we shall need to begin by rebuilding social capital in our communities, by renewing our civic connections.

4

THE DEMOCRATIC VIRTUES

C. Douglas Lummis

Public Trust

DEMOCRATIC ORDER finds a congenial ally in the natural order of nonoppressive work, but in itself it is a political order, not an economic one. It is distinguished from other forms of order by the nature of the bond which holds it together. It is not founded on such "guarantees" as state violence, indoctrination, fear of God, or bureaucratic management. It is also not founded on a set of "essential" first principles from which its necessity can be infallibly deduced. In a democratic situation, people are bound together into a state of order not by necessity but by trust. The possibility of a social order grounded in trust depends on the peculiar human ability to make promises, "the only alternative," Arendt wrote, "to a mastery which relies on domination of one's self and rule over others."[1]

The possibility of order created by trust is often expressed in political philosophy through the myth of the social contract. When Rousseau asked his famous question, How is it possible for people to live in an orderly community and still be "free as before," his answer was the social contract. A contract is of course a promise. And promises do establish order without violating freedom. That is, a promise is not a promise unless it is made freely. Keeping a promise means doing the thing we said we would because we said we would: standing by our words. Of course promises or contracts may be strengthened by added guarantees: rewards if they are kept, punishments or vengeance if they are not. But these guarantees are the beginning of an evolution from promises to something else. We rely on rewards and punishments when we do not trust one another.

Trusting that a promise will be kept is different from believing a fact or a theory to be true or predicting that something will happen tomorrow. The appropriate object of trust is not a thing, fact, theory, or event, but a person. Trust means expecting that a person will do something or refrain from doing something. But it is trust only when the person has the freedom to do otherwise. Trust presupposes the freedom of the other. It is not trust if I expect you to digest your dinner. It is not trust if I lock you in an iron cage and expect that you will still be there tomorrow. It is not trust if, putting a knife to your throat and saying, "Your money or your life!" I expect that you will hand me your wallet. It is not trust if I brainwash you and expect you to act accordingly. It is trust if I expect that you will not betray me when you could.

The phenomenon of trust in human relations is not fully captured by the image of the contract, nor is it limited to the keeping of actual promises. Most of the things we trust each other about are never articulated in specific contracts or promises. When we say a person is trustworthy, we mean that the person can be expected not to betray others even in matters that no one has thought to put into words. The greater part of the "contract" that holds societies together is tacit, embedded in common sense; only a small part is disembedded and put into specific words.

Still, the contract, in addition to being a useful form of promise making, is a good metaphor that can help us to see the nature of all trust relations. The negation of trust is not sin but betrayal. We consider trustworthiness a virtue, but it is different in character from moral goodness. If, for example, we were confronted with a perfect saint, that is, a person all of whose actions are governed by an absolute principle of goodness, we would not trust this person in the ordinary sense, though we would be able to predict his or her behavior if we knew the principle. And it is doubtful that a true saint would be capable of making promises in the ordinary sense. A promise with another saint would not be necessary, and a promise with one of us ordinary people would risk the saint's saintly status. In the real world it often turns out that not all of the things we need to do to keep promises are in accord with perfect morality. On the other hand, ordinary humans with spouses and children who make promises with the Absolute can find themselves involved in bloody horrors, as Abraham learned.

Consider the figure of the totally just monad proposed by Glaucon in Book I of Plato's *Republic*. In that story, Glaucon demands that Socrates show that justice is good not for its reputation but in itself, and he refuses to accept anything less than a demonstration that justice would be good for a person even if that person suffered under the reputation of being totally unjust.[2] The peculiarity, not mentioned by Plato, of the totally-just-person-with-the-reputation-of-being-totally-unjust is that such a person would be incapable of making promises. No one would trust you, and no one would expect anything good of you. With no promises you could neither keep nor break them; with no trust relations you could neither betray people nor be faithful to their expectations. Socrates' argument may be correct that his justice, in the sense that it is the state of health of the soul, is good-in-itself. But deprived of its capacity to generate trust in others it is, socially, good-for-nothing.

Trust relations are not arrived at by deduction from moral first principles. They are established in the web of human relations by thousands of promises and contracts, some explicit but most not, which people make in their daily dealings with one another over the years and over generations. Trust is not morality, but it produces virtuous behavior and virtuous persons. True, we sometimes say things like, "You can trust that man to stab you in the back every time he gets a chance," but this is only turning the word upside-down for the purpose of sarcasm. It is also true that people sometimes make promises to do evil together, the paradox we call "honor among thieves." . . . Augustine considered this paradox the essence of the secular state, providing justice to its citizens and pillage to its neighbors . . . [but] this dual consciousness is not stable, and there is the continual danger that, to borrow Burke's phrase . . ., the breakers of law in India will return to become the makers of law in England; that the thief part will overpower the justice part. And to be sure, there are times when breaking promises and deserting comrades may be the best thing to do, as for a person in an army on the wrong side of an imperialist war, or in a government that tortures prisoners, or in a company that poisons the sea. Be that as it may, the only point in this context is that, other things being equal, keeping promises is . . . itself good behavior; if it were not, "honor among thieves" would not be a paradox.

Nietzsche writes, "To breed an animal with the right to make promises—is not this the paradoxical problem nature has set itself with regard to man?"[3] Promises produce order through time. You promise to do something tomorrow, and you do it; you have to that degree put order into your action. Making promises and keeping them is the direct opposite to doing what you feel like. Keeping a promise means exactly doing what you said you would do whether you still feel like it or not. Does this mean that keeping promises is self-repressive, the action of the dictatorial superego crushing the free play of human emotions? Not according to

Nietzsche. The very man who saw "bad conscience" as a sickness of the soul, a weakness produced by the self attacking the self, saw the making and keeping of promises as acts of power, freedom, and health:

> I do not mean a purely passive succumbing to past impressions, the indigestion of being unable to be done with a pledge once made, but rather an active not wishing to be done with it, a continuing to will what has been willed, a veritable "memory of the will"; so that, between the original determination and the actual performance of the thing willed, a whole world of new things, conditions, even volitional acts, can be interposed without snapping the long chain of the will.[4]

The act of making and keeping a promise is a conquest of the chaos that would come if each of us followed our individual passions from moment to moment wherever they lead. It is a conquest that establishes order without placing humankind under a punishing God, a punishing leviathan, a punishing conscience, or a punishing order of exploitative work. In Rousseau's words, it leaves us "free as before." There is no need to ask why making a promise is an act of freedom: we make promises only where there is freedom. Where there is no freedom there is no need for a promise. True, we sometimes say things like, "I promise to be hungry by dinner time"; the point, again, is that this is a joke. Through promises, people faced with more than one choice can create order by collectively willing one. (Of course order can also be created when one person with power issues an order, which is why an "order" is called that.) The specific content of a promise need not, as mentioned above, be moral or honorable. But even when it is indifferent ("I will meet you at 7:00 P.M. in front of the post office"), keeping it takes on moral weight. This weight does not come from some metaphysical source: god, transcendent law, absolute reason, the form of the good. It comes from the people themselves, and their act of promising.

Trust in a Brutal World

Trust is different from all metaphysical sources of morality in that no one would think of grounding it in proof. Again, where the behavior of the other can be predicted with certainty, there is no need for trust. When we trust a person, however, we usually do so on the basis of evidence: the person's actions up to now. We hope that people who have proved trustworthy thus far will continue so. But when we say that democracy is an order based on trust, do we mean that we must somehow be willing to trust people we have never met? This might not be a problem if we lived in some kind of democratic utopia, where for generations there had been none but trustworthy people. But where we do live the idea sounds like plain foolishness. We have no experience suggesting that we can safely trust people we don't know, or people in general. On the contrary, experience teaches us that people are sometimes trustworthy and sometimes not, that we should be selective in whom we trust, and that we should not trust people without guarantees.

One must begin with the world as it is. We dream of trust; we live in a world where, in the words of Bob Marley's song, "everywhere is war"— a world in which unwillingness to drop atomic bombs on people would disqualify a person for the office of head of state of any of the major powers, unwillingness to exploit people would disqualify a person for work in the business world, and unwillingness to shoot people or beat them with clubs would disqualify a person from work in the police force of any country. There is no call for a lengthy argument demonstrating the brutal gap between the dream of a world of trust and the world we actually live in. Rather, let us take this gap as the starting point. From this starting point, what are the moves we might make?

One move is sentimentalism, a flight from reality into the fantasy world of well-meaning politicians, charitable capitalists, kindly soldiers and policemen. The particular advantage of wearing rose-colored glasses is that you can't see the blood. Another move is despair. Despair has the advantage over sentimentalism that it is realistic; from despairing writers we can sometimes get a picture of the world which has an almost scientific clarity. Anyone who knows despair, however, knows that it is to be avoided if possible. From the position of despair we cannot do anything, which means we cannot live.

A third move is cynicism. Cynicism shares with despair the advantage of being realistic. As with despairing writers, cynical writers can teach us much truth about the world and provide a good antidote to sentimentalism. Moreover, cynicism has the advantage over despair that it allows us to act. It also allows for humor, which matters much. But it has the very great disadvantage that it includes oneself among the things it is cynical about. Cynicism is a complex arrangement by which our condemnation of the evils of the world is somehow used to justify our participation in those evils. No matter how convoluted its evasions may become it can never escape its beginning, which is self-contempt. The cynic maintains a divided self: the critic and the actor. The critical cynic through his contempt for the corruption of the world maintains the power of criticism and the values on which it is based. The acting cynic is liberated by the very same cynicism from the necessity to act on the basis of these values.

In his wonderful analysis of modern cynicism Peter Sloterdijk writes, "This is the essential point in modern cynicism: the ability of its bearers to work—in spite of everything that might happen, and especially, after anything that might happen."[5] This is the state of consciousness of the great majority of the people working in managerial and bureaucratic positions in the rich industrial countries. Cynicism keeps them at this work: when I said the cynic can act, I meant only that. The cynic can continue to work in the system that he or she condemns as meaningless or worse, and will do nothing to change it. A person who has fallen into cynicism can rarely be talked out of it: the cynical consciousness has heard everything and has a place within itself to file away any new fact or argument. I shall attempt no such refutation of cynicism here but limit myself to the comment that a consciousness grounded in self-contempt is not a happy one.

A fourth move is religious faith. This takes many forms, but if I understand Sören Kierkegaard and other commentators correctly, its essence is positing that there is a transcendent good that justifies the horrors of this world and believing in it without understanding it. In the Jewish and Christian traditions, faith is presented as the highest form of trust. In the Old Testament God takes the form of a person—that is, a being capable of making a promise—and the origin of faith is expressed through the image of a promise—a covenant—between him and Abraham. As God is omnipotent and his purposes are unknown to Abraham and his descendants, they have no way of enforcing the covenant or of checking to see if God's side of it has been fulfilled. So their belief in the promise and in the good faith of the other party becomes a new form of trust, trust raised to a higher power. I shall not attempt here an analysis of the phenomenon of faith; all I wish to do is to point out some of the advantages and disadvantages of this move in the context of this discussion. The first of its advantages is that it permits a realistic view of this world. There are of course pseudofaiths based on sentimentalism, but there is no trace of sentimentalism in the great heroes of faith, Abraham and Job, or in the great theologians such as Augustine and Aquinas. On the contrary, faith in the Absolute gives one a chillingly clear picture of how far humankind has Fallen. At the same time, faith prevents one from falling into the agony of despair. Like cynicism, it permits one to go on living and acting; unlike cynicism it allows one to live in hope. Moreover, unlike the cynic, the faithful person will seek to be better. The faithful, however, will never be able to be as good as the Absolute demands; this inevitable gap is the origin of bad conscience. The self-criticism of bad conscience is different from the self-contempt of the cynic. It is based on something living and active: a conscience. In the case of the cynic, it is one's own atrophied conscience that is the chief object of contempt. The conscience is the great achievement of faith. This list of advantages is impressive: realism about the world, combined with a reason to keep on living and acting and even to try to act well and in hope. The great disadvantage is that while it offers some degree (the degree depends on the theologist) of hope in this world, its ultimate hope is not for this world.

After Ludwig Feuerbach—and after Marx, after Kierkegaard, after Nietzsche—we know that faith is, indeed, a "move." We know, that is, that if we want to understand faith we must look at it as an act taken in this world, not as something provided us from outside this world. This view includes understanding that the object of faith is also a human construction and a human choice. If religious readers object to this formulation, I am ready to rephrase it and to say only that at least this essay proceeds from that position, to say with Feuerbach (*The Fiery Brook*)[6] that "religion is the dream of the human mind" (p. 258). In the case of the Jewish religion, as well as of its two major offshoots Christianity and Islam, this dream has contained a large element of nightmare for both the believers and their victims. But without judging whether on the whole it was worth the cost (a judgment surely no human being is qualified to make) we can say that the invention of faith, in that it gave people a power to be "better, braver, and more active" was a great achievement.

Feuerbach argues that the attributes people have given to God are actually their own: "You believe in love as a divine attribute because you yourself love, and believe that God is a wise and benevolent being because you know nothing better in yourself than wisdom and benevolence" (p. 115). But though God is created in man's image, he is also clearly different: he is perfect and man is not. On the other hand, this difference can be stood on its head with the observation that there is one virtue of which human beings are capable and God is not: faith itself. Faith requires imperfect knowledge, but God is omniscient; besides, what could God have faith *in*? According to Feuerbach, this difference leads human beings into self-contempt: "In order to enrich God, man must become poor; that God may be all, man must be nothing" (p. 124). His project is to redirect this religious impulse, to shift its gaze from an imagined object to a real one: from God to humankind: "What I . . . do to religion—and to speculative philosophy and theology as well—is nothing else than to *open its eyes* or rather to turn *outward* its *inwardly directed eyes*; in other words, I only lead the object from its existence in the imagination to its existence in reality" (p. 258).

Feuerbach's project is noble but filled with dangers. As an object for the religious impulse God has great advantages over human beings. He is a safe place in which to put our faith, for the simple reason that he is posited as such. The affair is arranged so that no matter what happens to us on earth we can never say that God has betrayed us or that our faith has been misplaced. Presumably the Book of Job was included in the Old Testament to hammer this lesson home. God's nature is ineffable and his purposes are beyond our understanding, so there can never be a reason for us to follow the advice of Job's wife, to "curse God, and die."

But what of human beings? Feuerbach's celebration ("The Divine Being is nothing other than the being of man himself"; p. 111) is marvelous and brave, but is it wise? God is defined so as never to betray us, but can we say the same of human beings? We do not know what God does or thinks, but we do know something of what human beings do and think, including ourselves. Is Feuerbach asking us to place our faith *there*? Does he not realize that placing our full trust in human beings would require a faith even beyond the imagination of Abraham? Wasn't it the untrustworthiness of human beings which led to the positing of "God" in the first place?

Replacing God with man as the object of faith is a dangerous move; it can cause one to pass rapidly through the stages of sentimental humanism to disillusion and despair and finally to cynicism. This transition is no mere speculation; who would deny the relationship between the massive secularization of Western culture since Feuerbach and the deep cynicism by which it is characterized today?

There is a position halfway between religious faith and cynicism which can stop, or at least delay, the slide from the former to the latter: belief in "progress." This move has the advantage that it follows Feuerbach's program of secularization while avoiding the worst dangers of that program. The believer may dispense with the metaphysical entity "God" while retaining one of his alleged effects on the world: providence. It is easier to live without the hypothesis of a divine being if we can convince ourselves that the world is anyway constructed *as if* it were the creation of a divine intelligence and that history progresses *as if* it were the unfolding of a divine plan. This belief permits us to put our faith in human beings without that faith's being threatened by anything human beings actually do. We put our faith in the human beings of the future, and "the human beings of the future" will never let us down because they are, like God, the products of our imagination. They are an abstraction, and we can construct them any way we like. Again our faith is deposited in a safe place, where none of the crimes, stupidities, or failures of the people living in our own Dark Times can get at it. This safety gives us hope, and a reason to act. These are great advantages.

But there are disadvantages. If faith in progress, and in the human of the future, is immune to betrayal by the actual human beings living in the present, at the same time it gives us no particular reason to be loyal to them either. If the human of the future is the goal, it is perfectly consistent to treat the human of the present with sublime contempt, as stepping stones, building blocks, "human resources," or cannon fodder, that is, as *means* to the future. Faith in progress allows us to maintain two very different attitudes side by side. With regard to the human of the future we can be idealists, dreamers. With regard to the humans of the present we are able to behave just like the cynics. The believer in progress can have it both ways, being Abel later and Cain now. Of course ordinary people do not usually carry this form of faith to such an extreme, but in this century we have witnessed some of the chilling forms this position can take. Just as the deep faith of the Middle Ages could produce, with no logical inconsistency, the faithful inquisitor and the *auto-da-fé* (Portuguese for "act of faith"), so the historical faith of the twentieth century could produce, with equal consistency, progressive idealists such as Stalin, Truman, Robert McNamara, and Pol Pot.

The peculiar brutality that faith in progress has brought to our era grows from the fact that it is faith placed both in the wrong time and in the wrong sort of object. Faith is trust raised to a higher power, and the proper object for both is human beings. Faith in the humans of the future is faith in an abstraction; it is trust that cannot be reciprocated or grounded in any real promise. It is an evasion of the real task, the one thing needful, which is to work for a world founded on real trust among real humans, now. Just as its object is an abstraction, so its enactment becomes an abstraction; it is fulfilled not by the keeping of promises but by the operation of "laws of motion" and "historical forces." In short, in being transferred from God to Progress, faith is transformed from religion to superstition.

Democratic Faith: Choosing Isaac

The reintroduction of real persons as the original and only proper object of faith is the starting point for democratic thinking. As I have said, this step is not easy—its difficulty is the very reason we have invented so many ways of escaping it. Faith, the decision to continue to believe despite the evidence, has the power to raise us out of despair and to cure cynicism. At the same time faith in the wrong object has the power to make us into stupid, intolerant, and brutal "true believers." The only faith that can make us "better, braver, and more active" without the danger of also making us stupid and intolerant is faith in real human beings: democratic faith.

Faith in human beings is the hardest faith, yet we all have it in some degree. We have to, to live. It is the very stuff out of which our personal lives are shaped; it is so common we barely notice it. When people die or sacrifice their personal happiness for a Cause we are dazzled; when they do the same for their family or friends we admire them but are not so surprised. We do not reward them with fame and glory or establish national holidays in their honor. To do so would be embarrassing. Still, this faith is a tremendous power in history, far more powerful than all the force that has so far been held by states, armies, and other violence-wielding organizations. The proof of this power is that, despite these organizations, civilization still exists.

This view returns us to the point made earlier, that radical democracy does not require the introduction of some heroic new ethic into the world: it requires only that we put to better use some of the common-sense virtues we already have. To do so we need to gain new confidence in these common-sense virtues. We have a political mythology that denigrates them. Political order, we are taught, was established by men (meaning males) who were ready to sacrifice personal loyalty to do so. Cain killed Abel and built a city; Romulus killed Remus and founded Rome; Brutus killed his sons and founded the Roman Republic; Abraham held the knife over his son and founded the Hebrew people and became the Father of Faith. Democratic faith, common-sense faith, is founded differently, by the people who do *not* kill their brothers and children. It is founded by the people who will say calmly, with E. M. Forster, "If I had to choose between betraying my country and betraying my friend, I hope that I should have the guts to betray my country."[7]

One may push the point further and say that from the standpoint of democratic faith Abraham's act was a failure of faith. Had he the true faith of a *father*, he would have had perfect confidence that God would not punish him for refusing to kill the boy. Any *mother* would have understood that. If he had a covenant with his God he had another with his son, the tacit covenant one enters into by bringing a child into this world. From the standpoint of common-sense faith, he should have kept that covenant, the one with the weaker party, whom it was his duty to protect. Think of the horror and despair of Isaac when he saw his father raise the knife over his bound body—could anything that came after ever make things all right again? Are we to say that faith is the belief in a God who would hate Abraham for refusing to submit his son to that? Should we not reinterpret the entire myth and say that actually Abraham failed the test, that an amazed and horrified God mercifully stopped him from carrying out the despicable act and then punished Abraham and all his descendants by laying on them the Curse of Abraham's Faith, under the yoke of which we have been sacrificing our parents, children, brothers, sisters, and comrades to the State, the Party, the True Religion, and other Higher Causes ever since?

For a new beginning, we need an Abraham who would not kill the boy. But we need not look far to find him: most fathers in the world, I believe, would not, and neither would most mothers. Most would think, I do not believe that God will really punish me for refusing; If he does he is not really God; Even if he is God and he punishes me I will take the punishment before I will kill the boy. Or they would think nothing at all, but simply be unable to raise their arms to do the deed. It is because the world is mainly made up of people like these that there is hope.

The common-sense democrat will find this big talk embarrassing. Faith is a heavy word. We need it to give the argument here sufficient weight. Later we can substitute some more modest term like "tenacity" or "decency." But here let us call it faith and make the argument straight out: democratic faith is the true faith of which all other faiths are evasions; it is the faith of which all other faiths are imitations or indirect expressions or distorted forms; it is *radical* faith, at once the most natural and the most difficult.

The naturalness and the difficulty of democratic faith are rooted in the essential paradox of trust. The only proper object of trust is people, *because* people are capable of untrustworthiness; only people are capable of untrustworthiness, *because* they are trusted. We do not trust a rock to be hard, or a hen to lay eggs, or a falling object to accelerate at 32 ft./sec.[2] Trust—and trustworthiness—was invented as a way of dealing with the uncertainties of human beings, who are free. It does not change the uncertainties into certainties. Trust is not a proof but a judgment and a choice.

Democratic faith is not simply trusting everybody equally; it is not sentimental foolishness. It is grounded on a lucid understanding of the weaknesses, follies, and horrors people are capable of. It is precisely because of those weaknesses, follies, and horrors that something so weighty as faith is called for. Democratic faith is the decision to believe that a world of democratic trust is possible because we can see it in each person sometimes. It is the decision to believe in what people can be on the basis of what they sometimes are. It is the decision to believe that each polity and each person contains the possibility of a democratic version of itself. It is the belief that as people are free, they are free to become that, too. None of this has been proved, but neither can it be disproved. One is free to believe either way. The move to embrace democratic faith gives one hope and the ability to act, without self-deception about the actual state of things. The gap between the possibility in which the democrat believes and the reality that we have is a wide one; among leaps of faith, this is a long one. That is why, of all faiths, it needs to be the strongest.

So the democrat is not impressed with the Abraham who puts his faith in God the Omnipotent, the Omniscient, the Unchangeable, the Eternal, as against the little boy who, for all we know, sometimes steals cakes from the kitchen, dreams forbidden dreams, and is now wishing he had any other father in the world but this one. Obeying the omnipotent is no great feat compared with gambling on the boy.

The business turns another shade darker if we think of it from the standpoint of Feuerbach. For then we must see the God of Abraham as created by Abraham, for the purpose of giving himself and posterity an unshakable basis for faith, which he is unable to find in human beings. Abraham has created this homunculus and taught it to command him to sacrifice the boy, in order to raise himself above the uncertainties of mere human trust. The democrat does not join the theologians in applauding this attempt to evade the complexities of seeking to establish an honest order among human beings, using only human strength and wit. It is the worst possible beginning for a quest for the promised land. Feuerbach argues that human beings created God out of the best human qualities. But this God has another, inhuman quality: moral certainty. Human beings cannot arrive at moral certainty on their own. The story of Abraham and Isaac is a parable of this idea as well: it teaches how a person possessed of moral certainty passes outside the realm of the human and becomes a terrifying and incomprehensible force. There is no way we can think our way to that degree of certainty with merely human thoughts. Faith only among human beings, none of whom is "absolute," can never yield so mighty a consequence. The voice of the people is not the voice of God; democracy has no need of that hypothesis. It is only the voice of the people.

The State of Public Hope and the Art of the Possible

In the spring of 1985, in the last months of the Marcos dictatorship, I visited the Philippines on what they call there an "exposure tour," sponsored by a loose alliance of anti-Marcos movement organizations. The nine-day visit put me in a state of shock. It was not culture shock, or poverty shock. The only name I could think of for it was hope shock.

In Japan, where I live, most people have private hope. They believe that privately their lives will go well—that they will find work, earn adequate money, and live in comfort. Few of them fear that they or their children will fall into poverty, suffer malnutrition, be forced to turn to crime, or die violent deaths.

Most, however, have no public hope. Their attitude about the future of their country, or the future of the world, is typically one of bland despair. They talk easily and vaguely about the probable continuation of the destruction of nature, of the unlikelihood that they will ever achieve popular control over the entrenched political cliques that run their government, about the inevitable death of freedom in the technomanagerial society of the future. The belief that none of these things can be avoided by the action of mere human beings (which is to say, the belief that democracy is impossible) has become common sense.

In the Philippines in 1985 there were few objective reasons for hope. Under the Marcos development dictatorship, the economy was starving the people and the government was murdering them. Privately most young people, except those from very rich families, faced bleak futures. But everybody I talked to was filled with hope. Of course we will win, they told us. We will drive out this dictator. We will drive out the predatory foreign capitalists. We will drive out the U.S. bases. We will make the Philippines into a just and prosperous country. By the actions of ordinary people, they told us, these things will be done.

There was an atmosphere of freedom everywhere. We heard people sing forbidden anti-Marcos songs in public restaurants. We attended rallies and participated in marches. We walked with ten thousand people, mostly workers from the Battaan Export Processing Zone, where only a few years before union activity had been unthinkable, in a march from Mariveles to Batanga which took two days. Only once I saw government soldiers: three army jeeps whizzed by looking like hedgehogs with rifles sticking out all around, and the marchers hooted at them. We all camped in a public schoolyard. I remember thinking, What kind of dictatorship is this? If ten thousand antigovernment demonstrators set up camp in a public schoolyard in Japan or the United States or any other of the "democratic" countries, the riot police would drive them out in less than half an hour.

This was the shock: to be transferred suddenly from a society in a state of public despair into a society in a state of public hope. The "Miracle of EDSA" was not a sudden phenomenon; the process leading up to it had been well under way a year earlier. The tragedy of that "miracle" was that it turned into a ritual for transferring the people's public faith from People's Power to state power. Has there ever been a clearer illustration of the antidemocratic potential of "democratic elections"? The election of Corazon Aquino to the presidency marked not the beginning but the end of People's Power in the Philippines—at least for the time being. The country was freer in the last days of the Marcos regime than it is today. (I suppose the same could be said of Poland in the days when Solidarity had all the power except state power, compared to later with Lech Walesa in the presidency.) Today, the Philippines is a country struggling with despair.

Nevertheless, in their moment of public hope the Philippine people accomplished a deed that will be remembered throughout that country's history. And the possibility remains that it can be repeated.

The state of public hope is difficult to analyze or account for in the technical language of ordinary political science, and major people's movements and revolutions always catch the experts by surprise. Political science searches for causes. But the state of public hope is in a sense self-causing. The same is true for the state of public despair. When people will not join together in public action because they believe it is doomed to failure, then it is doomed to failure. The subjective belief creates the objective fact that proves the belief to be "correct." This state of things we commonly call "political realism."

In the state of public hope this vicious cycle is reversed. People begin to believe that public action can succeed. It doesn't matter why they believe—it could be for the wrong reason. When hope is shared by many, it becomes its own reason. Public hope is itself grounds for hope. When many people, filled with hope, take part in public action, hope is transformed from near-groundless faith (which it was in the state of public despair) to plain common sense. It is this capacity seemingly to defy the law of cause and effect, to create something out of nothing, which leads people to use the expression "miracle" to describe public action. It is also the reason movements sometimes unexpectedly turn into revolutions, going beyond their original goals: as the movement grows it becomes realistic to make demands that were unthinkable at the beginning. (Even something so unpolitical as the spontaneous growth of mutual-aid organizations out of people's efforts to survive the effects of an earthquake can be the catalyst for a new democratic movement, as happened in Mexico.)

In the Philippines, it is true, many people believed that success in throwing out Marcos was possible because of the power of the New People's Army (NPA). This belief was not groundless; the NPA was crucial in the delegitimization of the Marcos dictatorship and in the alteration of the balance of power in the country. But the self-generating dynamic of public hope soon developed into a tornado of power which far surpassed, albeit briefly, the military power of the guerrilla army and achieved something that army could not do, the overthrow of the dictator. The NPA is still there and still has military power, but public hope and people's power are not.

The expression "Politics is the art of the possible" is attributed to Otto von Bismarck. It is usually understood in a Bismarckian fashion: politics should be limited to *realpolitik*; it should rid itself of its utopian and idealistic elements and stick to a possible agenda. To enter politics is to give up being a dreamer, to abandon one's highest hopes, and to resign oneself to the realities of power. In this sense, "Politics is the art of the possible" has been the slogan of cynical politics.

The democrat, however, will take it in a different sense. In democratic politics, the art of the possible means the art of extending the possible, the art of creating the possible out of the impossible. It is true that the logic of *realpolitik* is the only logic that is effective in the context of the state of public despair. Democratic politics has the power to bring about a political change of state and make possible what was impossible before. This is not sentimental idealism but plain realism: it can happen and it does happen. If all the soldiers refuse to fight, the war is over; if all the citizens take to the streets, the dictatorship is out of power; if all the unions strike on the same day, they are in control of industry; if all the indebted nations simultaneously abrogate their debts, the International Monetary Fund and the World Bank are abolished. This is the *realpolitik* of democratic politics.

We have been taught by Hobbes to fear the state of nature. In this state where each wars against all in an endless agony of despair, public hope has vanished altogether. The state of nature is not a time in the far past; it is an ever-present possibility, a specter that follows us all through history and is always just a hairsbreadth away, ready to spring into reality any time we make the mistake of challenging the power of Leviathan. This miserable image, always just on the other side of the looking glass from political reality, operates as the constant killer of hope on this side too.

Against this image the democrat posits the image of the state of public hope, the state of democracy. This state, we say, is also an ever-present possibility, also just a hairsbreadth away. Knowing this gives us a reason not to lose hope even in the worst of political situations, even now. . . .

NOTES

1. Hannah Arendt, *The Human Condition* (New York: Anchor, 1959), p. 220.

2. Plato, *Republic* 2.360e–61d.

3. Friedrich Nietzsche, "The Genealogy of Morals," *"The Birth of Tragedy" and "The Genealogy of Morals,"* trans. Francis Golffing (New York: Anchor, 1956), p. 189.

4. Ibid., p. 196.

5. Peter Sloterdijk, *Critique of Cynical Reason,* trans. Michael Eldred, foreword by Andreas Huyssen (Minneapolis: University of Minnesota Press, 1987), p. 5.

6. Ludwig Feuerbach, *The Fiery Brook: Selected Writings of Ludwig Feuerbach,* trans. and introd. by Zawar Hanfi (New York: Anchor, 1972).

7. E. M. Forster, *Two Cheers for Democracy* (London: Edward Arnold, 1951), p. 78.

5

WAS DEMOCRACY
JUST A MOMENT?

Robert D. Kaplan

IN THE FOURTH CENTURY A.D. Christianity's conquest of Europe and
the Mediterranean world gave rise to the belief that a peaceful era in
world politics was at hand, now that a consensus had formed around an
ideology that stressed the sanctity of the individual. But Christianity was,
of course, not static. It kept evolving, into rites, sects, and "heresies" that
were in turn influenced by the geography and cultures of the places where
it took root. Meanwhile, the church founded by Saint Peter became a rit-
ualistic and hierarchical organization guilty of long periods of violence
and bigotry. This is to say nothing of the evils perpetrated by the Orthodox churches in the East. Christianity made the world not more peaceful
or, in practice, more moral but only more complex. Democracy, which is
now overtaking the world as Christianity once did, may do the same.

The collapse of communism from internal stresses says nothing about
the long-term viability of Western democracy. Marxism's natural death in
Eastern Europe is no guarantee that subtler tyrannies do not await us,
here and abroad. History has demonstrated that there is no final triumph
of reason, whether it goes by the name of Christianity, the Enlightenment,
or, now, democracy. To think that democracy as we know it will triumph—or is even here to stay—is itself a form of determinism, driven by
our own ethnocentricity. Indeed, those who quote Alexis de Tocqueville
in support of democracy's inevitability should pay heed to his observation
that Americans, because of their (comparative) equality, exaggerate "the

scope of human perfectibility." Despotism, Tocqueville went on, "is more particularly to be feared in democratic ages," because it thrives on the obsession with self and one's own security which equality fosters.

I submit that the democracy we are encouraging in many poor parts of the world is an integral part of a transformation toward new forms of authoritarianism; that democracy in the United States is at greater risk than ever before, and from obscure sources; and that many future regimes, ours especially, could resemble the oligarchies of ancient Athens and Sparta more than they do the current government in Washington. History teaches that it is exactly at such prosperous times as these that we need to maintain a sense of the tragic, however unnecessary it may seem. The Greek historian Polybius, of the second century B.C., interpreted what we consider the Golden Age of Athens as the beginning of its decline. To Thucydides, the very security and satisfactory life that the Athenians enjoyed under Pericles blinded them to the bleak forces of human nature that were gradually to be their undoing in the Peloponnesian War.

My pessimism is, I hope, a foundation for prudence. America's Founders were often dismal about the human condition. James Madison: "Had every Athenian citizen been a Socrates, every Athenian assembly would still have been a mob." Thomas Paine: "Society is produced by our wants and government by our wickedness." It was the "crude" and "reactionary" philosophy of Thomas Hobbes, which placed security ahead of liberty in a system of enlightened despotism, from which the Founders drew philosophical sustenance. Paul A. Rahe, a professor of history at the University of Tulsa, shows in his superb three-volume *Republics Ancient and Modern* (1992) how the Founders partly rejected the ancient republics, which were based on virtue, for a utilitarian regime that channeled man's selfish, materialistic instincts toward benign ends. Man, Benjamin Franklin said in an apparent defense of Hobbesian determinism, is "a tool-making animal."

Democracies Are Value-Neutral

Hitler and Mussolini each came to power through democracy. Democracies do not always make societies more civil—but they do always mercilessly expose the health of the societies in which they operate.

In April of 1985 I found myself in the middle of a Sudanese crowd that had just helped to overthrow a military regime and replace it with a new government, which the following year held free and fair elections. Sudan's newly elected democracy led immediately to anarchy, which in turn led to the most brutal tyranny in Sudan's postcolonial history: a military regime that broadened the scope of executions, persecuted women, starved non-Muslims to death, sold kidnapped non-Muslim children back to their parents for $200, and made Khartoum the terrorism capital of the Arab world, replacing Beirut. In Sudan only 27 percent of the population (and only 12 percent of the women) could read. If a society is not in reasonable health, democracy can be not only risky but disastrous: during the last phases of the post–First World War German and Italian democracies, for example, the unemployment and inflation figures for Germany and the amount of civil unrest in Italy were just as abysmal as Sudan's literacy rates.

As an unemployed Tunisian student once told me, "In Tunisia we have a twenty-five percent unemployment rate. If you hold elections in such circumstances, the result will be a fundamentalist government and violence like in Algeria. First create an economy, then worry about elections." There are many differences between Tunisia and its neighbor Algeria, including the fact that Tunisia has been peaceful without democracy and Algeria erupted in violence in 1992 after its first election went awry and the military canceled the second. In Kurdistan and Afghanistan, two fragile tribal societies in which the United States encouraged versions of democracy in the 1990s, the security vacuums that followed the failed attempts at institutionalizing pluralism were filled by Saddam Hussein for a time in Kurdistan and by Islamic tyranny in much of Afghanistan. In Bosnia democracy legitimized the worst war crimes in Europe since the Nazi era. In sub-Saharan Africa democracy has weakened institutions and services in some states, and elections have been manipulated to restore dictatorship in others. In Sierra Leone and Congo-Brazzaville elections have led to chaos. In Mali, which Africa-watchers have christened a democratic success story, recent elections were boycotted by the opposition and were marred by killings and riots. Voter turnout was less than 20 percent. Even in Latin America, the Third World's most successful venue for democracy, the record is murky. Venezuela has enjoyed elected civilian governments since 1959, whereas for most of the 1970s and 1980s Chile was effectively under military rule. But Venezuela is a society in turmoil, with periodic coup attempts, rampant crime, and an elite that invests most of its savings outside the country; as a credit risk Venezuela ranks behind only Russia and Mexico. Chile has become a stable middle-class society whose economic growth rate compares to those of the Pacific Rim. Democratic Colombia is a pageant of bloodletting, and many members of the middle class are attempting to leave the country.

Then there is Peru, where, all the faults of the present regime notwith-standing, a measure of stability has been achieved by a retreat from democracy into quasi-authoritarianism.

Throughout Latin America there is anxiety that unless the middle classes are enlarged and institutions modernized, the wave of democrati-zation will not be consolidated. Even in an authentically democratic nation like Argentina, institutions are weak and both corruption and un-employment are high. President Carlos Menem's second term has raised questions about democracy's sustainability—questions that the success of his first term seemed to have laid to rest. In Brazil and other countries democracy faces a backlash from millions of badly educated and newly urbanized dwellers in teeming slums, who see few palpable benefits to Western parliamentary systems. Their discontent is a reason for the multifold increases in crime in many Latin American cities over the past decade.

Because both a middle class and civil institutions are required for suc-cessful democracy, democratic Russia, which inherited neither from the Soviet regime, remains violent, unstable, and miserably poor despite its 99 percent literacy rate. Under its authoritarian system China has dra-matically improved the quality of life for hundreds of millions of its peo-ple. My point, hard as it may be for Americans to accept, is that Russia may be failing in part because it is a democracy and China may be suc-ceeding in part because it is not. Having traveled through much of west-ern China, where Muslim Turkic Uighurs (who despise the Chinese) often predominate, I find it hard to imagine a truly democratic China without at least a partial breakup of the country. Such a breakup would lead to chaos in western China, because the Uighurs are poorer and less educated than most Chinese and have a terrible historical record of governing them-selves. Had the student demonstrations in 1989 in Tiananmen Square led to democracy, would the astoundingly high economic growth rates of the 1990s still obtain? I am not certain, because democracy in China would have ignited turmoil not just in the Muslim west of the country but else-where, too; order would have decreased but corruption would not have. The social and economic breakdowns under democratic rule in Albania and Bulgaria, where the tradition of pre-communist bourgeois life is weak or nonexistent (as in China), contrasted with more-successful democratic venues like Hungary and the Czech Republic, which have had well-estab-lished bourgeoisie, constitute further proof that our belief in democracy regardless of local conditions amounts to cultural hubris.

Look at Haiti, a small country only ninety minutes by air from Miami, where 22,000 American soldiers were dispatched in 1994 to restore "democracy." Five percent of eligible Haitian voters participated in an election last April, chronic instability continues, and famine threatens. Those who think that America can establish democracy the world over should heed the words of the late American theologian and political philosopher Reinhold Niebuhr:

> The same strength which has extended our power beyond a continent has also . . . brought us into a vast web of history in which other wills, running in oblique or contrasting directions to our own, inevitably hinder or contradict what we most fervently desire. We cannot simply have our way, not even when we believe our way to have the "happiness of mankind" as its promise.

The lesson to draw is not that dictatorship is good and democracy bad but that democracy emerges successfully only as a capstone to other social and economic achievements. In his "Author's Introduction" to *Democracy in America,* Tocqueville showed how democracy evolved in the West not through the kind of moral fiat we are trying to impose throughout the world but as an organic outgrowth of development. European society had reached a level of complexity and sophistication at which the aristocracy, so as not to overburden itself, had to confer a measure of equality upon other citizens and allocate some responsibility to them: a structured division of the population into peacefully competing interest groups was necessary if both tyranny and anarchy were to be averted.

The very fact that we retreat to moral arguments—and often moral arguments only—to justify democracy indicates that for many parts of the world the historical and social arguments supporting democracy are just not there. Realism has come not from us but from, for example, Uganda's President Yoweri Museveni, an enlightened Hobbesian despot whose country has posted impressive annual economic growth rates—10 percent recently—despite tribal struggles in the country's north. In 1986 Museveni's army captured the Ugandan capital of Kampala without looting a single shop; Museveni postponed elections and saw that they took place in a manner that ensured his victory. "I happen to be one of those people who do not believe in multi-party democracy," Museveni has written. "In fact, I am totally opposed to it as far as Africa today is concerned. . . . If one forms a multi-party system in Uganda, a party cannot win elections unless it finds a way of dividing the ninety-four percent of the electorate [that consists of peasants], and this is where the main problem comes up: tribalism, religion, or regionalism becomes the basis for intense partisanship." In other words, in a society that has not reached the level of development Tocqueville described, a multi-party system merely hardens and institutionalizes established ethnic and regional divisions. Look at Armenia and Azerbaijan, where democratic processes brought national-ists to power upon the demise of the Soviet Union: each leader furthered his country's slide into war. A coup in Azerbaijan was necessary to restore peace and, by developing Azerbaijan's enormous oil resources, foster eco-nomic growth. Without the coup Western oil companies would not have gained their current foothold, which has allowed the United States to increase pressure on neighboring Iran at the same time that we attempt to normalize relations with Iran "on our terms."

Certainly, moral arguments in support of democracy were aired at the 1787 Constitutional Convention in Philadelphia, but they were tempered by the kind of historical and social analysis we now abjure. "The Consti-tution of the United States was written by fifty-five men—and one ghost," writes retired Army Lieutenant General Dave R. Palmer in *1794: Amer-ica, Its Army, and the Birth of the Nation* (1994). The ghost was that of Oliver Cromwell, the archetypal man on horseback who, in the course of defending Parliament against the monarchy in the mid seventeenth cen-tury, devised a tyranny worse than any that had ever existed under the English Kings. The Founders were terrified of a badly educated populace that could be duped by a Cromwell, and of a system that could allow too much power to fall into one person's hands. That is why they constructed a system that filtered the whims of the masses through an elected body and dispersed power by dividing the government into three branches.

The ghosts of today we ignore—like the lesson offered by Rwanda, where the parliamentary system the West promoted was a factor in the murder of hundreds of thousands of Tutsis by Hutu militias. In 1992, responding partly to pressure from Western governments, the Rwandan regime established a multi-party system and transformed itself into a coalition government. The new political parties became masks for ethnic groups that organized murderous militias, and the coalition nature of the new government helped to prepare the context for the events that led to the genocide in 1994. Evil individuals were certainly responsible for the mass murder. But they operated within a fatally flawed system, which our own ethnocentric hubris helped to construct. Indeed, our often moralistic attempts to impose Western parliamentary systems on other countries are not dissimilar to the attempts of nineteenth-century West-ern colonialists—many of whom were equally idealistic—to replace well-functioning chieftaincy and tribal patronage systems with foreign administrative practices.

The demise of the Soviet Union was no reason for us to pressure Rwanda and other countries to form political parties—though that is what our post–Cold War foreign policy has been largely about, even in parts of the world that the Cold War barely touched. The Eastern European countries liberated in 1989 already had, in varying degrees, the historical and social preconditions for both democracy and advanced industrial life: bourgeois traditions, exposure to the Western Enlightenment, high literacy rates, low birth rates, and so on. The post–Cold War effort to bring democracy to those countries has been reasonable. What is less reasonable is to put a gun to the head of the peoples of the developing world and say, in effect, "Behave as if you had experienced the Western Enlightenment to the degree that Poland and the Czech Republic did. Behave as if 95 percent of your population were literate. Behave as if you had no bloody ethnic or regional disputes."

States have never been formed by elections. Geography, settlement patterns, the rise of literate bourgeoisie, and, tragically, ethnic cleansing have formed states. Greece, for instance, is a stable democracy partly because earlier in the century it carried out a relatively benign form of ethnic cleansing—in the form of refugee transfers—which created a monoethnic society. Nonetheless, it took several decades of economic development for Greece finally to put its coups behind it. Democracy often weakens states by necessitating ineffectual compromises and fragile coalition governments in societies where bureaucratic institutions never functioned well to begin with. Because democracy neither forms states nor strengthens them initially, multi-party systems are best suited to nations that already have efficient bureaucracies and a middle class that pays income tax, and where primary issues such as borders and power-sharing have already been resolved, leaving politicians free to bicker about the budget and other secondary matters.

Social stability results from the establishment of a middle class. Not democracies but authoritarian systems, including monarchies, create middle classes—which, having achieved a certain size and self-confidence, revolt against the very dictators who generated their prosperity. This is the pattern today in the Pacific Rim and the southern cone of South America, but not in other parts of Latin America, southern Asia, or sub-Saharan Africa. A place like the Democratic Republic of Congo (formerly Zaire), where the per capita gross national product is less than $200 a year and the average person is either a rural peasant or an urban peasant; where there is little infrastructure of roads, sewers, and so on; and where reliable bureaucratic institutions are lacking, needs a leader like Bismarck or Jerry Rawlings—the Ghanaian ruler who stabilized his country through dictatorship and then had himself elected democratically—in place for years before he is safe from an undisciplined soldiery.

Foreign correspondents in sub-Saharan Africa who equate democracy with progress miss this point, ignoring both history and centuries of political philosophy. They seem to think that the choice is between dictators and democrats. But for many places the only choice is between bad dictators and slightly better ones. To force elections on such places may give us some instant gratification. But after a few months or years a bunch of soldiers with grenades will get bored and greedy, and will easily topple their fledgling democracy. As likely as not, the democratic government will be composed of corrupt, bickering, ineffectual politicians whose weak rule never had an institutional base to start with: modern bureaucracies generally require high literacy rates over several generations. Even India, the great exception that proves the rule, has had a mixed record of success as a democracy, with Bihar and other poverty-wracked places remaining in semi-anarchy. Ross Munro, a noted Asia expert, has documented how Chinese autocracy has better prepared China's population for the economic rigors of the post-industrial age than Indian democracy has prepared India's.

Of course, our post–Cold War mission to spread democracy is partly a pose. In Egypt and Saudi Arabia, America's most important allies in the energy-rich Muslim world, our worst nightmare would be free and fair elections, as it would be elsewhere in the Middle East. The end of the Cold War has changed our attitude toward those authoritarian regimes that are not crucial to our interests—but not toward those that are. We praise democracy, and meanwhile we are grateful for an autocrat like King Hussein, and for the fact that the Turkish and Pakistani militaries have always been the real powers behind the "democracies" in their countries. Obviously, democracy in the abstract encompasses undeniably good things such as civil society and a respect for human rights. But as a matter of public policy it has unfortunately come to focus on elections. What is in fact happening in many places requires a circuitous explanation.

The New Authoritarianism

The battle between liberal and neoconservative moralists who are concerned with human rights and tragic realists who are concerned with security, balance-of-power politics, and economic matters (famously, Henry Kissinger) is a variation of a classic dispute between two great English philosophers—the twentieth-century liberal humanist Isaiah Berlin and the seventeenth-century monarchist and translator of Thucydides, Thomas Hobbes.

In May of 1953, while the ashes of the Nazi Holocaust were still smoldering and Stalin's grave was fresh, Isaiah Berlin delivered a spirited lecture against "historical inevitability"—the whole range of belief, advocated by Hobbes and others, according to which individuals and their societies are determined by their past, their civilization, and even their biology and environment. Berlin argued that adherence to historical inevitability, so disdainful of the very characteristics that make us human, led to Nazism and communism—both of them extreme attempts to force a direction onto history. Hobbes is just one of many famous philosophers Berlin castigated in his lecture, but it is Hobbes's bleak and elemental philosophy that most conveniently sums up what Berlin and other moralists so revile. Hobbes suggested that even if human beings are nobler than apes, they are nevertheless governed by biology and environment. According to Hobbes, our ability to reason is both a mask for and a slave to our passions, our religions arise purely from fear, and theories about our divinity must be subordinate to the reality of how we behave. Enlightened despotism is thus preferable to democracy: the masses require protection from themselves. Hobbes, who lived through the debacle of parliamentary rule under Cromwell, published his translation of Thucydides in order, he said, to demonstrate how democracy, among other factors, was responsible for Athens's decline. Reflecting on ancient Athens, the philosopher James Harrington, a contemporary and follower of Hobbes, remarked that he could think of "nothing more dangerous" than "debate in a crowd."

Though the swing toward democracy following the Cold War was a triumph for liberal philosophy, the pendulum will come to rest where it belongs—in the middle, between the ideals of Berlin and the realities of Hobbes. Where a political system leans too far in either direction, realignment or disaster awaits.

In 1993 Pakistan briefly enjoyed the most successful period of governance in its history. The government was neither democratic nor authoritarian but a cross between the two. The unelected Prime Minister, Moin Qureshi, was chosen by the President, who in turn was backed by the military. Because Qureshi had no voters to please, he made bold moves that restored political stability and economic growth. Before Qureshi there had been violence and instability under the elected governments of Benazir Bhutto and Nawaz Sharif. Bhutto's government was essentially an ethnic-Sindhi mafia based in the south; Sharif's was an ethnic-Punjabi mafia from the geographic center. When Qureshi handed the country back to "the people," elections returned Bhutto to power, and chaos resumed. Finally, in November of last year, Pakistan's military-backed President again deposed Bhutto. The sigh of relief throughout the country was audible. Recent elections brought Sharif, the Punjabi, back to power. He is governing better than the first time, but communal violence has returned to Pakistan's largest city, Karachi. I believe that Pakistan must find its way back to a hybrid regime like the one that worked so well in 1993; the other options are democratic anarchy and military tyranny. (Anarchy and tyranny, of course, are closely related: because power abhors a vacuum, the one necessarily leads to the other. One day in 1996 Kabul, the Afghan capital, was ruled essentially by no one; the next day it was ruled by Taliban, an austere religious movement.)

Turkey's situation is similar to Pakistan's. During the Cold War, Turkey's military intervened when democracy threatened mass violence, about once every decade. But Turkish coups are no longer tolerated by the West, so Turkey's military has had to work behind the scenes to keep civilian governments from acting too irrationally for our comfort and that of many secular Turks. As elected governments in Turkey become increasingly circumscribed by the army, a quieter military paternalism is likely to evolve in place of periodic coups. The crucial element is not the name the system goes by but how the system actually works.

Peru offers another version of subtle authoritarianism. In 1990 Peruvian voters elected Alberto Fujimori to dismantle parts of their democracy. He did, and as a consequence he restored a measure of civil society to Peru. Fujimori disbanded Congress and took power increasingly into his own hands, using it to weaken the Shining Path guerrilla movement, reduce inflation from 7,500 percent to 10 percent, and bring investment and jobs back to Peru. In 1995 Fujimori won re-election with three times as many votes as his nearest challenger. Fujimori's use of deception and corporate-style cost-benefit analyses allowed him to finesse brilliantly the crisis caused by the terrorist seizure of the Japanese embassy in Lima. The commando raid that killed the terrorists probably never could have taken place amid the chaotic conditions of the preceding Peruvian government. Despite the many problems Fujimori has had and still has, it is hard to argue that Peru has not benefited from his rule.

In many of these countries Hobbesian realities—in particular, too many young, violence-prone males without jobs—have necessitated radical action. In a York University study published last year the scholars Christian G. Mesquida and Neil I. Wiener demonstrate how countries with young populations (young poor males especially) are subject to political violence. With Third World populations growing dramatically (albeit at slowing rates) and becoming increasingly urbanized, democrats must be increasingly ingenious and dictators increasingly tyrannical in order to rule successfully. Surveillance, too, will become more important on an urbanized planet; it is worth noting that the etymology of the word "police" is *polis,* Greek for "city." Because tottering democracies and despotic militaries frighten away the investors required to create jobs for violence-prone youths, more hybrid regimes will perforce emerge. They will call themselves democracies, and we may go along with the lie—but, as in Peru, the regimes will be decisively autocratic. (Hobbes wrote that Thucydides "praiseth the government of Athens, when . . . it was democratical in name, but in effect monarchical under Pericles." Polybius, too, recommended mixed regimes as the only stable form of government.) Moreover, if a shortage of liquidity affects world capital markets by 2000, as Klaus Schwab, the president of the World Economic Forum, and other experts fear may happen, fiercer competition among developing nations for scarcer investment money will accelerate the need for efficient neo-authoritarian governments.

The current reality in Singapore and South Africa, for instance, shreds our democratic certainties. Lee Kuan Yew's offensive neo-authoritarianism, in which the state has evolved into a corporation that is paternalistic, meritocratic, and decidedly undemocratic, has forged prosperity from abject poverty. A survey of business executives and economists by the World Economic Forum ranked Singapore No. 1 among the fifty-three most advanced countries appearing on an index of global competitiveness. What is good for business executives is often good for the average citizen: per capita wealth in Singapore is nearly equal to that in Canada, the nation that ranks No. 1 in the world on the United Nations' Human Development Index. When Lee took over Singapore, more than thirty years ago, it was a mosquito-ridden bog filled with slum quarters that frequently lacked both plumbing and electricity. Doesn't liberation from filth and privation count as a human right? Jeffrey Sachs, a professor of international trade at Harvard, writes that "good government" means relative safety from corruption, from breach of contract, from property expropriation, and from bureaucratic inefficiency. Singapore's reputation in these regards is unsurpassed. If Singapore's 2.8 million citizens ever demand democracy, they will just prove the assertion that prosperous middle classes arise under authoritarian regimes before gaining the confidence to dislodge their benefactors. Singapore's success is frightening, yet it must be acknowledged.

Democratic South Africa, meanwhile, has become one of the most violent places on earth that are not war zones, according to the security firm Kroll Associates. The murder rate is six times that in the United States, five times that in Russia. There are ten private-security guards for every policeman. The currency has substantially declined, educated people continue to flee, and international drug cartels have made the country a new transshipment center. Real unemployment is about 33 percent, and is probably much higher among youths. Jobs cannot be created without the cooperation of foreign investors, but assuaging their fear could require the kind of union-busting and police actions that democracy will not permit. The South African military was the power behind the regime in the last decade of apartheid. And it is the military that may yet help to rule South Africa in the future. Like Pakistan but more so, South Africa is destined for a hybrid regime if it is to succeed. The abundant coverage of South Africa's impressive attempts at coming to terms with the crimes of apartheid serves to obscure the country's growing problems. There is a sense of fear in such celebratory, backward-looking coverage, as if writing too much about difficulties in that racially symbolic country would expose the limits of the liberal humanist enterprise worldwide.

Burma, too, may be destined for a hybrid regime, despite the deification of the opposition leader and Nobel Peace laureate Aung San Suu Kyi by Western journalists. While the United States calls for democracy in and economic sanctions against Burma, those with more immediate clout—that is, Burma's Asian neighbors, and especially corporate-oligarchic militaries like Thailand's—show no compunction about increasing trade links with Burma's junta. Aung San Suu Kyi may one day bear the title of leader of Burma, but only with the tacit approval of a co-governing military. Otherwise Burma will not be stable. A rule of thumb is that governments are determined not by what liberal humanists wish but rather by what business people and others require. Various democratic revolutions failed in Europe in 1848 because what the intellectuals wanted was not what the emerging middle classes wanted. For quite a few parts of today's world, which have at best only the beginnings of a middle class, the Europe of the mid nineteenth century provides a closer comparison than the Europe of the late twentieth century. In fact, for the poorest countries where we now recommend democracy, Cromwell's England may provide the best comparison.

As with the Christian religion (whose values are generally different for Americans than for Bosnian Serbs or for Lebanese Phalangists, to take only three examples), the nominal system of a government is less significant than the nature of the society in which it operates. And as democracy sinks into the soils of various local cultures, it often leaves less-than-nourishing deposits. "Democracy" in Cambodia, for instance, began evolving into something else almost immediately after the UN-sponsored elections there, in 1993. Hun Sen, one of two Prime Ministers in a fragile coalition, lived in a fortified bunker from which he physically threatened journalists and awarded government contracts in return for big bribes. His coup last summer, which toppled his co–Prime Minister and ended the democratic experiment, should have come as no surprise.

"World Government"

Authoritarian or hybrid regimes, no matter how illiberal, will still be treated as legitimate if they can provide security for their subjects and spark economic growth. And they will easily find acceptance in a world driven increasingly by financial markets that know no borders.

For years idealists have dreamed of a "world government." Well, a world government has been emerging—quietly and organically, the way vast developments in history take place. I do not refer to the United Nations, the power of which, almost by definition, affects only the poorest countries. After its peacekeeping failures in Bosnia and Somalia—and its $2 billion failure to make Cambodia democratic—the UN is on its way to becoming a supranational relief agency. Rather, I refer to the increasingly dense ganglia of international corporations and markets that are becoming the unseen arbiters of power in many countries. It is much more important nowadays for the leader of a developing country to get a hearing before corporate investors at the World Economic Forum than to speak before the UN General Assembly. Amnesty International now briefs corporations, just as it has always briefed national governments. Interpol officials have spoken about sharing certain kinds of intelligence with corporations. The Prime Minister of Malaysia, Mahathir Mohamad, is recognizing the real new world order (at least in this case) by building a low-tax district he calls a "multimedia super-corridor," with two new cities and a new airport designed specifically for international corporations. The world's most efficient peacemaking force belongs not to the UN or even to the great powers but to a South African corporate mercenary force called Executive Outcomes, which restored relative stability to Sierra Leone in late 1995. (This is reminiscent of the British East India Company, which raised armies transparently for economic interests.) Not long after Executive Outcomes left Sierra Leone, where only 20.7 percent of adults can read, that country's so-called model democracy crumbled into military anarchy, as Sudan's model democracy had done in the late 1980s.

Of the world's hundred largest economies, fifty-one are not countries but corporations. While the 200 largest corporations employ less than three fourths of one percent of the world's work force, they account for

28 percent of world economic activity. The 500 largest corporations account for 70 percent of world trade. Corporations are like the feudal domains that evolved into nation-states; they are nothing less than the vanguard of a new Darwinian organization of politics. Because they are in the forefront of real globalization while the overwhelming majority of the world's inhabitants are still rooted in local terrain, corporations will be free for a few decades to leave behind the social and environmental wreckage they create—abruptly closing a factory here in order to open an unsafe facility with a cheaper work force there. Ultimately, as technological innovations continue to accelerate and the world's middle classes come closer together, corporations may well become more responsible to the cohering global community and less amoral in the course of their evolution toward new political and cultural forms.

For instance, ABB Asea Brown Boveri Ltd. is a $36 billion-a-year multinational corporation divided into 1,300 companies in 140 countries; no one national group accounts for more than 20 percent of its employees. ABB's chief executive officer, Percy Barnevik, recently told an interviewer that this diversity is so that ABB can develop its own "global ABB culture—you might say an umbrella culture." Barnevik explains that his best managers are moved around periodically so that they and their families can develop "global personalities" by living and growing up in different countries. ABB management teams, moreover, are never composed of employees from any one country. Barnevik says that this encourages a "cross-cultural glue." Unlike the multiculturalism of the left, which masks individual deficiencies through collective—that is, ethnic or racial—self-esteem, a multinational corporation like ABB has created a diverse multicultural environment in which individuals rise or fall completely on their own merits. Like the hybrid regimes of the present and future, such an evolving corporate community can bear an eerie resemblance to the oligarchies of the ancient world. "Decentralization goes hand in hand with central monitoring," Barnevik says.

The level of social development required by democracy as it is known in the West has existed in only a minority of places—and even there only during certain periods of history. We are entering a troubling transition, and the irony is that while we preach our version of democracy abroad, it slips away from us at home.

The Shrinking Domain of "Politics"

I put special emphasis on corporations because of the true nature of politics: who does and who doesn't have power. To categorize accurately the political system of a given society, one must define the significant elements of power within it. Supreme Court Justice Louis Brandeis knew this instinctively, which is why he railed against corporate monopolies. Of course, the influence that corporations wield over government and the economy is so vast and obvious that the point needs no elaboration. But there are other, more covert forms of emerging corporate power.

The number of residential communities with defended perimeters that have been built by corporations went from 1,000 in the early 1960s to more than 80,000 by the mid-1980s, with continued dramatic increases in the 1990s. ("Gated communities" are not an American invention. They are an import from Latin America, where deep social divisions in places like Rio de Janeiro and Mexico City make them necessary for the middle class.) Then there are malls, with their own rules and security forces, as opposed to public streets; private health clubs as opposed to public playgrounds; incorporated suburbs with strict zoning; and other mundane aspects of daily existence in which—perhaps without realizing it, because the changes have been so gradual—we opt out of the public sphere and the "social contract" for the sake of a protected setting. Dennis Judd, an urban-affairs expert at the University of Missouri at St. Louis, told me recently, "It's nonsense to think that Americans are individualists. Deep down we are a nation of herd animals: micelike conformists who will lay at our doorstep many of our rights if someone tells us that we won't have to worry about crime and our property values are secure. We have always put up with restrictions inside a corporation which we would never put up with in the public sphere. But what many do not realize is that life within some sort of corporation is what the future will increasingly be about."

Indeed, a number of American cities are re-emerging as Singapores, with corporate enclaves that are dedicated to global business and defended by private security firms adjacent to heavily zoned suburbs. For instance, in my travels I have looked for St. Louis and Atlanta and not found them. I found only hotels and corporate offices with generic architecture, "nostalgic" tourist bubbles, zoned suburbs, and bleak urban wastelands; there was nothing distinctive that I could label "St. Louis" or "Atlanta." [The 1996] Olympics in Atlanta will most likely be judged by future historians as the first of the postmodern era, because of the use of social façades to obscure fragmentation. Peace and racial harmony were continually proclaimed to be Olympic themes—even though whites and blacks in Atlanta live in separate enclaves and the downtown is a fortress of office blocks whose streets empty at dusk. During the games a virtual army was required to protect visitors from terrorism, as at previous Olympics, and also from random crime. All this seems normal. It is both wonderful and frightening how well we adapt.

Universities, too, are being redefined by corporations. I recently visited Omaha, where the corporate community made it possible for the Omaha branch of the University of Nebraska to build an engineering school— even after the Board of Regents vetoed the project. Local corporations, particularly First Data Resources, wanted the school, so they worked with the Omaha branch of the university to finance what became less a school than a large information-science and engineering complex. "This is the future," said the chancellor of the Omaha campus, Del Weber. "Universities will have to become entrepreneurs, working with corporations *on curriculum* [Kaplan's emphasis] and other matters, or they will die." The California state university system, in particular the San Diego campus, is perhaps the best example of corporate-academic synergy, in which a school rises in prestige because its curriculum has practical applications for nearby technology firms.

Corporations, which are anchored neither to nations nor to communities, have created strip malls, edge cities, and Disneyesque tourist bubbles. Developments are not necessarily bad: they provide low prices, convenience, efficient work forces, and, in the case of tourist bubbles, safety. We need big corporations. Our society has reached a level of social and technological complexity at which goods and services must be produced for a price and to a standard that smaller businesses cannot manage. We should also recognize, though, that the architectural reconfiguration of our cities and towns has been an undemocratic event—with decisions in effect handed down from above by an assembly of corporate experts.

"The government of man will be replaced by the administration of things," the Enlightenment French philosopher Henri de Saint-Simon prophesied. We should worry that experts will channel our very instincts and thereby control them to some extent. For example, while the government fights drug abuse, often with pathetic results, pharmaceutical corporations have worked *through* the government and political parties to receive sanction for drugs such as stimulants and anti-depressants, whose consciousness-altering effects, it could be argued, are as great as those of outlawed drugs.

The more appliances that middle-class existence requires, the more influence their producers have over the texture of our lives. Of course, the computer in some ways enhances the power of the individual, but it also depletes our individuality. A degree of space and isolation is required for a healthy sense of self, which may be threatened by the constant stream of other people's opinions on computer networks.

Democratic governance, at the federal, state, and local levels, goes on. But its ability to affect our lives is limited. The growing piles of our material possessions make personal life more complex and leave less time for communal matters. And as communities become liberated from geography, as well as more specialized culturally and electronically, they will increasingly fall outside the realm of traditional governance. Democracy loses meaning if both rulers and ruled cease to be part of a community tied to a specific territory. In this historical transition phase, lasting perhaps a century or more, in which globalization has begun but is not complete and loyalties are highly confused, civil society will be harder to maintain. How and when we vote during the next hundred years may be a minor detail for historians.

True, there are strong similarities between now and a century ago. In the 1880s and 1890s America experienced great social and economic upheaval. The combination of industrialization and urbanization shook the roots of religious and family life: sects sprouted, racist Populists ranted, and single women, like Theodore Dreiser's Sister Carrie, went to work in filthy factories. Racial tensions hardened as the Jim Crow system took hold across the South. "Gadgets" like the light bulb and the automobile brought an array of new choices and stresses. "The city was so big, now, that people disappeared into it unnoticed," Booth Tarkington lamented in *The Magnificent Ambersons*.

A hundred years ago millionaires' mansions arose beside slums. The crass accumulation of wealth by a relatively small number of people gave the period its name—the Gilded Age, after a satire by Mark Twain and Charles Dudley Warner about financial and political malfeasance. Around the turn of the century 12 percent of all American households controlled about 86 percent of the country's wealth.

But there is a difference, and not just one of magnitude. The fortunes made from the 1870s through the 1890s by John D. Rockefeller, Andrew Carnegie, J. P. Morgan, and others were *American* fortunes, anchored to a specific geographic space. The Gilded Age millionaires financed an economy of scale to fit the vast landscape that Abraham Lincoln had secured by unifying the nation in the 1860s. These millionaires funded libraries and universities and founded symphony orchestras and historical societies to consolidate their own civilization in the making. Today's fortunes are being made in a global economic environment in which an affluent global civilization and power structure are being forged even as a large stratum of our society remains rooted in place. A few decades hence it may be hard to define an "American" city.

Even J. P. Morgan was limited by the borders of the nation-state. But in the future who, or what, will limit the likes of Disney chairman Michael Eisner? The UN? Eisner and those like him are not just representatives of the "free" market. Neither the Founders nor any of the early modern philosophers ever envisioned that the free market would lead to the concentration of power and resources that many corporate executives already embody. Whereas the liberal mistake is to think that there is a program or policy to alleviate every problem in the world, the conservative flaw is to be vigilant against concentrations of power in government only—not in the private sector, where power can be wielded more secretly and sometimes more dangerously.

Umpire Regimes

This rise of corporate power occurs more readily as the masses become more indifferent and the elite less accountable. Material possessions not only focus people toward private and away from communal life but also encourage docility. The more possessions one has, the more compromises one will make to protect them. The ancient Greeks said that the slave is someone who is intent on filling his belly, which can also mean someone who is intent on safeguarding his possessions. Aristophanes and Euripides, the late-eighteenth-century Scottish philosopher Adam Ferguson, and Tocqueville in the nineteenth century all warned that material prosperity would breed servility and withdrawal, turning people into, in Tocqueville's words, "industrious sheep."

In moderate doses, apathy is not necessarily harmful. I have lived and traveled in countries with both high voter turnouts and unstable politics; the low voter turnouts in the United States do not by themselves worry me. The philosopher James Harrington observed that the very indifference of most people allows for a calm and healthy political climate. Apathy, after all, often means that the political situation is healthy enough to be ignored. The last thing America needs is more voters—particularly badly educated and alienated ones—with a passion for politics. But when voter turnout decreases to around 50 percent at the same time that the middle class is spending astounding sums in gambling casinos and state lotteries, joining private health clubs, and using large amounts of stimulants and anti-depressants, one can legitimately be concerned about the state of American society.

I recently went to a basketball game at the University of Arizona. It was just a scrimmage, not even a varsity game. Yet the stadium was jammed, and three groups of cheerleaders performed. Season tickets were almost impossible to obtain, even before the team won the national championship. Donating $10,000 to $15,000 to the university puts one in a good position to accumulate enough points to be eligible for a season ticket, though someone could donate up to $100,000 and still not qualify. I have heard that which spouse gets to keep tickets can be a primary issue in Tucson divorce cases. I noticed that almost everyone in the stands was white; almost everyone playing was black. Gladiators in Rome were almost always of racial or ethnic groups different from the Romans. "There may be so little holding these southwestern communities together that a basketball team is all there is," a Tucson newspaper editor told me. "It's a sports team, a symphony orchestra, and a church rolled into one." Since neither Tucson nor any other southwestern city with a big state university can find enough talent locally, he pointed out, community self-esteem becomes a matter of which city can find the largest number of talented blacks from far away to represent it.

We have become voyeurs and escapists. Many of us don't play sports but love watching great athletes with great physical attributes. The fact that basketball and football and baseball have become big corporate business has only increased the popularity of spectator sports. Basketball in particular—so fluid, and with the players in revealing shorts and tank tops—provides the artificial excitement that mass existence "against instinct," as the philosopher Bertrand Russell labeled our lives, requires.

Take the new kind of professional fighting, called "extreme fighting," that has been drawing sellout crowds across the country. Combining boxing, karate, and wrestling, it has nothing fake about it—blood really flows. City and state courts have tried, often unsuccessfully, to stop it. The spectators interviewed in a CNN documentary on the new sport all appeared to be typical lower-middle and middle-class people, many of whom brought young children to the fights. Asked why they came, they said that they wanted to "see blood." The mood of the Colosseum goes together with the age of the corporation, which offers entertainment in place of values. The Nobel laureate Czeslaw Milosz provides the definitive view on why Americans degrade themselves with mass culture: "Today man believes that there is *nothing* in him, so he accepts *anything*, even if he knows it to be bad, in order to find himself at one with others, in order not to be alone." Of course, it is because people find so little in themselves that they fill their world with celebrities. The masses avoid important national and international news because much of it is tragic, even as they show an unlimited appetite for the details of Princess Diana's death. This willingness to give up self and responsibility is the sine qua non for tyranny.

The classicist Sir Moses Finley ended his austere and penetrating work *Politics in the Ancient World* (1983) with these words:

The ideology of a ruling class is of little use unless it is accepted by those who are being ruled, and so it was to an extraordinary degree in Rome. Then, when the ideology began to disintegrate within the elite itself, the consequence was not to broaden the political liberty among the citizenry but, on the contrary, to destroy it for everyone.

So what about our ruling class?

I was an expatriate for many years. Most expatriates I knew had utopian liberal beliefs that meant little, since few of them had much of a real stake in any nation. Their patriotism was purely nostalgic: a French friend would become tearful when her national anthem was played, but whenever she returned to France, she complained nonstop about the French. Increasingly, though, one can be an expatriate without living abroad. One can have Oriental rugs, foreign cuisines, eclectic tastes, exposure to foreign languages, friends overseas with whom one's life increasingly intertwines, and special schools for the kids—all at home. Resident expatriatism, or something resembling it, could become the new secular religion of the upper-middle and upper classes, fostered by communications technology. Just as religion was replaced by nationalism at the end of the Middle Ages, at the end of modern times nationalism might gradually be replaced by a combination of traditional religion, spiritualism, patriotism directed toward the planet rather than a specific country, and assorted other organized emotions. Resident expatriates might constitute an elite with limited geographic loyalty beyond their local communities, which provide them with a convenient and aesthetically pleasing environment.

An elite with little loyalty to the state and a mass society fond of gladiator entertainments form a society in which corporate Leviathans rule and democracy is hollow. James Madison in *The Federalist* considered a comparable situation. Madison envisioned an enormously spread-out nation, but he never envisioned a modern network of transportation that would allow us psychologically to inhabit the same national community. Thus his vision of a future United States was that of a vast geographic space with governance but without patriotism, in which the state would be a mere "umpire," refereeing among competing interests. Regional, religious, and communal self-concern would bring about overall stability. This concept went untested, because a cohesive American identity and culture did take root. But as Americans enter a global community, and as class and racial divisions solidify, Madison's concept is relevant anew.

There is something postmodern about this scenario, with its blend of hollow governance and fragmentation, and something ancient, too.

Because of suburbanization, American communities will be increasingly segregated by race and class. The tendency both toward compromise and toward trusting institutions within a given community will be high, as in small and moderately sized European countries today, or as in ancient Greek city-states. Furthermore, prosperous suburban sprawls such as western St. Louis and western Omaha, and high-technology regions such as the Tucson-Phoenix corridor, North Carolina's Research Triangle, and the Portland-Seattle-Vancouver area will compete with one another and with individual cities and states for overseas markets, as North America becomes a more peaceful and productive version of chaotic, warring city-state Greece.

A continental regime must continue to function, because America's edge in information warfare requires it, both to maintain and to lead a far-flung empire of sorts, as the Athenians did during the Peloponnesian War. But trouble awaits us, if only because the "triumph" of democracy in the developing world will cause great upheavals before many places settle into more practical—and, it is to be hoped, benign—hybrid regimes. In the Middle East, for instance, countries like Syria, Iraq, and the Gulf sheikhdoms—with artificial borders, rising populations, and rising numbers of working-age youths—will not instantly become stable democracies once their absolute dictators and medieval ruling families pass from the scene. As in the early centuries of Christianity, there will be a mess.

Given the surging power of corporations, the gladiator culture of the masses, and the ability of the well-off to be partly disengaged from their own countries, what will democracy under an umpire regime be like?

The Return of Oligarchy?

Surprisingly, the Founders admired the military regime of Sparta. Only in this century has Sparta been seen as the forerunner of a totalitarian state. Why shouldn't men like Madison and George Washington have admired Sparta? Its division of power among two Kings, the elders, and the *ephors* ("overseers") approximated the system of checks and balances that the Founders desired in order to prevent the emergence of another Cromwell. Of course, Sparta, like Athens, was a two-tiered system, with an oligarchic element that debated and decided issues and a mass—*helots* ("serfs") in Sparta, and slaves and immigrants in Athens—that had few or no rights. Whether Sparta was a monarchy, an oligarchy, or a limited democracy— and whether Athens was oligarchic or democratic—still depends on one's viewpoint. According to Aristotle, "Whether the few or the many rule is accidental to oligarchy and democracy—the rich are few everywhere, the poor many." The real difference, he wrote, is that "oligarchy is to the advantage of the rich, democracy to the advantage of the poor." By "poor" Aristotle meant laborers, landowning peasants, artisans, and so on—essentially, the middle class and below.

Is it not conceivable that corporations will, like the rulers of both Sparta and Athens, project power to the advantage of the well-off while satisfying the twenty-first-century servile populace with the equivalent of bread and circuses? In other words, the category of politics we live with may depend more on power relationships and the demeanor of our society than on whether we continue to hold elections. Just as Cambodia was never really democratic, despite what the State Department and the UN told us, in the future we may not be democratic, despite what the government and media increasingly dominated by corporations tell us.

Indeed, the differences between oligarchy and democracy and between ancient democracy and our own could be far subtler than we think. Modern democracy exists within a thin band of social and economic conditions, which include flexible hierarchies that allow people to move up and down the ladder. Instead of clear-cut separations between classes there are many gray shades, with most people bunched in the middle. Democracy is a fraud in many poor countries outside this narrow band: Africans want a better life and instead have been given the right to vote. As new and intimidating forms of economic and social stratification appear in a world based increasingly on the ability to handle and analyze large quantities of information, a new politics might emerge for us, too—less like the kind envisioned by progressive reformers and more like the pragmatic hybrid regimes that are bringing prosperity to developing countries.

The classicist Sir Moses Finley has noted that what really separated the rulers from the ruled in the ancient world was literacy: the illiterate masses were subject to the elite's interpretation of documents. Analogous gulfs between rulers and ruled may soon emerge, not only because of differing abilities to process information and to master technology but also because of globalization itself. Already, barely literate Mexicans on the U.S. border, working in dangerous, Dickensian conditions to produce our VCRs, jeans, and toasters, earn less than 50 cents an hour, with no rights or benefits. Is that Western democracy or ancient-Greek-style oligarchy?

As the size of the U.S. population and the complexity of American life spill beyond the traditional national community, creating a new world of city-states and suburbs, the distance will grow between the citizens of the new city-states and the bureaucratic class of overseers in Washington. Those overseers will manage an elite volunteer military armed with information-age weapons, in a world made chaotic by the spread of democracy and its attendant neo-authoritarian heresies. We prevented the worst excesses of a "military-industrial complex" by openly fearing it, as President Dwight Eisenhower told us to do. It may be equally wise to fear a high-tech military complex today.

Precisely because the technological future in North America will provide so much market and individual freedom, this productive anarchy will require the supervision of tyrannies—or else there will be no justice for anyone. Liberty, after all, is inseparable from authority, as Henry Kissinger observed in *A World Restored: Metternich, Castlereagh, and the Problems of Peace 1812–1822* (1957). A hybrid regime may await us all. The future of the Third World may finally be our own.

And that brings us to a sober realization. If democracy, the crowning political achievement of the West, is gradually being transfigured, in part because of technology, then the West will suffer the same fate as earlier civilizations. Just as Rome believed it was giving final expression to the republican ideal of the Greeks, and just as medieval Kings believed they were giving final expression to the Roman ideal, we believe, as the early Christians did, that we are bringing freedom and a better life to the rest of humankind. But as the nineteenth-century Russian liberal intellectual Alexander Herzen wrote, "Modern Western thought will pass into history and be incorporated in it . . . just as our body will pass into the composition of grass, of sheep, of cutlets, and of men." I do not mean to say that the United States is in decline. On the contrary, at the end of the twentieth century we are the very essence of creativity and dynamism. We are poised to transform ourselves into something perhaps quite different from what we imagine.

PART THREE

CITIZENSHIP
AND CHARACTER

THIS SECTION presents three very different chapters by three very different philosophers. Each author makes a valuable contribution toward developing our understanding of the notion of democratic character.

The first of these authors is conservative British political philosopher Michael Oakeshott. In "The Masses in Representative Democracy," a chapter that originally appeared in 1961, Oakeshott offers us a look at the "mass man," someone who is marked by so exiguous an individuality that when he encounters "a powerful experience of individuality" he resorts to what Oakeshott calls "anti-individuality." Distinguished by his character (rather than by numbers), the "mass man," Oakeshott tells us, "has generated for himself an appropriate morality, an appropriate understanding of the office of government, and appropriate modifications of 'parliamentary government.'"

Oakeshott wrote in the shadow of the Cold War. Drawing on a vast sweep of European history, his argument may not be as accessible as some of the others presented in this volume. And because he is a cautious and meticulous philosopher, he must be read with particular care. But such an approach yields considerable rewards. In the end we are left to ask, If this "mass man" does indeed exist, what does his existence mean with respect to efforts to develop democratic character in the young?

Originally presented in an abbreviated version at Kappa Delta Pi's annual dinner in February 1937, Boyd H. Bode's "Reorientation in Education," reproduced in Chapter Seven, approaches democracy quite differently. In this piece, Bode, a philosopher and educator who was critical of the turn-of-the-century progressive education movement for failing to focus adequately on democracy as a way of life, argues that schools have an obligation not only to practice democracy but also to "develop the doctrine so as to make it serviceable as an intellectual basis for the organization of life."

Bode probably comes as close as anyone to exploring the essence of democratic character and the role of public education in a democratic society: "The school is, *par excellence,* the institution to which a democratic society is entitled to look for clarification of the meaning of democracy. In other words, the school is peculiarly the institution in which democracy becomes conscious of itself."

To Oakeshott's concept of the "mass man," and to Bode's recognition of democracy as "an intellectual basis for the organization of life," we add Martin Buber's idea of the "great character." Chapter Eight was originally presented as an address to the National Conference of Palestinian Teachers in Tel Aviv in 1939. A year earlier, Buber had been forced to migrate from Germany (where he had been the editor of *Der Jude,* the leading journal of German-speaking Jewish intellectuals) to Palestine because of his opposition to the Nazis. A philosopher and theologian, Buber begins "The Education of Character" with the bold assertion that "Education worthy of the name is essentially education of character." Although Buber does not speak specifically of democratic character, the connection is implied when he states, "Genuine education of character is genuine education for community."

To help develop our understanding of character, Buber introduces us to what he calls the "great character," whom he describes as someone "who by his actions and attitudes satisfies the claim of situations out of deep readiness to respond with his whole life, and in such a way that the sum of his actions and attitudes expresses at the same time the unity of his being in its willingness to accept responsibility." Buber's "great character" appears in many ways indistinguishable from what many of us are calling democratic character.

6

THE MASSES IN REPRESENTATIVE DEMOCRACY

Michael Oakeshott

One

THE COURSE OF MODERN EUROPEAN HISTORY has thrown up a character whom we are accustomed to call the "mass man." His appearance is spoken of as the most significant and far-reaching of all the revolutions of modern times. He is credited with having transformed our way of living, our standards of conduct and our manners of political activity. He is, sometimes regretfully, acknowledged to have become the arbiter of taste, the dictator of policy, the uncrowned king of the modern world. He excites fear in some, admiration in others, wonder in all. His numbers have made him a giant; he proliferates everywhere; he is recognized either as a locust who is making a desert of what was once a fertile garden, or as the bearer of a new and more glorious civilization.

All this I believe to be a gross exaggeration. And I think we should recognize what our true situation is in this respect, what precisely we owe to this character, and the extent of his impact, if we understood more clearly who this "mass man" is and where he has come from. And with a view to answering these questions, I propose to engage in a piece of historical description.

It is a long story, which has too often been made unintelligible by being abridged. It does not begin (as some would have us understand) with the French Revolution or with the industrial changes of the late eighteenth century; it begins in those perplexing centuries which, because of their illegibility, no historian can decide whether they should properly be regarded as a conclusion or a preface, namely the fourteenth and fifteenth centuries. And it begins, not with the emergence of the "mass man," but with an emergence of a very different kind, namely, that of the human individual in his modern idiom. You must bear with me while I set the scene for the entry of the character we are to study, because we shall mistake him unless we prepare ourselves for his appearance.

Two

There have been occasions, some of them in the distant past, when, usually as a consequence of the collapse of a closely integrated manner of living, human individuality has emerged and has been enjoyed for a time. An emergence of this sort is always of supreme importance; it is the modification not only of all current activities, but also of all human relationships from those of husband, wife and children to those of ruler and subject. The fourteenth and fifteenth centuries in western Europe were an occasion of this kind. What began to emerge, then, was conditions so preeminently favourable to a very high degree of human individuality, and human beings enjoying (to such a degree and in such numbers) the experience of "self-determination" in conduct and belief, that it overshadows all earlier occasions of the sort. Nowhere else has the emergence of individuals (that is, persons accustomed to making choices for themselves) either modified human relationships so profoundly, or proved so durable an experience, or provoked so strong a reaction, or explained itself so elaborately in the idiom of philosophical theory.

Like everything else in modern Europe, achievement in respect of human individuality was a modification of medieval conditions of life or thought. It was not generated in claims and assertions on behalf of individuality, but in sporadic divergencies from a condition of human circumstance in which the opportunity for choice was narrowly circumscribed. To know oneself as the member of a family, a group, a corporation, a church, a village community, as the suitor at a court or as the occupier of a tenancy, had been, for the vast majority, the circumstantially possible sum of self-knowledge. Not only were ordinary activities, those concerned with getting a living, communal in character, but so also were decisions, rights and responsibilities. Relationships and allegiances normally sprang from status and rarely extricated themselves from the analogy of kinship. For the most part anonymity prevailed; individual human character was rarely observed because it was not there to be observed. What differentiated one man from another was insignificant when compared with what was enjoyed in common as members of a group of some sort.

This situation reached something of a climax in the twelfth century. It was modified slowly, sporadically and intermittently over a period of about seven centuries, from the thirteenth to the twentieth century. The change began earlier and went more rapidly in some parts of Europe than in others; it penetrated some activities more readily and more profoundly than others; it affected men before it touched women; and during these seven centuries there have been many local climaxes and corresponding recessions. But the enjoyment of the new opportunities of escape from communal ties gradually generated a new idiom of human character.

It emerged first in Italy: Italy was the first home of the modern individual who sprang from the break-up of medieval communal life. "At the close of the thirteenth century," writes Burckhardt, "Italy began to swarm with individuality; the ban laid upon human personality was dissolved; a thousand figures meet us, each in his own special shape and dress." The *uomo singolare,* whose conduct was marked by a high degree of self-determination and a large number of whose activities expressed personal preferences, gradually detached himself from his fellows. And together with him appeared, not only the *libertine* and the *dilettante,* but also the *uomo unico,* the man who, in the mastery of his circumstances, stood alone and was a law to himself. Men examined themselves and were not dismayed by their own want of perfection. This was the character which Petrarch dramatized for his generation with unmatched skill and unrivalled energy. A new image of human nature appeared—not Adam, not Prometheus, but Proteus—a character distinguished from all others on account of his multiplicity and of his endless power of self-transformation.

North of the Alps, events took a similar course, though they moved more slowly and had to contend with larger hindrances. In England, in France, in the Netherlands, in Spain, in Switzerland, in Poland, Hungary and Bohemia, and particularly in all centres of municipal life, conditions favourable to individuality, and individuals to exploit them, appeared. There were few fields of activity untouched. By the middle of the sixteenth century they had been so firmly established that they were beyond the range of mere suppression: not all the severity of the Calvinist *régime* in Geneva was sufficient to quell the impulse to think and behave as an independent individual. The disposition to regard a high degree of individuality in conduct and in belief as the condition proper to mankind and as the main ingredient of human "happiness," had become one of the significant dispositions of modern European character. What Petrarch did for one century, Montaigne did for another.

The story of the vicissitudes of this disposition during the last four centuries is exceedingly complex. It is a story, not of steady growth, but of
climaxes and anti-climaxes, of diffusion to parts of Europe at first relatively ignorant of it, of extension to activities from which it was at first
excluded, of attack and defence, of confidence and of apprehension. But,
if we cannot pursue it in all its detail, we may at least observe how profoundly this disposition imposed itself upon European conduct and belief.
In the course of a few hundred years, it was magnified into an ethical and
even into a metaphysical theory, it gathered to itself an appropriate understanding of the office of government, it modified political manners and
institutions, it settled itself upon art, upon religion, upon industry and
trade and upon every kind of human relationship.

In the field of intellectual speculation the clearest reflection of this profound experience of individuality is to be seen in ethical theory. Almost
all modern writing about moral conduct begins with the hypothesis of an
individual human being choosing and pursuing his own directions of
activity. What appeared to require explanation was not the existence
of such individuals, but how they could come to have duties to others of
their kind and what was the nature of those duties, just as the existence
of other minds became a problem to those who understood knowledge as
the residue of sense experience. This is unmistakable in Hobbes, the first
moralist of the modern world to take candid account of the current experience of individuality. He understood a man as an organism governed by
an impulse to avoid destruction and to maintain itself in its own characteristic and chosen pursuits. Each individual has a natural right to independent existence: the only problem is how he is to pursue his own chosen
course with the greatest measure of success, the problem of his relation
to "others" of his kind. And a similar view of things appeared, of course,
in the writings of Spinoza. But even where an individualistic conclusion
was rejected, this autonomous individual remained as the starting point
of ethical reflection. Every moralist in the seventeenth and eighteenth centuries is concerned with the psychological structure of this assumed "individual": the relation of "self" and "others" is the common form of all
moral theory of the time. And nowhere is this seen more clearly to be the
case than in the writings of Kant. Every human being, in virtue of not being subject to natural necessity, is recognized by Kant to be a Person, an
end in himself, absolute and autonomous. To seek his own happiness is
the natural pursuit of such a person; self-love is the motive of the choices
which compose his conduct. But as a rational human being he will recognize in his conduct the universal conditions of autonomous personality; and the chief of these conditions is to use humanity, as well in himself

as in others, as an end and never as a means. Morality consists in the recognition of individual personality whenever it appears. Moreover, personality is so far sacrosanct that no man has either a right or a duty to promote the moral perfection of another: we may promote the "happiness" of others, but we cannot promote their "good" without destroying their "freedom" which is the condition of moral goodness.

In short, whatever we may think of the moral theories of modern Europe, they provide the clearest evidence of the overwhelming impact of this experience of individuality.

But this pursuit of individuality, and of the conditions most favourable to its enjoyment, was reflected also in an understanding of the proper office of government and in appropriate manners of governing and being governed, both modifications of an inheritance from the Middle Ages. We have time only to notice them in their most unqualified appearance, namely, in what we have come to call "modern representative democracy." This manner of governing and being governed appeared first in England, in the Netherlands and in Switzerland, and was later (in various idioms) extended to other parts of Western Europe and the United States of America. It is not to be understood either as an approximation to some ideal manner of government, or as a modification of a manner of government (with which it has no connection whatever) current for a short while in certain parts of the ancient world. It is simply what emerged in Western Europe where the impact of the aspirations of individuality upon medieval institutions of government was greatest.

The first demand of those intent upon exploring the intimations of individuality was for an instrument of government capable of transforming the interests of individuality into rights and duties. To perform this task government required three attributes. First, it must be single and supreme; only by a concentration of all authority at one centre could the emergent individual escape from the communal pressures of family and guild, of church and local community, which hindered his enjoyment of his own character. Secondly, it must be an instrument of government not bound by prescription and therefore with authority to abolish old rights and create new: it must be a "sovereign" government. And this, according to current ideas, means a government in which all who enjoyed rights were partners, a government in which the "estates" of the realm were direct or indirect participants. Thirdly, it must be powerful—able to preserve the order without which the aspirations of individuality could not be realized, but not so powerful as itself to constitute a new threat to individuality. In an earlier time, the recognized methods of transforming interests into rights had been judicial; the "parliaments" and "councils" of the middle ages had been pre-eminently judicial bodies. But from these "courts of law" emerged an instrument with more emphatic authority to recognize new interests by converting them into new rights and duties; there emerged legislative bodies. Thus, a ruler, and a parliament representative of his subjects, came to share the business of "making" law. And the law they made was favourable to the interests of individuality: it provided the detail of what became a well-understood condition of human circumstance, commonly denoted by the word "freedom." In this condition every subject was secured of the right to pursue his chosen directions of activity as little hindered as might be by his fellows or by the exactions of government itself, and as little distracted by communal pressures. Freedom of movement, of initiative, of speech, of belief and religious observance, of association and disassociation, of bequest and inheritance, security of person and property; the right to choose one's own occupation and dispose of one's labour and goods; and over all the "rule of law": the right to be ruled by a known law, applicable to all subjects alike. And these rights, appropriate to individuality, were not the privileges of a single class; they were the property of every subject alike. Each signified the abrogation of some feudal privilege.

This manner of governing, which reached its climax in the "parliamentary" government which emerged in England and elsewhere in the late eighteenth and early nineteenth centuries, was concurrently theorized in an understanding of the proper office of government. What had been a "community" came to be recognized as an "association" of individuals: this was the counterpart in political philosophy of the individualism that had established itself in ethical theory. And the office of government was understood to be the maintenance of arrangements favourable to the interests of individuality, arrangements (that is) which emancipated the subject from the "chains" (as Rousseau put it) of communal allegiancies, and constituted a condition of human circumstance in which the intimations of individuality might be explored and the experience of individuality enjoyed.

Briefly, then, my picture is as follows. Human individuality is an historical emergence, as "artificial" and as "natural" as the landscape. In modern Europe this emergence was gradual, and the specific character of the individual who emerged was determined by the manner of his generation. He became unmistakable when the habit appeared of engaging in activities identified as "private"; indeed, the appearance of "privacy" in human conduct is the obverse of the desuetude of the communal arrangements from which modern individuality spring. This experience of individuality provoked a disposition to explore its own intimations, to place the highest value upon it, and to seek security in its enjoyment. To enjoy it came to be recognized as the main ingredient of "happiness." The experience was magnified into an ethical theory, it was reflected in manners of governing and being governed, in newly acquired rights and duties and in a whole pattern of living. The emergence of this disposition to be an individual is the pre-eminent event in modern European history.

Three

There were many modest manners in which this disposition to be an individual might express itself. Every practical enterprise and every intellectual pursuit revealed itself as an assemblage of opportunities for making choices: art, literature, philosophy, commerce-industry and politics each came to partake of this character. Nevertheless, in a world being transformed by the aspirations and activities of those who were excited by these opportunities, there were some people, by circumstance or by temperament, less ready than others to respond to this invitation; and for many the invitation to make choices came before the ability to make them and was consequently recognized as a burden. The old certainties of belief, of occupation and of status were being dissolved, not only for those who had confidence in their own power to make a new place for themselves in an association of individuals, but also for those who had no such confidence. The counterpart of the agricultural and industrial *entrepreneur* of the sixteenth century was the displaced labourer; the counterpart of the *libertine* was the dispossessed believer. The familiar warmth of communal pressures was dissipated for all alike—an emancipation which excited some, depressed others. The familiar anonymity of communal life was replaced by a personal identity which was burdensome to those who could not transform it into an individuality. What some recognized as happiness, appeared to others as discomfort. The same condition of human circumstance was identified as progress and as decay. In short, the circumstances of modern Europe, even as early as the sixteenth century, bred, not a single character, but two obliquely opposed characters: not only that of the individual, but also that of the "individual *manqué*." And this "individual *manqué*" was not a relic of a past age; he was a "modern" character, the product of the same dissolution of communal ties as had generated the modern European individual.

We need not speculate upon what combination of debility, ignorance, timidity, poverty or mischance operated in particular cases to provoke this character; it is enough to observe his appearance and his efforts to accommodate himself to his hostile environment. He sought a protector who would recognize his predicament, and he found what he sought, in some measure, in "the government." From as early as the sixteenth century the governments of Europe were being modified, not only in response to the demands of individuality, but in response also to the needs of the "individual *manqué*." The "godly prince" of the Reformation and his lineal descendant, the "enlightened despot" of the eighteenth century, were political inventions for making choices for those indisposed to make choices for themselves; the Elizabethan Statute of Labourers was designed to take care of those who were left behind in the race.

The aspirations of individuality had imposed themselves upon conduct and belief and upon the constitutions and activities of governments, in the first place, as demands emanating from a powerful and confident disposition. There was little attempt to moralize these demands, which in the sixteenth century were clearly in conflict with current moral sentiment, still fixed in its loyalty to the morality of communal ties. Nevertheless, from the experience of individuality there sprang, in the course of time, a morality appropriate to it—a disposition not only to explore individuality but to approve of the pursuit of individuality. This constituted a considerable moral revolution: but such was its force and vigour that it not only swept aside the relics of the morality appropriate to the defunct communal order, but left little room for any alternative *to itself*. And the weight of this moral victory bore heavily upon the "individual *manqué*." Already outmanoeuvred in the field (in conduct), he now suffered a defeat at home, in his own character. What had been no more than a doubt about his ability to hold his own in a struggle for existence, became a radical self-distrust; what had been merely a hostile prospect, disclosed itself as an abyss; what had been the discomfort of ill-success was turned into the misery of guilt.

In some, no doubt, this situation provoked resignation; but in others it bred envy, jealousy and resentment. And in these emotions a new disposition was generated: the impulse to escape from the predicament by imposing it upon all mankind. From the frustrated "individual *manqué*" there sprang the militant "anti-individual," disposed to assimilate the world to his own character by deposing the individual and destroying his moral prestige. No promise, or even offer, of self-advancement could tempt this "anti-individual"; he knew his individuality was too poorly furnished to be explored or exploited with any satisfaction whatever. He was moved solely by the opportunity of complete escape from the anxiety of not being an individual, the opportunity of removing from the world all that convicted him of his own inadequacy. His situation provoked him to seek release in separatist communities, insulated from the moral pressure of individuality. But the opportunity he sought appeared fully when he recognized that, so far from being alone, he belonged to the most numerous class in modern European society, the class of those who had no choices of their own to make. Thus, in the recognition of his numerical superiority the "anti-individual" at once recognized himself as the "mass man" and discovered the way of escape from his predicament. For, although the "mass man" is specified by his dispositions—a disposition to allow in others only a replica of himself, to impose upon all a uniformity of belief and conduct that leaves no room for either the pains or the pleasures of choice—and not by his numbers, he is confirmed in this disposition by the support of others of his kind. He can have no friends (because friendship is a relation between individuals), but he has comrades. The "masses" as they appear in modern European history are not composed of individuals, they are composed of "anti-individuals" united in a revulsion from individuality. Consequently, although the remarkable growth of population in Western Europe during the last four hundred years is a condition of the success with which this character has imposed itself, it is not a condition of the character itself.

Nevertheless, the "anti-individual" had feelings rather than thoughts, impulses rather than opinions, inabilities rather than passions, and was only dimly aware of his power. Consequently, he required "leaders": indeed, the modern concept of "leadership" is a concomitant of the "anti-individual," and without him it would be unintelligible. An association of individuals requires a ruler, but it has no place for a "leader." The "anti-individual" needed to be told what to think; his impulses had to be transformed into desires, and these desires into projects; he had to be made aware of his power; and these were the tasks of his leaders. Indeed, from one point of view, "the masses" must be regarded as the invention of their leaders.

The natural submissiveness of the "mass man" may itself be supposed to have been capable of prompting the appearance of appropriate leaders. He was unmistakably an instrument to be played upon, and no doubt the instrument provoked the *virtuoso*. But there was, in fact, a character ready to occupy this office. What was required was a man who could at once appear as the image and the master of his followers; a man who could more easily make choices for others than for himself; a man disposed to mind other people's business because he lacked the skill to find satisfaction in minding his own. And these, precisely, were the attributes of the "individual *manqué*," whose achievements and whose failures in respect of individuality exactly fitted him for this task of leadership. He was enough of an individual to seek a personal satisfaction in the exercise of individuality, but too little to seek it anywhere but in commanding others. He loved himself too little to be anything but an egoist; and what his followers took to be a genuine concern for their salvation was in fact nothing more than the vanity of the almost selfless. No doubt the "masses" in modern Europe have had other leaders than this cunning frustrate who has led always by flattery and whose only concern is the exercise of power; but they have had none more appropriate—for he only had never prompted them to be critical of their impulses. Indeed, the "anti-individual" and his leader were the counterparts of a single moral situation; they relieved one another's frustrations and supplied one another's wants. Nevertheless, it was an uneasy partnership: moved by impulses rather than by desires, the "mass man" has been submissive but not loyal to his leaders: even the exiguous individuality of the leader has easily aroused his suspicion. And the leader's greed for power has disposed him to raise hopes in his followers which he has never been able to satisfy.

Of all the manners in which the "anti-individual" has imposed himself upon Western Europe two have been pre-eminent. He has generated a morality designed to displace the current morality of individuality; and he has evoked an understanding of the proper office of government and manners of governing appropriate to his character.

The emergence of the morality of the "anti-individual," a morality, namely, not of "liberty" and "self-determination," but of "equality" and "solidarity" is, of course, difficult to discern, but it is already clearly visible in the seventeenth century. The obscurity of its beginnings is due in part to the fact that its vocabulary was at first that of the morality of the defunct communal order; and there can be little doubt that it derived strength and plausibility from its deceptive affinity to that morality. But it was, in fact, a new morality, generated in opposition to the hegemony of individuality and calling for the establishment of a new condition of human circumstance reflecting the aspirations of the "anti-individual."

The nucleus of this morality was the concept of a substantive condition of human circumstance represented as the "common" or "public" good, which was understood not to be composed of the various goods that might be sought by individuals on their own account, but to be an independent entity. "Self-love," which was recognized in the morality of individuality as a legitimate spring of human activity, the morality of the "anti-individual" pronounced to be evil. But it was to be replaced, not by the love of "others," or by "charity" or by "benevolence" (which would have entailed a relapse into the vocabulary of individuality), but by the love of "the community."

Round this nucleus revolved a constellation of appropriate subordinate beliefs. From the beginning, the designers of this morality identified private property with individuality, and consequently connected its abolition with the condition of human circumstances appropriate to the "mass man." And further, it was appropriate that the morality of the "anti-individual" should be radically equalitarian: how should the "mass man," whose sole distinction was his resemblance to his fellows and whose salvation lay in the recognition of others as merely replicas of himself, approve of any divergence from an exact uniformity? All must be equal and anonymous units in a "community." And, in the generation of this morality, the character of this "unit" was tirelessly explored. He was understood as a "man" *per se,* as a "comrade," as a "citizen." But the most acute diagnosis, that of Proudhon, recognized him as a "debtor"; for in this notion what was asserted was not only the absence of distinction between the units who composed the "community" (all are alike "debtors"), but also a debt owed, not to "others" to but to the "community" itself: at birth he enters into an inheritance which he had played no part in accumulating, and whatever the magnitude of his subsequent contribution, it never equals what he has enjoyed: he dies necessarily insolvent.

This morality of the "anti-individual," the morality of a *solidarité commune,* began to be constructed in the sixteenth century. Its designers were mostly visionaries, dimly aware of their purposes, and lacking a large audience. But a momentous change occurred when the "anti-individual" recognized himself as the "mass man," and perceived the power that his numerical superiority gave him. The recognition that the morality of the "anti-individual" was, in the first place, the morality not of a sect of aspirants, but of a large ready-made class in society (the class, not of the "poor," but of those who by circumstance or by occupation had been denied the experience of individuality), and that in the interests of this class it must be imposed upon all mankind, appears unmistakably first in the writings of Marx and Engels.

Before the end of the nineteenth century, then, a morality of "anti-individualism" had been generated in response to the aspirations of the "mass man." It was, in many respects, a rickety construction: it never achieved a design comparable to that which Hobbes or Kant or Hegel gave the morality of individuality; and it has never been able to resist relapse into the inappropriate concepts of individuality. Nevertheless it throws back a tolerably clear reflection of the "mass man," who by this means became more thoroughly acquainted with himself. But we are not concerned with its merits or defects, we are concerned only to notice it as evidence of the

power with which the "mass man" has imposed himself on modern
Europe over a period of about four centuries. "Anti-individuality," long
before the nineteenth century, had established itself as one of the major
dispositions of the modern European moral character. And this disposition was evident enough for it to be recognized unequivocally by Sorel,
and to be identified by writers such as Nietzsche, Kierkegaard and
Burckhardt as the image of a new barbarism.

From the beginning (in the sixteenth century) those who exerted themselves on behalf of the "anti-individual" perceived that his counterpart, a
"community" reflecting his aspirations, entailed a "government" active in
a certain manner. To govern was understood to be the exercise of power
in order to impose and maintain the substantive condition of human circumstance identified as "the public good"; to be governed was, for the
"anti-individual," to have made for him the choices he was unable to
make for himself. Thus, "government" was cast for the rôle of architect
and custodian, not of "public order" in an "association" of individuals
pursuing their own activities, but of "the public good" of a "community."
The ruler was recognized to be, not the referee of the collisions of individuals, but the moral leader and managing director of "the community."
And this understanding of government has been tirelessly explored over
a period of four and a half centuries, from Thomas More's *Utopia* to the
Fabian Society, from Campanella to Lenin. But the leaders who served
the "mass man" were not merely theorists concerned to make his character intelligible in a moral doctrine and in an understanding of the office
of government; they were also practical men who revealed to him his
power and the manner in which the institutions of modern democratic
government might be appropriated to his aspirations. And if we call the
manner of government that had been generated by the aspirations of individuality "parliamentary government," we may call the modification of
it under the impact of the "mass man," "popular government." But it is
important to understand that these are two wholly different manners of
government.

The emergent individual in the sixteenth century had sought new rights,
and by the beginning of the nineteenth century the rights appropriate to
his character had, in England and elsewhere, been largely established. The
"anti-individual" observed these rights, and he was persuaded that his circumstances (chiefly his poverty) had hitherto prevented him from sharing
them. Hence the new rights called for on his behalf were, in the first place,
understood as the means by which he might come to participate in the
rights won and enjoyed by those he thought of as his better placed fellows. But this was a great illusion; first, because in fact he had these rights,

and secondly because he had no use for them. For the disposition of the "mass man" was not to become an individual, and the enterprise of his leaders was not to urge him in this direction. And what, in fact, prevented him enjoying the rights of individuality (which were as available to him as to anyone else) was not his "circumstances" but his character—his "anti-individuality." The rights of individuality were necessarily such that the "mass man" could have no use for them. And so, in the end, it turned out: what he came to demand were rights of an entirely different *kind*, and of a kind which entailed the abolition of the rights appropriate to individuality. He required the right to enjoy a substantive condition of human circumstance in which he would not be asked to make choices for himself. He had no use for the right to "pursue happiness"—that could only be a burden to him: he needed the right to "enjoy happiness." And looking into his own character he identified this with Security—but again, not security against arbitrary interference in the exercise of his preferences, but Security against having to make choices for himself and against having to meet the vicissitudes of life from his own resources. In short, the right he claimed, the right appropriate to his character, was the right to live in a social protectorate which relieved him from the burden of "self-determination."

But this condition of human circumstances was seen to be impossible unless it were imposed upon all alike. So long as "others" were permitted to make choices for themselves, not only would his anxiety at not being able to do so himself remain to convict him of his inadequacy and threaten his emotional security, but also the social protectorate which he recognized as his counterpart would itself be disrupted. The Security he needed entailed a genuine equality of circumstances imposed upon all. The condition he sought was one in which he would meet in others only a replica of himself: what he was, everybody must become.

He claimed this condition as a "right," and consequently he sought a government disposed to give it to him and one endowed with the power necessary to impose upon all activities the substantive pattern of activity called "the public good." "Popular government" is, precisely, a modification of "parliamentary government" designed to accomplish this purpose. And if this reading is correct, "popular government" is no more intimated in "parliamentary government" than the rights appropriate to the "anti-individual" are intimated in the rights appropriate to individuality: they are not complementary but directly opposed to one another. Nevertheless, what I have called "popular government" is not a concrete manner of government established and practised; it is a disposition to impose certain modifications upon "parliamentary government" in order to convert it into a manner of government appropriate to the aspirations of the "mass man."

This disposition has displayed itself in specific enterprises, and in less specific habits and manners in respect of government. The first great enterprise was the establishment of universal adult suffrage. The power of the "mass man" lay in his numbers, and this power could be brought to bear upon government by means of "the vote." Secondly, a change in the character of the parliamentary representative was called for: he must be not an individual, but a *mandataire* charged with the task of imposing the substantive condition of human circumstances required by the "mass man." "Parliament" must become a "work-shop," not a debating assembly. Neither of these changes was intimated in "parliamentary government"; both, in so far as they have been achieved, have entailed an assembly of a new character. Their immediate effect has been twofold: first, to confirm the authority of mere numbers (an authority alien to the practice of "parliamentary government"), and secondly, to give governments immensely increased power.

But the institutions of "parliamentary government" proved to have only a limited eligibility for conversion into institutions appropriate to serve the aspirations of the "mass man." And an assembly of instructed delegates was seen to be vulnerable to a much more appropriate contrivance—the *plébiscite.* Just as it lay in the character of the "mass man" to see everyman as a "public official," an agent of "the public good," and to see his representatives not as individuals but instructed delegates, so he saw every voter as the direct participant in the activity of governing: and the means of this was the *plébiscite.* An assembly elected on a universal adult suffrage, composed of instructed delegates and flanked by the device of the *plébiscite* was, then, the counterpart of the "mass man." They gave him exactly what he wanted: the illusion without the reality of choice; choice without the burden of having to choose. For, with universal suffrage have appeared the massive political parties of the modern world, composed not of individuals but of "anti-individuals." And both the instructed delegate and the *plébiscite* are devices for avoiding the necessity for making choices. The "mandate" from the beginning was an illusion. The "mass man," as we have seen, is a creature of impulses, not desires; he is utterly unable to draw up instructions for his representative to follow. What in fact has happened, whenever the disposition of "popular government" has imposed itself, is that the prospective representative has drawn up his own mandate and then, by a familiar trick of ventriloquism, has put it into the mouth of his electors: as an instructed delegate he is not an individual, and as a "leader" he relieves his followers of the need to make choices for themselves. And similarly, the *plébiscite* is not a method by which the "mass man" imposes his choices upon his rulers, it is a method of generating a government with unlimited authority to make choices on his behalf. In the *plébiscite* the "mass man" achieved final release from the burden of individuality: he was told emphatically what to choose.

Thus, in these and other constitutional devices, and in less formal habits of political conduct, was generated a new art of politics: the art, not of "ruling" (that is, of seeking the most practicable adjustments for the collisions of "individuals"), nor even of maintaining the support of a majority of individuals in a "parliamentary" assembly, but of knowing what offer will collect most votes and making it in such a manner that it appears to come from "the people"; the art, in short, of "leading" in the modern idiom. Moreover, it is known in advance what offer will collect the most votes: the character of the "mass man" is such that he will be moved only by the offer of release from the burden of making choices for himself, the offer of "salvation." And anyone who makes this offer may confidently demand unlimited power; it will be given him.

The "mass man," as I understand him, then, is specified by his character, not by his numbers. He is distinguished by so exiguous an individuality that when it meets a powerful experience of individuality it revolts into "anti-individuality." He has generated for himself an appropriate morality, an appropriate understanding of the office of government, and appropriate modifications of "parliamentary government." He is not necessarily "poor," nor is he envious only of "riches"; he is not necessarily "ignorant," often he is a member of the so-called *intelligentsia*; he belongs to a class which corresponds exactly with no other class. He is specified primarily by a moral, not an intellectual, inadequacy. He wants "salvation"; and in the end will be satisfied only with release from the burden of having to make choices for himself. He is dangerous, not on account of his opinions or desires, for he has none: but on account of his submissiveness. His disposition is to endow government with power and authority such as it has never before enjoyed: he is utterly unable to distinguish a "ruler" from a "leader." In short, the disposition to be an "anti-individual" is one to which every European man has a propensity; the "mass man" is merely one in whom this propensity is dominant.

Four

Of the many conclusions which follow from this reading of the situation the most important is to dispose of the most insidious of our current political delusions. It has been said, and it is commonly believed, that the event of supreme importance in modern European history is "the accession of the masses to complete social power." But that no such event has taken place is evident when we consider what it would entail. If it is true (as I have contended) that modern Europe enjoys two opposed moralities (that of individuality and that of the "anti-individual"), that it enjoys two opposed understandings of the office of government, and two corresponding interpretations of the current institutions of government, then, for the "mass man" to have won for himself a position of undisputed sovereignty would entail the complete suppression of what, in any reading, must be considered the strongest of our moral and political dispositions and the survival of the weakest. A world in which the "mass man" exercised "complete social power" would be a world in which the activity of governing was understood *solely* as the imposition of a single substantive condition of human circumstance, a world in which "popular government" had altogether displaced "parliamentary government," a world in which the "civil" rights of individuality had been abrogated by the "social" rights of anti-individuality—and there is no evidence that we live in such a world. Certainly the "mass man" has emerged and has signified his emergence in an appropriate morality and an appropriate understanding of the office of government. He has sought to transform the world into a replica of himself, and he has not been entirely unsuccessful. He has sought to enjoy what he could not create for himself, and nothing he has appropriated remains unchanged. Nevertheless, he remains an unmistakably derivative character, an emanation of the pursuit of individuality, helpless, parasitic and able to survive only in opposition to individuality. Only in the most favourable circumstances, and then only by segregating him from all alien influences, have his leaders been able to suppress in him an unquenched propensity to desert at the call of individuality. He has imposed himself emphatically only where the relics of a morality of communal ties survived to make plausible his moral and political impulses. Elsewhere, the modifications he has provoked in political manners and moral beliefs have been extensive, but the notion that they have effaced the morality of individuality and "parliamentary government" is without foundation. He loves himself too little to be able to dispose effectively of the only power he has, namely, his numerical superiority. He lacks passion rather than reason. He has had a past in which he was taught to admire himself and his antipathies; he has a present in which he is often the object of the ill-concealed contempt of his "leaders"; but the heroic future forecast him is discrepant with his own character. He is no hero.

On the other hand, if we judge the world as we find it (which includes, of course, the emergence of the "mass man") the event of supreme and seminal importance in modern European history remains the emergence of the human individual in his modern idiom. The pursuit of individuality has evoked a moral disposition, an understanding of the office of government and manners of governing, a multiplicity of activity and opinion and a notion of "happiness," which have impressed themselves indelibly upon European civilization. The onslaught of the "mass man" has shaken but not destroyed the moral prestige of individuality; even the "anti-individual," whose salvation lies in escape, has not been able to escape it. The desire of "the masses" to enjoy the products of individuality has modified their destructive urge. And the antipathy of the "mass man" to the "happiness" of "self-determination" easily dissolves into self-pity. At all important points the individual still appears as the substance and the "anti-individual" only as the shadow.

7

REORIENTATION IN EDUCATION

Boyd H. Bode

IT IS AGREED ON ALL HANDS that education is more than just a matter of learning facts and skills. The public interest is poorly served if attitudes and appreciations do not receive at least equal consideration. The things that are learned must translate themselves into terms of emotion and conduct if they are to be significant. Social theory must become a part of the bone and tissue of everyday life if it is to be more than an academic showpiece. In other words, education must make provision for the application of social theory to conduct if it is to escape from futility and frustration. Teaching democracy in the abstract is on a par with teaching swimming by correspondence.

This, however, raises a difficulty. If we grant that the present social order is still dominated extensively by the aristocratic tradition, it follows that the pupils in our schools, by the mere fact of living in this social order, are being nurtured in attitudes and habits that are incompatible with a genuinely democratic philosophy. The influences by which pupils are surrounded in their out-of-school life and which relate to their beliefs and standards of value are all but overpowering. How, as a matter of sober fact, can the schools hope to combat an enemy of this kind?

The question is not new. Even Plato in the dim and distant past struggled for an answer. The solution at which he arrived was sufficiently extraordinary to be classed as an emergency measure. To rid young people of the attitudes and beliefs which they had already acquired, he recommended the "royal lie." By means of pious and heroic prevarication, so Plato suggested, it is perhaps possible to convince young people that their previous experience never really happened at all, but was just a dream. The slate would then be wiped clean. In the language of physiology, it is supposed that the effects of previous experience can be wiped out of the nervous system of the pupils through the utterance of certain well-chosen words, and that the schools will then have their chance to build up desirable habits. A procedure of this kind would hardly be considered realistic at the present time. But what is the alternative?

Perhaps there is no completely satisfactory answer to this question, but we must do the best we can. Leaving aside for the moment the problem of what to do about the beliefs and attitudes which the pupil brings with him when he comes to school, we are bound to endorse Plato's insistence that the school must build up the attitudes and appreciations which are appropriate to its underlying philosophy. If this philosophy is a philosophy of democracy, the school must undertake to exemplify, in its organization and procedures, its conception of democratic living. This is necessary, not merely to promote a better intellectual understanding of democracy, but to create the conditions for transforming democratic precepts into established habits of feeling and willing. In brief, the school must be a place where pupils go, not merely to learn, but to carry on a way of life.

For present purposes the character of this way of life is all-important. It is precisely at this point that the progressive movement in education has shown its greatest weakness. It has indeed recognized and emphasized the central fact that learning and doing are knit together in an organic relationship, that education is not merely a preparation for future living but a form of present living. Its conception of present living, however, has been disturbingly obscure. To be significant, a way of life must be the expression of an inclusive outlook on life, of what the Germans call *Weltanschauung*. In the earlier American communities this *Weltanschauung* was embodied in the general patterns which formed the basis of community life. These patterns claimed absolute authority; and in order to escape from this rigidity progressive education had recourse to the device of converting the school into a separate community for the cultivation of a distinctive way of life. In organizing this way of life, however, progressive education has tended to take its clews, not from a distinctive social theory, but from what it conceived to be needs and interests of individual pupils. Or, to put it differently, it was so concerned to liberate pupils from the domination of dictatorial patterns that it was disposed to regard the elimination of this domination as the chief aim of education. There was no adequate social theory or "frame of reference" for judging and guiding educational procedures, and so ideas inevitably tended to run wild.

The reaction against dictatorial regimentation grew into a pious hostility against the whole idea of discipline; interest and freedom became identified with action guided by spontaneous impulse; "social development" was supposed to be achieved by playing up group activities, even to the point of making dependence on the group a substitute for personal development and self-reliance; and continuity of program in the curriculum went by the board for lack of a guiding principle. The undertow was in the direction of making the school, not a way of life, but a combination of clinic and playroom. It is true, of course, that the more sober minds in the movement checked these extravagancies by keeping in view considerations of common sense. But common sense is a name for the ability to maintain perspective, and the question at issue just now is, not how our perspective is to be maintained, but how it is to be changed and made more adequate.

The shift of emphasis from a one-sided preoccupation with the individual pupil to a concern for promoting a democratic way of life opens up a new approach, since it enables us to deal with education in terms of what community and individual owe to each other. The primary obligation of a democratic community to its members is to provide for each the opportunity to share in the common life according to interest and capacity. This is about what is meant by the doctrine of individual differences. Interest is of major importance as an indication of the road along which the initiation of the pupil into the larger surrounding life may best be achieved. But the concept of interest may never be converted into an excuse for permitting the pupil to ignore his responsibilities as a member of his group. He may not willfully disturb others; he may not be careless in handling school property; he may not permit himself to be undependable in his relations to others.

Obligations of this kind are in principle as binding on the child as they are on the adult. It is equally true, of course, that in dealing with offenses we must never lose sight of the fact that a child is not an adult. But appropriate "punishment" has a legitimate place. In the main, to be sure, the average young person learns to shape his conduct by reference to a continuously widening circle of experiences and he does so of his own initiative and not from fear of punishment. Instead of spending his pennies, for example, as fast as he acquires them, he learns to resist temptation so as to save them for some great occasion or to help out the family budget. This is "internal control," which is another name for self-discipline and which is at the heart of the educative process. It is no more true, however, of the child than it is of the adult that this is the only kind of discipline which can be tolerated. A willful offender tends to become incapable of seeing his conduct in true perspective if he invariably "gets away with it." Punishment of an appropriate kind enables the offender to see how his conduct is regarded by others, and for this reason it may be highly educative. Perhaps it is pertinent to mention that the Prodigal Son formed an entirely different opinion of himself after he had been thoroughly "disciplined" by fate. No community has ever been able to get along without taking some measures against those who willfully refuse to see the light. To justify itself punishment must, of course, "fit the crime," and it must be made for the enforcement of a principle which the offender can understand and of which he inwardly approves. If freedom consists in the power of acting with reference to a "widening circle of considerations," then the fact that a person is held to accountability for what he does is not inherently an interference with his freedom but may become a means for the realization of freedom.

The democratic school, in brief, is an institution which aims to promote the ideal of "free and equal" by taking proper account of individual differences and by reliance on the principle of community living. It is an artificial community in the sense that it does not spring up naturally but is created for a special purpose. This distinctive institution is necessary, both because the life outside of the school is too complex to be understood without some kind of simplification and reorganization, and also because this outside life is very far from being an ideal democratic social order. On the contrary, it tends to promote many beliefs and attitudes which are essentially undemocratic or anti-democratic. The materials of the school are drawn from the surrounding environment; the organization of these materials and the procedures of the school are designed with reference both to the discovery and exploitation of individual capacity and to a continuously deepening sense of membership in the social order. These two elements are indispensable in an educational application of the democratic doctrine that men are created free and equal.

There still remains, however, the problem raised by Plato, *viz.*, how we are to deal with the attitudes and appreciations which are fostered in young people by the life outside of the school. The more we insist on the contrast between adult society and the ideal society within a democratic school, the more serious this problem becomes. If we ignore the problem we are likely to find that pupils will develop two sets of habits, one for the school and one for out-of-school, pretty much as a businessman may develop different habits for his office and for his club. Many such men would be greatly surprised, and perhaps even offended, if they were expected to show the same courtesy and geniality and generosity toward their employees as they spontaneously exhibit at the club. They would point out promptly that business is not conducted that way. Perhaps it would not even occur to many pupils that the organization of the school is intended to give an indication [of] how the rest of society should be organized. The school in that case becomes a place where people behave in a distinctive way, just as they do in church or at the bathing beach. Unless such an outcome is prevented, the purpose of the school is largely defeated.

To adopt the alternative course by stressing the contrast between the organization of the school and the organization of the outside order likewise has its difficulties. The school in that case becomes a constant and annoying critic of the existing social order. Collisions in every direction become inevitable. To encourage immature pupils in habits of precocious criticism will hardly be tolerated. It is to be foreseen that society will not give continued support to an institution which it regards as hostile to itself.

Apparently we are confronted with a dilemma. The school can either resign itself to trivial nurse-maiding or it can accept the invitation to commit suicide. Either alternative means a confession of defeat. To attack the social order head-on and go down with the flag nailed to the mast may have its meed of glory, but it may easily do more harm than good. There must be some way around the difficulty, or else there is nothing left for the school except to continue its age-old function of drilling into the minds of the younger generation those patterns which are best adapted to the interests of the ruling class.

Let us remind ourselves that our problem centers on the fact that pupils bring to school certain beliefs and attitudes which have been built up in the outside environment and which do not fit acceptably into the philosophy that is adopted and practiced by a democratic school. These beliefs and attitudes all relate to fixed patterns or absolute standards of value, and so they have more kinship with the spirit of dictatorship than with the spirit of democracy. This discrepancy can neither be ignored nor can it be construed as a justification for an evangelistic campaign on the part of the schools. If the schools should start on a crusade for social reform, the irate citizen and parent would have reason for inquiring by what right the schoolmasters of the nation consider themselves commissioned to take the affairs of the whole country into their own hands. Perhaps the function of a teacher is not altogether clear, but at any rate the appointment to a teaching position does not mean either that the teacher must teach as he is told to teach by some power wielding legal authority nor that the teacher, by virtue of his office, must make it his business to impose his own personal philosophy on his pupils and on the social order.

Is there no other alternative? We can at least hold that the pupils coming to school are entitled to learn what the issue of fixed versus flexible patterns is all about. The cultural outlook which they unconsciously absorb is dominated throughout by fixed patterns—fixed patterns in religion, in ethics, in art, in science, in economics, and in government. They are in no position to realize that any other point of view is possible. If our present contention is sound, *viz.*, that the democratic point of view is a challenge to the whole mass of tradition, it follows that no school can claim to be truly democratic if it does not accept the clarification of this issue as a major responsibility.

The mistake that is likely to be made at this point is to assume that a pupil has achieved insight if he has become hostile to the existing order. The rejection of a fixed pattern or set of patterns is not the same as an understanding of the function of patterns in individual and collective living. Old habits are not laid aside so easily. The new doctrine becomes simply the raw material for the old habit of insisting that life must be ordered according to immutable patterns. Hence the typical revolutionist is likely to be as fiercely intolerant of any deviation from the true faith as the most violent reactionary. He has no patience with the slow process of evolution and no faith in it. White is white and black is black to him and so the whole present order stands condemned, while revolution becomes the only sensible method of progress. As the goal of revolution he envisages only the establishment of a new orthodoxy with all the old trimmings of supervision and control. "'We have come to bring you Liberty and Equality,' Marshal Lefebvre thundered the slogan of the Republic at the terrified burgomasters of Franconia, 'but don't let that go to your heads,' he warned, 'for the first one of you who makes a move without my permission will be shot.'"[*]

Perhaps something of this spirit is necessary for the successful conduct of a revolution. But it is basically opposed to the spirit of democracy, which is as hostile to one kind of tyranny as to another. As applied to education, the moral of the story is that progress lies not in the substitution of new names for old habits but in the transformation of old habits into a new quality of mind and heart. This is a much longer and harder undertaking than a summary brushing aside of old beliefs and old forms of conduct, but it cuts deeper and it marks off the most distinctive trait of a democratic system of education.

This process of reconstruction naturally must find its point of departure in the discovery by the pupil that the beliefs or patterns which he happens

---

[*] J. J. Smertenko, "The Radical's Betrayal," *Harper's Magazine,* July, 1935, p. 129.

to have acquired are inadequate, at least in the form in which they exist in his mind. Our previous discussion of democracy affords a convenient illustration. The tradition that government must govern as little as possible is still strong. This tradition, indeed, does not prevent us from having recourse to governmental interference in particular situations whenever this seems desirable in order to achieve specific ends. We levy tariffs, we forbid polygamy, we legislate for schools, and we view with equanimity the presence in Washington of a vast array of lobbies which represent all kinds of private interests. All this may be right and proper, but it hardly squares with the notion that the government is merely a kind of umpire or referee charged with the duty of seeing to it that the game is played according to the rules. The pattern does not cover the facts in the case. What, then, is the proper conception of government? Let us grant, at least for the moment, that the school is not authorized to answer this question. The school at least has the obligation to clear away the vagueness or obscurity which prevents us from seeing straight. No other social agency has quite the same obligation in this respect. To ignore this obligation is to defraud the pupil of his right to become intelligent and to enter into a conspiracy to support the good things as they are.

From government to citizenship is but a step. The true American, so the pupil has somehow learned, gives whole-hearted loyalty to our American institutions. But what the pupil has not yet learned is that he does not know what that means. In its extreme form it may be taken to mean that there must be no changes in such matters as the public control of private property, in the status of women, in the regulation of competition, of marriage and divorce and of labor disputes, or that Catholics, Jews and Negroes must be suppressed. All this is going rather far. But if the principle of regulation and of toleration is admitted, there must be some standard for distinguishing between sound and unsound regulation or toleration, just as there must be some standard for determining the proper functions of government. Reliance on "loyalty" means that the unsuspecting pupil is left holding the bag.

Essentially the same situation prevails all along the line. The average American holds to a pattern of "supernaturalism," which he assumes to be essential to religion. Just what this means, however, he does not know; and, what is much worse, he does not know that he does not know. He is quite unable to tell the difference between the "natural" and the "supernatural," and so he finds it necessary, in specific situations, to depend for guidance on familiar labels. The notion of art is associated in his mind with a certain body of materials which are accepted as "classical" and which, if he is properly docile, he struggles uncomplainingly to learn to like. Other materials have no claim on him until they have been properly certified by recognized authority. The upshot of it all is that he is governed by his habits and not by his intelligence. He may admire the great figures of history because they were rebels, against the tradition of their day, and at the same time regard every present-day rebel as a nuisance and a danger that should be suppressed. Thus tradition, like conscience, makes cowards of us all. The escape from this bondage does not lie in the substitution of one set of beliefs for another, but in providing the conditions for the free play of intelligence in the reconstruction of patterns. In educational terms this is the issue between dictatorship and democracy.

This emphasis on the reconstruction of habits does not conflict with specialization in any given field, but provides specialization with a new context and a new importance. Historical perspective takes on a new meaning and becomes quite indispensable. The scientific organization of subject matter in the natural sciences ceases to be a peculiarity to which research specialists are somehow addicted and becomes a way of viewing the universe which is seriously at variance with the assumptions of tradition. Each in its own way serves to set intelligence free for the improvement of human life.

But something more is still needed. It is not enough for a pupil to discover that his inherited attitudes or "patterns" are inadequate for the conditions of his social environment. Unless something more is offered, this discovery will either render him completely paralyzed or else will drive him back to a kind of desperate loyalty to old patterns as his only port in time of storm. At its worst this loyalty will take the form of refusing to think at all; at its best it will cling to the assumption that fixed patterns of an improved kind must somehow be obtained. Let us grant that for some, perhaps many, thoughtful pupils this will seem to be the best course to take. They will then emerge with a reconstructed outlook or way of life which is still based on fixed patterns but of a less narrow and bigoted kind. As a rule this will be a gain for democratic values, even though it does not mean the adoption of a genuinely democratic point of view. The result of such reconstruction will ordinarily mean that a greater range of human values is taken into account. Moreover, the pupil will have had valuable practice in the art of using his intelligence when confronted with new situations instead of relying on blind habit. A result of this kind must be accepted with good grace in a democratic school if the doctrine that the enduring values of education have to do with independent reconstruction of beliefs and attitudes is to be taken seriously. But it is hardly fair to the pupil to leave him no choice. He is entitled to have it pointed out to him that there is an alternative way of life which does not involve fixed patterns at all.

The school, therefore, is clearly under the obligation to show that democracy is a way of life which breaks sharply with the past. It must not merely practice democracy but must develop the doctrine so as to make it serviceable as an intellectual basis for the organization of life. To achieve this end it must utilize the concept of democracy so as to secure continuity of program, which up to the present has been so conspicuously lacking in the progressive movement. The idea of democracy, consequently, cannot be disposed of by dealing with it in a separate course and at some fixed point in the curriculum. Just as the reconstruction of patterns or outlook is a constant concern throughout the school program, so the meaning of democracy as a way of life must be developed progressively and inwoven with everything else, but without sacrifice of clarity. The school is, *par excellence,* the institution to which a democratic society is entitled to look for clarification of the meaning of democracy. In other words, the school is peculiarly the institution in which democracy becomes conscious of itself.

8

THE EDUCATION
OF CHARACTER

Martin Buber

1

EDUCATION WORTHY OF THE NAME is essentially education of character. For the genuine educator does not merely consider individual functions of his pupil, as one intending to teach him only to know or be capable of certain definite things; but his concern is always the person as a whole, both in the actuality in which he lives before you now and in his possibilities, what he can become. But in this way, as a whole in reality and potentiality, a man can be conceived either as personality, that is, as a unique spiritual-physical form with all the forces dormant in it, or as character, that is, as the link between what this individual is and the sequence of his actions and attitudes. Between these two modes of conceiving the pupil in his wholeness there is a fundamental difference. Personality is something which in its growth remains essentially outside the influence of the educator; but to assist in the moulding of character is his greatest task. Personality is a completion, only character is a task. One may cultivate and enhance personality, but in education one can and one must aim at character.

However—as I would like to point out straightaway—it is advisable not to over-estimate what the educator can even at best do to develop character. In this more than in any other branch of the science of teaching it is important to realize, at the very beginning of the discussion, the fundamental limits to conscious influence, even before asking what character is and how it is to be brought about.

If I have to teach algebra I can expect to succeed in giving my pupils an idea of quadratic equations with two unknown quantities. Even the slowest-witted child will understand it so well that he will amuse himself by solving equations at night when he cannot fall asleep. And even one with the most sluggish memory will not forget, in his old age, how to play with x and y. But if I am concerned with the education of character, everything becomes problematic. I try to explain to my pupils that envy is despicable, and at once I feel the secret resistance of those who are poorer than their comrades. I try to explain that it is wicked to bully the weak, and at once I see a suppressed smile on the lips of the strong. I try to explain that lying destroys life, and something frightful happens: the worst habitual liar of the class produces a brilliant essay on the destructive power of lying. I have made the fatal mistake of *giving instruction* in ethics, and what I said is accepted as current coin of knowledge; nothing of it is transformed into character-building substance.

But the difficulty lies still deeper. In all teaching of a subject I can announce my intention of teaching as openly as I please, and this does not interfere with the results. After all, pupils do want, for the most part, to learn something, even if not overmuch, so that a tacit agreement becomes possible. But as soon as my pupils notice that I want to educate their characters I am resisted precisely by those who show most signs of genuine independent character: they will not let themselves be educated, or rather, they do not like the idea that somebody wants to educate them. And those, too, who are seriously labouring over the question of good and evil, rebel when one dictates to them, as though it were some long established truth, what is good and what is bad; and they rebel just because they have experienced over and over again how hard it is to find the right way. Does it follow that one should keep silent about one's intention of educating character, and act by ruse and subterfuge? No; I have just said that the difficulty lies deeper. It is not enough to see that education of character is not introduced into a lesson in class; neither may one conceal it in cleverly arranged intervals. Education cannot tolerate such politic action. Even if the pupil does not notice the hidden motive it will have its negative effect on the actions of the teacher himself by depriving him of the directness which is his strength. Only in his whole being, in all his spontaneity can the educator truly affect the whole being of his pupil. For educating characters you do not need a moral genius, but you do need a man who is wholly alive and able to communicate himself directly to his fellow beings. His aliveness streams out to them and affects them most strongly and purely when he has no thought of affecting them.

The Greek word character means *impression*. The special link between man's being and his appearance, the special connexion between the unity of what he is and the sequence of his actions and attitudes is impressed on his still plastic substance. Who does the impressing? Everything does: nature and the social context, the house and the street, language and custom, the world of history and the world of daily news in the form of rumour, of broadcast and newspaper, music and technical science, play and dream—everything together. Many of these factors exert their influence by stimulating agreement, imitation, desire, effort; others by arousing questions, doubts, dislike, resistance. Character is formed by the interpenetration of all those multifarious, opposing influences. And yet, among this infinity of form-giving forces the educator is only one element among innumerable others, but distinct from them all by his *will* to take part in the stamping of character and by his *consciousness* that he represents in the eyes of the growing person a certain *selection* of what is, the selection of what is "right," of what *should* be. It is in this will and this consciousness that his vocation as an educator finds its fundamental expression. From this the genuine educator gains two things: first, humility, the feeling of being only one element amidst the fullness of life, only one single existence in the midst of all the tremendous inrush of reality on the pupil; but secondly, self-awareness, the feeling of being therein the only existence that *wants* to affect the whole person, and thus the feeling of responsibility for the selection of reality which he represents to the pupil. And a third thing emerges from all this, the recognition that in this realm of the education of character, of wholeness, there is only *one* access to the pupil: his *confidence*. For the adolescent who is frightened and disappointed by an unreliable world, confidence means the liberating insight that there is human truth, the truth of human existence. When the pupil's confidence has been won, his resistance against being educated gives way to a singular happening: he accepts the educator as a person. He feels he may trust this man, that this man is not making a business out of him, but is taking part in his life, accepting him before desiring to influence him. And so he learns to *ask*.

The teacher who is for the first time approached by a boy with somewhat defiant bearing, but with trembling hands, visibly opened-up and fired by a daring hope, who asks him what is the right thing in a certain situation—for instance, whether in learning that a friend has betrayed a secret entrusted to him one should call him to account or be content with entrusting no more secrets to him—the teacher to whom this happens realizes that this is the moment to make the first conscious step towards education of character; he has to answer, to answer under a responsibility, to give an answer which will probably lead beyond the alternatives of the question by showing a third possibility which is the right one. To dictate what is good and evil in general is not his business. His business is to answer a concrete question, to answer what is right and wrong in a given situation. This, as I have said, can only happen in an atmosphere of confidence. Confidence, of course, is not won by the strenuous endeavour to win it, but by direct and ingenuous participation in the life of the people one is dealing with—in this case in the life of one's pupils—and by assuming the responsibility which arises from such participation. It is not the educational intention but it is the meeting which is educationally fruitful. A soul suffering from the contradictions of the world of human society, and of its own physical existence, approaches me with a question. By trying to answer it to the best of my knowledge and conscience I help it to become a character that actively overcomes the contradictions.

If this is the teacher's standpoint towards his pupil, taking part in his life and conscious of responsibility, then everything that passes between them can, without any deliberate or politic intention, open a way to the education of character: lessons and games, a conversation about quarrels in the class, or about the problems of a world-war. Only, the teacher must not forget the limits of education; even when he enjoys confidence he cannot always expect agreement. Confidence implies a break-through from reserve, the bursting of the bonds which imprison an unquiet heart. But it does not imply unconditional agreement. The teacher must never forget that conflicts too, if only they are decided in a healthy atmosphere, have an educational value. A conflict with a pupil is the supreme test for the educator. He must use his own insight wholeheartedly; he must not blunt the piercing impact of his knowledge, but he must at the same time have in readiness the healing ointment for the heart pierced by it. Not for a moment may he conduct a dialectical manœuver instead of the real battle for truth. But if he is the victor he has to help the vanquished to endure defeat; and if he cannot conquer the self-willed soul that faces him (for victories over souls are not so easily won), then he has to find the word of love which alone can help to overcome so difficult a situation.

2

So far I have referred to those personal difficulties in the education of character which arise from the relation between educator and pupil, while for the moment treating character itself, the object of education, as a simple concept of fixed content. But it is by no means that. In order to penetrate to the real difficulties in the education of character we have to examine critically the concept of character itself.

Kerschensteiner in his well-known essay on *The Concept and Education of Character* distinguished between "character in the most general sense," by which he means "a man's attitude to his human surroundings, which is constant and is expressed in his actions," and real "ethical character," which he defines as "a special attitude, and one which in action gives the preference before all others to absolute values." If we begin by accepting this distinction unreservedly—and undeniably there is some truth in it—we are faced with such heavy odds in all education of character in our time that the very possibility of it seems doubtful.

The "absolute values" which Kerschensteiner refers to cannot, of course, be meant to have only subjective validity for the person concerned. Don Juan finds absolute and subjective value in seducing the greatest possible number of women, and the dictator sees it in the greatest possible accumulation of power. "Absolute validity" can only relate to universal values and norms, the existence of which the person concerned recognizes and acknowledges. But to deny the presence of universal values and norms of absolute validity—that is the conspicuous tendency of our age. This tendency is not, as is sometimes supposed, directed merely against the sanctioning of the norms by religion, but against their universal character and absolute validity, against their claim to be of a higher order than man and to govern the whole of mankind. In our age values and norms are not permitted to be anything but expressions of the life of a group which translates its own needs into the language of objective claims, until at last the group itself, for example a nation, is raised to an absolute value—and moreover to the only value. Then this splitting up into groups so pervades the whole of life that it is no longer possible to re-establish a sphere of values common to mankind, and a commandment to mankind is no longer observed. As this tendency grows the basis for the development of what Kerschensteiner means by moral character steadily diminishes. How, under these circumstances, can the task of educating character be completed?

At the time of the Arab terror in Palestine, when there were single Jewish acts of reprisal, there must have been many discussions between teacher and pupils on the question: Can there be any suspension of the Ten Commandments, i.e. can murder become a good deed if committed in the interest of one's own group? One such discussion was once repeated to me. The teacher asked: "When the commandment tells you 'Thou shalt not bear false witness against thy neighbour,' are we to interpret it with the condition, 'provided that it does not profit you'?" Thereupon one of the pupils said, "But it is not a question of my profit, but of the profit of my people." The teacher: "And how would you like it, then, if we put our condition this way: 'Provided that it does not profit your family'?" The pupil: "But family—that is still something more or less like myself; but the people—that is something quite different; there all question of *I* disappears." The teacher: "Then if you are thinking, 'we want victory,' don't you feel at the same time, 'I want victory'?" The pupil: "But the people, that is something infinitely more than just the people of to-day. It includes all past and future generations." At this point the teacher felt the moment had come to leave the narrow compass of the present and to invoke historical destiny. He said: "Yes; all past generations. But what was it that made those past generations of the Exile live? What made them outlive and overcome all their trials? Wasn't it that the cry 'Thou shalt not' never faded from their hearts and ears?" The pupil grew very pale. He was silent for a while, but it was the silence of one whose words threatened to stifle him. Then he burst out: "And what have we achieved that way? This!" And he banged his fist on the newspaper before him, which contained the report on the British White Paper. And again he burst out with "Live? Outlive? Do you call that life? We want to live!"

I have already said that the test of the educator lies in conflict with his pupil. He has to face this conflict and, whatever turn it may take, he has to find the way through it into life, into a life, I must add, where confidence continues unshaken—more, is even mysteriously strengthened. But the example I have just given shows the extreme difficulty of this task, which seems at times to have reached an impassable frontier. This is no longer merely a conflict between two generations, but between a world which for several millennia has believed in a truth superior to man, and an age which does not believe in it any longer—will not or cannot believe in it any longer.

But if we now ask, "How in this situation can there be any education of character?" something negative is immediately obvious: it is senseless to want to prove by any kind of argument that nevertheless the denied absoluteness of norms exists. That would be to assume that the denial is the result of reflection, and is open to argument, that is, to material for renewed reflection. But the denial is due to the disposition of a dominant human type of our age. We are justified in regarding this disposition as a sickness of the human race. But we must not deceive ourselves by believing that the disease can be cured by formulae which assert that nothing is really as the sick person imagines. It is an idle undertaking to call out, to a mankind that has grown blind to eternity: "Look! the eternal values!" To-day host upon host of men have everywhere sunk into the slavery of collectives, and each collective is the supreme authority for its own slaves; there is no longer, superior to the collectives, any universal sovereignty in idea, faith, or spirit. Against the values, decrees and decisions of the collective no appeal is possible. This is true, not only for the totalitarian countries, but also for the parties and party-like groups in the so-called democracies. Men who have so lost themselves to the collective Moloch cannot be rescued from it by any reference, however eloquent, to the absolute whose kingdom the Moloch has usurped. One has to begin by pointing to that sphere where man himself, in the hours of utter solitude, occasionally becomes aware of the disease through sudden pain: by pointing to the relation of the individual to his own self. In order to enter into a personal relation with the absolute, it is first necessary to be a person again, to rescue one's real personal self from the fiery jaws of collectivism which devours all selfhood. The desire to do this is latent in the pain the individual suffers through his distorted relation to his own self. Again and again he dulls the pain with a subtle poison and thus suppresses the desire as well. To keep the pain awake, to waken the desire—that is the first task of everyone who regrets the obscuring of eternity. It is also the first task of the genuine educator in our time.

The man for whom absolute values in a universal sense do not exist cannot be made to adopt "an attitude which in action gives the preference over all others to absolute values." But what one can inculcate in him is the desire to attain once more to a real attitude, and that is, the desire to become a person following the only way that leads to this goal to-day.

But with this the concept of character formulated by Kerschensteiner and deriving, as we know, from Kant is recognized to be useless for the specifically modern task of the education of character. Another concept has to be found if this task is to be more precisely defined.

We cannot conceal from ourselves that we stand to-day on the ruins of the edifice whose towers were raised by Kant. It is not given to us living to-day to sketch the plan for a new building. But we can perhaps begin by laying the first foundations without a plan, with only a dawning image before our mind's eye.

3

According to Kerschensteiner's final definition character is "fundamentally nothing but voluntary obedience to the maxims which have been moulded in the individual by experience, teaching, and self-reflection, whether they have been adopted and then completely assimilated or have originated in the consciousness through self-legislation." This voluntary obedience "is, however, only a form of self-control." At first, love or fear of other people must have produced in man "the *habit* of self-conquest." Then, gradually, "this outer obedience must be transformed into inner obedience."

The concept of habit was then enlarged, especially by John Dewey in his book, *Human Nature and Conduct.* According to him character is "the interpenetration of habits." Without "the continued operation of all habits in every act" there would be no unified character, but only "a juxtaposition of disconnected reactions to separated situations."

With this concept of character as an organization of self-control by means of the accumulation of maxims, or as a system of interpenetrating habits, it is very easy to understand how powerless modern educational science is when faced by the sickness of man. But even apart from the special problems of the age, this concept can be no adequate basis for the construction of a genuine education of character. Not that the educator could dispense with employing useful maxims or furthering good habits. But in moments that come perhaps only seldom, a feeling of blessed achievement links him to the explorer, the inventor, the artist, a feeling of sharing in the revelation of what is hidden. In such moments he finds himself in a sphere very different from that of maxims and habits. Only on this, the highest plane of his activity, can he fix his real goal, the real concept of character which is his concern, even though he might not often reach it.

For the first time a young teacher enters a class independently, no longer sent by the training college to prove his efficiency. The class before him is like a mirror of mankind, so multiform, so full of contradictions, so inaccessible. He feels "These boys—I have not sought them out; I have been put here and have to accept them as they are—but not as they now are in this moment, no, as they *really* are, as they can become. But how can I find out what is in them and what can I do to make it take shape?" And the boys do not make things easy for him. They are noisy, they cause trouble, they stare at him with impudent curiosity. He is at once tempted to check this or that trouble-maker, to issue orders, to make compulsory the rules of decent behaviour, to say No, to say No to everything rising against him from beneath: he is at once tempted to start from beneath. And if one starts from beneath one perhaps never arrives above, but everything comes down. But then his eyes meet a face which strikes him. It is not a beautiful face nor particularly intelligent; but it is a real face, or rather, the chaos preceding the cosmos of a real face. On it he reads a question which is something different from the general curiosity: "Who are you? Do you know something that concerns me? Do you bring me something? What do you bring?"

In some such way he reads the question. And he, the young teacher, addresses this face. He says nothing very ponderous or important, he puts an ordinary introductory question: "What did you talk about last in geography? The Dead Sea? Well, what about the Dead Sea?" But there was obviously something not quite usual in the question, for the answer he gets is not the ordinary schoolboy answer; the boy begins to *tell a story*. Some months earlier he had stayed for a few hours on the shores of the Dead Sea and it is of this he tells. He adds: "And everything looked to me as if it had been created a day before the rest of creation." Quite unmistakably he had only in this moment made up his mind to talk about it. In the meantime his face has changed. It is no longer quite as chaotic as before. And the class has fallen silent. They all listen. The class, too, is no longer a chaos. Something has happened. The young teacher has started from above.

The educator's task can certainly not consist in educating great characters. He cannot select his pupils, but year by year the world, such as it is, is sent in the form of a school class to meet him on his life's way as his destiny; and in this destiny lies the very meaning of his life's work. He has to introduce discipline and order, he has to establish a law, and he can only strive and hope for the result that discipline and order will become more and more inward and autonomous, and that at last the law will be written in the heart of his pupils. But his real goal which, once he has well recognized it and well remembers it, will influence all his work, is the great character.

The great character can be conceived neither as a system of maxims nor as a system of habits. It is peculiar to him to act from the whole of his substance. That is, it is peculiar to him to react in accordance with the uniqueness of every situation which challenges him as an active person. Of course there are all sorts of similarities in different situations; one can construct types of situations, one can always find to what section the particular situation belongs, and draw what is appropriate from the hoard of established maxims and habits, apply the appropriate maxim, bring into operation the appropriate habit. But what is untypical in the particular situation remains unnoticed and unanswered. To me that seems the same as if, having ascertained the sex of a new-born child, one were immediately to establish its type as well, and put all the children of one type into a common cradle on which not the individual name but the name of the type was inscribed. In spite of all similarities every living situation has, like a new-born child, a new face, that has never been before and will never come again. It demands of you a reaction which cannot be prepared beforehand. It demands nothing of what is past. It demands presence, responsibility; it demands you. I call a great character one who by his actions and attitudes satisfies the claim of situations out of deep readiness to respond with his whole life, and in such a way that the sum of his actions and attitudes expresses at the same time the unity of his being in its willingness to accept responsibility. As his being is unity, the unity of accepted responsibility, his active life, too, coheres into unity. And one might perhaps say that for him there rises a unity out of the situations he has responded to in responsibility, the indefinable unity of a moral destiny.

All this does not mean that the great character is beyond the acceptance of norms. No responsible person remains a stranger to norms. But the command inherent in a genuine norm never becomes a maxim and the fulfilment of it never a habit. Any command that a great character takes to himself in the course of his development does not act in him as part of his consciousness or as material for building up his exercises, but remains latent in a basic layer of his substance until it reveals itself to him in a concrete way. What it has to tell him is revealed whenever a situation arises which demands of him a solution of which till then he had perhaps no idea. Even the most universal norm will at times be recognized only in a very special situation. I know of a man whose heart was struck by the lightning flash of "Thou shalt not steal" in the very moment when he was moved by a very different desire from that of stealing, and whose heart was so struck by it that he not only abandoned doing what he wanted to do, but with the whole force of his passion did the very opposite. Good and evil are not each other's opposites like right and left. The evil approaches us as a whirlwind, the good as a direction. There is a direction, a "yes," a command, hidden even in a prohibition, which is revealed to us in moments like these. In moments like these the command addresses us really in the second person, and the Thou in it is no one else but one's own self. Maxims command only the third person, the each and the none.

One can say that it is the unconditioned nature of the address which distinguishes the command from the maxim. In an age which has become deaf to unconditioned address we cannot overcome the dilemma of the education of character from that angle. But insight into the structure of great character can help us to overcome it.

Of course, it may be asked whether the educator should really start "from above," whether, in fixing his goal, the hope of finding a great character, who is bound to be the exception, should be his starting-point; for in his methods of educating character he will always have to take into

consideration the others, the many. To this I reply that the educator would
not have the right to do so if a method inapplicable to these others were to
result. In fact, however, his very insight into the structure of a great character helps him to find the way by which alone (as I have indicated) he
can begin to influence also the victims of the collective Moloch, pointing
out to them the sphere in which they themselves suffer—namely, their
relation to their own selves. From this sphere he must elicit the values
which he can make credible and desirable to his pupils. That is what insight into the structure of a great character helps him to do.

A section of the young is beginning to feel today that, because of their
absorption by the collective, something important and irreplaceable is lost
to them—personal responsibility for life and the world. These young people, it is true, do not yet realize that their blind devotion to the collective,
e.g. to a party, was not a genuine act of their personal life; they do not
realize that it sprang, rather, from the fear of being left, in this age of confusion, to rely on themselves, on a self which no longer receives its direction from eternal values. Thus they do not yet realize that their devotion
was fed on the unconscious desire to have responsibility removed from
them by an authority in which they believe or want to believe. They do
not yet realize that this devotion was an escape. I repeat, the young people I am speaking of do not yet realize this. But they are beginning to
notice that he who no longer, with his whole being, decides what he does
or does not, and assumes responsibility for it, becomes sterile in soul. And
a sterile soul soon ceases to be a soul.

This is where the educator can begin and should begin. He can help the
feeling that something is lacking to grow into the clarity of consciousness
and into the force of desire. He can awaken in young people the courage
to shoulder life again. He can bring before his pupils the image of a great
character who denies no answer to life and the world, but accepts responsibility for everything essential that he meets. He can show his pupils this
image without the fear that those among them who most of all need discipline and order will drift into a craving for aimless freedom: on the contrary, he can teach them in this way to recognize that discipline and order
too are starting-points on the way towards self-responsibility. He can
show that even the great character is not born perfect, that the unity of
his being has first to mature before expressing itself in the sequence of his
actions and attitudes. But unity itself, unity of the person, unity of the
lived life, has to be emphasized again and again. The confusing contradictions cannot be remedied by the collectives, not one of which knows
the taste of genuine unity and which if left to themselves would end up,
like the scorpions imprisoned in a box, in the witty fable, by devouring

one another. This mass of contradictions can be met and conquered only by the rebirth of personal unity, unity of being, unity of life, unity of action—unity of being, life and action together. This does not mean a static unity of the uniform, but the great dynamic unity of the multiform in which multiformity is formed into unity of character. Today the great characters are still "enemies of the people," they who love their society, yet wish not only to preserve it but to raise it to a higher level. To-morrow they will be the architects of a new unity of mankind. It is the longing for personal unity, from which must be born a unity of mankind, which the educator should lay hold of and strengthen in his pupils. Faith in this unity and the will to achieve it is not a "return" to individualism, but a step beyond all the dividedness of individualism and collectivism. A great and full relation between man and man can only exist between unified and responsible persons. That is why it is much more rarely found in the totalitarian collective than in any historically earlier form of society; much more rarely also in the authoritarian party than in any earlier form of free association. Genuine education of character is genuine education for community. . . .

PART FOUR

DEMOCRACY AND ITS TROUBLES

WE BEGIN THIS SECTION with Chapter Nine, an address delivered by Noam Chomsky, a political activist, writer, and professor of linguistics at the Massachusetts Institute of Technology, to an audience at the University of Cape Town in South Africa in 1997. Among other things, "Market Democracy in a Neoliberal Order" serves to remind us that democracy is not exclusively an American ideal. Nor are the impacts of our actions strictly limited to American shores. Like it or not, the United States is part of a global human matrix. This interconnectivity with peoples, places, and things beyond our national borders is far more likely to increase than to decrease in coming years. Although this circumstance may offer unprecedented opportunities to do good, it also increases the potential to do harm.

While it appears (in this post–Cold War period) that democracy and the free market are rapidly spreading across the globe, there is considerable disagreement as to whether recent events signal the arrival of a world that is more just and more free. If we are ever to move closer to realizing our social and political ideals, we cannot do so without confronting, first and foremost, the realities of power and privilege.

Although his focus is closer to home, the issues addressed in Chapter Ten by Howard Zinn, professor emeritus of political science at Boston University, are no less global. "It is a deception of the citizenry to claim that the 'rule of law' has replaced the 'rule of men,'" he argues in his look at the relationship between law and justice. "It is still men (women are mostly kept out of the process)," he adds, "who enact the laws, who sit on the bench and interpret them, who occupy the White House or the Governor's mansion, and have the job of enforcing them." Expanding on the theme of power and privilege, Zinn forces us to think seriously about what we mean when we use words such as *patriotism* and *duty*—in the name of each of which much good as well as much harm has been done. The implications for schooling in a democratic society become clear when he reminds us that obligation to government "is not natural. It must be taught to every generation." How we think about that obligation is crucial to how we think about ourselves and our democracy.

As we endeavor to grapple with the issues raised by Chomsky, Zinn, and others, we must also consider the ways in which our educational goals have shifted over time. The differences between earlier ideals and contemporary realities serve as a basis for Chapter Eleven, "Jefferson, Morrill, and the Upper Crust," by Wendell Berry, which centers on the history of the land-grant colleges.

Berry, a writer, a farmer, and a philosopher who taught for many years at the University of Kentucky, explains that land-grant colleges were originally intended to "promote the stabilization of farming populations and communities" and to "establish in that way a 'permanent' agriculture, enabled by better education to preserve both the land and the people. The failure of this intention, and the promotion by the land-grant colleges of an impermanent agriculture destructive of land and people, was caused in part by the lowering of the educational standard from Jefferson's ideal of public or community responsibility to the utilitarianism of Morrill, insofar as this difference in the aims of the two men represented a shift of public value." Written in 1977, Berry's chapter remains as relevant today as it was when it first appeared—and arguably more so.

Much as democracy, free markets, and globalization provide opportunities to do both good and harm, so too does education itself. Laying the groundwork for a later discussion (in Part Six) of education in a democratic society, Berry notes that experimental intelligence, as emphasized by the modern university, can be far from neutral or democratic. "It is," he cautions, "at least potentially totalitarian. To think or act without cultural value, and the restraints invariably implicit in cultural value, is simply to wait upon force. This sort of behavior is founded in the cultural disintegration and despair which are also the foundation of political totalitarianism."

9

MARKET DEMOCRACY IN
A NEOLIBERAL ORDER

Noam Chomsky

I HAVE BEEN ASKED TO SPEAK on some aspect of academic or human freedom, an invitation that offers many choices. I will keep to some simple ones.

Freedom without opportunity is a devil's gift, and the refusal to provide such opportunities is criminal. The fate of the more vulnerable offers a sharper measure of the distance from here to something that might be called "civilization." While I am speaking, 1,000 children will die from easily preventable disease, and almost twice that many women will die or suffer serious disability in pregnancy or childbirth for lack of simple remedies and care.[1] UNICEF estimates that to overcome such tragedies, and to ensure universal access to basic social services, would require a quarter of the annual military expenditures of the "developing countries," about 10 percent of U.S. military spending. It is against the background of such realities as these that any serious discussion of human freedom should proceed.

It is widely held that the cure for such profound social maladies is within reach. This hope is not without foundation. The past few years have seen the fall of brutal tyrannies, the growth of scientific understanding that offers great promise, and many other reasons to look forward to a brighter future. The discourse of the privileged is marked by confidence and triumphalism: the way forward is known, and there is no other. The basic theme, articulated with force and clarity, is that "America's victory in the cold war was a victory for a set of political and economic principles: democracy and the free market." These principles are "the wave of the future—a future for which America is both the gatekeeper and the model." I am quoting the chief political commentator of the *New York Times,* but the picture is conventional, widely repeated throughout much of the world, and accepted as generally accurate even by critics. It was also enunciated as the "Clinton Doctrine," which declared that our new mission is to "consolidate the victory of democracy and open markets" that had just been won.

There remains a range of disagreement: at one extreme "Wilsonian idealists" urge continued dedication to the traditional mission of benevolence, and at the other, "realists" counter that we may lack the means to conduct these crusades of "global meliorism," and should not neglect our own interests in the service of others. Within this range lies the path to a better world.[2]

Reality seems to me rather different. The current spectrum of public policy debate has as little relevance to policy as its numerous antecedents: neither the United States nor any other power has been guided by "global meliorism." Democracy is under attack worldwide, including the leading industrial countries; at least, democracy in a meaningful sense of the term, involving opportunities for people to manage their own collective and individual affairs. Something similar is true of markets. The assaults on democracy and markets are furthermore related. Their roots lie in the power of corporate entities that are increasingly interlinked and reliant on powerful states, and largely unaccountable to the public. Their immense power is growing as a result of social policy that is globalizing the structural model of the third world, with sectors of enormous wealth and privilege alongside an increase in "the proportion of those who will labor under all the hardships of life, and secretly sigh for a more equal distribution of its blessings," as the leading framer of American democracy, James Madison, predicted 200 years ago.[3] These policy choices are most evident in the Anglo-American societies, but extend worldwide. They cannot be attributed to what "the free market has decided, in its infinite but mysterious wisdom,"[4] "the implacable sweep of 'the market revolution,'" "Reaganesque rugged individualism," or a "new orthodoxy" that "gives the market full sway." On the contrary, state intervention plays a decisive role, as in the past, and the basic outlines of policy are hardly novel. Current versions reflect "capital's clear subjugation of labor" for more than fifteen years, in the words of the business press,[5] which often accurately reports the perceptions of a highly class-conscious business community, dedicated to class war.

If these perceptions are valid, then the path to a world that is more just and more free lies well outside the range set forth by privilege and power. I cannot hope to establish such conclusions here, but only to suggest that they are credible enough to consider with care. And to suggest further that prevailing doctrines could hardly survive were it not for their contribution to "regimenting the public mind every bit as much as an army regiments the bodies of its soldiers," to quote . . . Edward Bernays[,] while presenting to the business world the lessons that had been learned from wartime propaganda. . . . [6]

Quite strikingly, in both of the world's leading democracies there was a growing awareness of the need to "apply the lessons" of the highly successful propaganda systems of World War I "to the organization of political warfare," as the chairman of the British Conservative party put the matter seventy years ago. Wilsonian liberals in the United States, including public intellectuals and prominent figures in the developing profession of political science, drew the same conclusions in the same years. In another corner of Western civilization, Adolf Hitler vowed that next time Germany would not be defeated in the propaganda war, and he also devised his own ways to apply the lessons of Anglo-American propaganda to political warfare at home.[7]

Meanwhile the business world warned of "the hazard facing industrialists" in "the newly realized political power of the masses," and the need to wage and win "the everlasting battle for the minds of men" and "indoctrinate citizens with the capitalist story" until "they are able to play back the story with remarkable fidelity"; and so on, in an impressive flow, accompanied by even more impressive efforts.[8]

To discover the true meaning of the "political and economic principles" that are declared to be "the wave of the future," it is of course necessary to go beyond rhetorical flourishes and public pronouncements and to investigate actual practice and the internal documentary record. Close examination of particular cases is the most rewarding path, but these must be chosen carefully to give a fair picture. There are some natural guidelines. One reasonable approach is to take the examples chosen by the proponents of the doctrines themselves, as their strongest case. Another is to investigate the record where influence is greatest and interference least, so that we see the operative principles in their purest form. If we want to determine what the Kremlin meant by "democracy" and "human rights," we will pay little heed to *Pravda's* solemn denunciations of racism in the United States or state terror in its client regimes, even less to protestation of noble motives. Far more instructive is the state of affairs in the "people's democracies" of Eastern Europe. The point is elementary, and applies to the self-designated "gatekeeper and model" as well. Latin America is the obvious testing ground, particularly the Central America-Caribbean region. Here Washington has faced few external challenges for almost a century, so the guiding principles of policy, and of today's neoliberal "Washington consensus," are revealed most clearly when we examine the state of the region, and how that came about.

It is of some interest that the exercise is rarely undertaken, and if proposed, castigated as extremist or worse. I leave it as an "exercise for the reader," merely noting that the record teaches useful lessons about the political and economic principles that are to be "the wave of the future."

Washington's "crusade for democracy," as it is called, was waged with particular fervor during the Reagan years, with Latin America serving as the chosen terrain. The results are commonly offered as a prime illustration of how the United States became "the inspiration for the triumph of democracy in our time," to quote the editors of a leading intellectual journal of American liberalism.[9] The most recent scholarly study of democracy describes "the revival of democracy in Latin America" as "impressive" but not unproblematic; the "barriers to implementation" remain "formidable," but can perhaps be overcome through closer integration with the United States. The author, Sanford Lakoff, singles out the "historic North American Free Trade Agreement (NAFTA)" as a potential instrument of democratization. In the region of traditional U.S. influence, he writes, the countries are moving toward democracy, having "survived military intervention" and "vicious civil war."[10]

Let us begin by looking more closely at these recent cases, the natural ones given overwhelming U.S. influence, and the ones regularly selected to illustrate the achievements and promise of "America's mission."

The primary "barriers to implementation" of democracy, Lakoff suggests, are efforts to protect "domestic markets"—that is, to prevent foreign (mainly U.S.) corporations from gaining even greater control over the society. We are to understand, then, that democracy is enhanced as significant decision making shifts even more into the hands of unaccountable private tyrannies, mostly foreign-based. Meanwhile the public arena is to shrink still further as the state is "minimized" in accordance with the neoliberal political and economic principles that have emerged triumphant. A study of the World Bank points out that the new orthodoxy represents "a dramatic shift away from a pluralist, participatory ideal of politics and towards an authoritarian and technocratic ideal," one that is very much in accord with leading elements of twentieth century liberal and progressive thought, and in another variant, the Leninist model; the two are more similar than often recognized.[11]

Thinking through the background, we gain some useful insight into the concepts of democracy and markets, in the operative sense.

Lakoff does not look into the "revival of democracy" in Latin America, but he does cite a scholarly source that includes a contribution on Washington's crusade in the 1980s. The author is Thomas Carothers, who combines scholarship with an "insider's perspective," having worked on "democracy enhancement" programs in Reagan's State Department.[12] Carothers regards Washington's "impulse to promote democracy" as "sincere," but largely a failure. Furthermore, the failure was systematic: where Washington's influence was least, in South America, there was real progress toward democracy, which the Reagan Administration generally opposed, later taking credit for it when the process proved irresistible. Where Washington's influence was greatest, progress was least, and where it occurred, the U.S. role was marginal or negative. His general conclusion is that the U.S. sought to maintain "the basic order of . . . quite undemocratic societies" and to avoid "populist-based change," "inevitably [seeking] only limited, top-down forms of democratic change that did not risk upsetting the traditional structures of power with which the United States has long been allied."

The last clause requires a gloss. The term *United States* is conventionally used to refer to structures of power within the United States; the "national interest" is the interest of these groups, which correlates only weakly with interests of the general population. So the conclusion is that Washington sought top-down forms of democracy that did not upset traditional structures of power with which the structures of power in the United States have long been allied. Not a very surprising fact, or much of a historical novelty.

Within the United States itself, "top-down democracy" is firmly rooted in the Constitutional system.[13] One may argue, as some historians do, that these principles lost their force as the national territory was conquered and settled. Whatever one's assessment of those years, by the late nineteenth century the founding doctrines took on a new and much more oppressive form. When James Madison spoke of "rights of persons," he meant *persons*. But the growth of the industrial economy, and the rise of corporate forms of economic enterprise, led to a completely new meaning of the term. In a current official document, "'Person' is broadly defined to include any individual, branch, partnership, associated group, association, estate, trust, corporation or other organization (whether or not organized under the laws of any State), or any government entity,"[14] a concept that would have shocked Madison and others with intellectual roots in the Enlightenment and classical liberalism.

These radical changes in the conception of human rights and democracy were introduced primarily not by legislation but by judicial decisions and intellectual commentary. Corporations, which previously had been considered artificial entities with no rights, were accorded all the rights of persons, and far more, since they are "immortal persons," and "persons" of extraordinary wealth and power. Furthermore, they were no longer bound to the specific purposes designated by State charter but could act as they chose, with few constraints.[15]

Conservative legal scholars bitterly opposed these innovations, recognizing that they undermine the traditional idea that rights inhere in individuals, and undermine market principles as well. But the new forms of authoritarian rule were institutionalized, and along with them the legitimation of wage labor, which was considered hardly better than slavery in mainstream American thought through much of the nineteenth century, not only by the rising labor movement but also by such figures as Abraham Lincoln, the Republican party, and the establishment media.[16]

These are topics with enormous implications for understanding the nature of market democracy. Again, I can only mention them here. The material and ideological outcome helps explain the understanding that "democracy" abroad must reflect the model sought at home; top-down forms of control, with the public kept to a spectator role, not participating in the arena of decision making, which must exclude these "ignorant and meddlesome outsiders," according to the mainstream of modern democratic theory. But the general ideas are standard and have solid roots in the tradition, radically modified, however, in the new era of "collectivist legal entities."

Returning to the "victory of democracy" under U.S. guidance, neither Lakoff nor Carothers asks how Washington maintained the traditional power structure of highly undemocratic societies. Their topic is not the terrorist wars that left tens of thousands of tortured and mutilated corpses, millions of refugees, and devastation perhaps beyond recovery—in large measure wars against the Church, which became an enemy when it adopted "the preferential option for the poor," trying to help suffering people to attain some measure of justice and democratic rights. It is more than symbolic that the terrible decade of the 1980s opened with the murder of an archbishop who had become "a voice for the voiceless," and closed with the assassination of six leading Jesuit intellectuals who had chosen the same path, in each case by terrorist forces armed and trained by the victors of the "crusade for democracy." One should take careful note of the fact that the leading Central American dissident intellectuals were doubly assassinated: both murdered and silenced. Their words, indeed their very existence, are scarcely known in the United States, unlike dissidents in enemy states, who are greatly honored and admired.

Such matters do not enter history as recounted by the victors. In Lakoff's study, which is not untypical in this regard, what survives are references to "military intervention" and "civil wars," with no external factor identified. These matters will not so quickly be put aside, however, by those who seek a better grasp of the principles that are to shape the future, if the structures of power have their way.

Particularly revealing is Lakoff's description of Nicaragua, again standard: "A civil war was ended following a democratic election, and a difficult effort is under way to create a more prosperous and self-governing society." In the real world, the superpower attacking Nicaragua escalated its assault after the country's first democratic election. The election of 1984 was closely monitored and recognized as legitimate by the professional association of Latin American scholars (LASA), Irish and British parliamentary delegations, and others, including a hostile Dutch government delegation that was remarkably supportive of Reaganite atrocities. The leading figure of Central American democracy, José Figueres of Costa Rica, also a critical observer, nevertheless regarded the elections as legitimate in this "invaded country," calling on Washington to allow the Sandinistas "to finish what they started in peace; they deserve it." The United States strongly opposed the holding of the elections and sought to undermine them, concerned that democratic elections might interfere with its terrorist war. But that concern was put to rest by the good behavior of the doctrinal system, which barred the reports with remarkable efficiency, reflexively adopting the state propaganda line that the elections were meaningless fraud.[17]

Overlooked as well is the fact that as the next election approached on schedule,[18] Washington left no doubt that unless the results came out the right way, Nicaraguans would continue to endure the illegal economic warfare and "unlawful use of force" that the World Court had condemned and ordered terminated, of course in vain. This time the outcome was acceptable, and hailed in the United States with an outburst of exuberance that is highly informative.[19]

At the outer limits of critical independence, columnist Anthony Lewis of the New York Times was overcome with admiration for Washington's "experiment in peace and democracy," which showed that "we live in a romantic age." The experimental methods were no secret. Thus Time magazine, joining in the celebration as "democracy burst forth" in Nicaragua, outlined them frankly: to "wreck the economy and prosecute a long and deadly proxy war until the exhausted natives overthrow the unwanted government themselves," with a cost to us that is "minimal," leaving the victim "with wrecked bridges, sabotaged power stations, and ruined farms," and providing Washington's candidate with "a winning issue," ending the "impoverishment of the people of Nicaragua," not to speak of the continuing terror, better left unmentioned. To be sure, the cost to *them* was hardly "minimal": Carothers notes that the toll "in per capita terms was significantly higher than the number of U.S. persons killed in the U.S. Civil War and all the wars of the twentieth century *combined*."[20] The outcome was a "Victory for U.S. Fair Play," a headline in the *New York Times* exulted, leaving Americans "United in Joy," in the style of Albania and North Korea.

The methods of this "romantic age," and the reaction to them in enlightened circles, tell us more about the democratic principles that have emerged victorious. They also shed some light on why it is such a "difficult effort" to "create a more prosperous and self-governing society" in Nicaragua. It is true that the effort is now under way, and is meeting with some success for a privileged minority, while most of the population faces social and economic disaster, all in the familiar pattern of Western dependencies.[21] Note that it is this example that led the *New Republic* editors to laud themselves as "the inspiration for the triumph of democracy in our time," joining the enthusiastic chorus.

We learn more about the victorious principles by recalling that these same representative figures of liberal intellectual life had urged that Washington's wars must be waged mercilessly, with military support for "Latin-style fascists . . . regardless of how many are murdered," because "there are higher American priorities than Salvadoran human rights." Elaborating, *New Republic* editor Michael Kinsley, who represented the left in mainstream commentary and television debate, cautioned against unthinking criticism of Washington's official policy of attacking undefended civilian targets. Such international terrorist operations cause "vast civilian suffering," he acknowledged, but they may be "perfectly legitimate" if "cost-benefit analysis" shows that "the amount of blood and misery that will be poured in" yields "democracy," as the world rulers define it. Enlightened opinion insists that terror is not a value in itself, but must meet the pragmatic criterion. Kinsley later observed that the desired ends had been achieved: "Impoverishing the people of Nicaragua was precisely the point of the contra war and the parallel policy of economic embargo and veto of international development loans," which "wreck[ed] the economy" and "creat[ed] the economic disaster [that] was probably the victorious opposition's best election issue." He then joined in welcoming the "triumph of democracy" in the "free election" of 1990.[22]

Client states enjoy similar privileges. Thus, commenting on yet another of Israel's attacks on Lebanon, foreign editor H.D.S. Greenway of the *Boston Globe,* who had graphically reported the first major invasion fifteen years earlier, commented that "if shelling Lebanese villages, even at the cost of lives, and driving civilian refugees north would secure Israel's border, weaken Hezbollah, and promote peace, I would say go to it, as would many Arabs and Israelis. But history has not been kind to Israeli adventures in Lebanon. They have solved very little and have almost always caused more problems." By the pragmatic criterion, then, the murder of many civilians, expulsion of hundreds of thousand of refugees, and devastation of southern Lebanon is a dubious proposition.[23]

Bear in mind that I am keeping to the dissident sector of tolerable opinion, what is called "the left," a fact that tells us more about the victorious principles and the intellectual culture within which they find their place.

Also revealing was the reaction to periodic Reagan Administration allegations of Nicaraguan plans to obtain jet interceptors from the Soviet Union (the United States having coerced its allies into refusing to sell them). Hawks demanded that Nicaragua be bombed at once. Doves countered that the charges must first be verified, but if they were, the United States would have to bomb Nicaragua. Sane observers understood why Nicaragua might want jet interceptors: to protect its territory from CIA overflights that were supplying the U.S. proxy forces and providing them with up-to-the-minute information so that they could follow the directive to attack undefended "soft targets." The tacit assumption is that no country has a right to defend civilians from U.S. attack, a doctrine that reigned virtually unchallenged in the mainstream.

The pretext for Washington's terrorist wars was self-defense, the standard official justification for just about any monstrous act, even the Nazi Holocaust. Indeed Ronald Reagan, finding "that the policies and actions of the government of Nicaragua constitute an unusual and extraordinary threat to the national security and foreign policy of the United States," declared "a national emergency to deal with that threat," arousing no ridicule.[24] By similar logic, the USSR had every right to attack Denmark, a far greater threat to its security, and surely Poland and Hungary when they took steps toward independence. The fact that such pleas can regularly be put forth is again an interesting comment on the intellectual culture of the victors, and another indication of what lies ahead. . . .

Let us return to the prevailing doctrine that "America's victory in the cold war" was a victory for democracy and the free market. With regard to democracy, the doctrine is partially true, though we have to understand what is meant by "democracy": top-down control "to protect the minority of the opulent against the majority." What about the free market? Here too, we find that doctrine is far removed from reality. . . .

Consider again the case of NAFTA, an agreement intended to lock Mexico into an economic discipline that protects investors from the danger of a "democracy opening." It is not a "free trade agreement." Rather, it is highly protectionist, designed to impede East Asian and European competitors. Furthermore, it shares with the global agreements such anti-market principles as "intellectual property rights" restrictions of an extreme sort that rich societies never accepted during their period of development, but that they now intend to use to protect home-based corporations: to destroy the pharmaceutical industry in poorer countries, for example—and, incidentally, to block technological innovations, such as improved production processes for patented products allowed under the traditional patent regime. Progress is no more a desideratum than markets, unless it yields benefits for those who count.

There are also questions about the nature of "trade." Over half of U.S. trade with Mexico is reported to consist of intrafirm transactions, up about 15 percent since NAFTA. Already a decade ago, mostly U.S.-owned plants in northern Mexico, employing few workers and with virtually no linkages to the Mexican economy, produced more than 33 percent of the engine blocks used in U.S. cars, and 75 percent of other essential components. The post-NAFTA collapse of the Mexican economy in 1994, exempting only the very rich and U.S. investors (protected by U.S. government bailouts), led to an increase of U.S.-Mexico trade as the new crisis, driving the population to still deeper misery, "transformed Mexico into a cheap [i.e., even cheaper] source of manufactured goods, with industrial wages one-tenth of those in the U.S.," the business press reports. According to some specialists, half of U.S. trade worldwide consists of such centrally managed transactions, and much the same is true of other industrial powers,[25] though one must treat with caution conclusions about institutions with limited public accountability. Some economists have plausibly described the world system as one of "corporate mercantilism," remote from the ideal of free trade. The OECD concludes that "oligopolistic competition and strategic interaction among firms and governments rather than the invisible hand of market forces condition today's competitive advantage and international division of labor in high-technology industries,"[26] implicitly adopting a similar view.

Even the basic structure of the domestic economy violates the neoliberal principles that are hailed. The main theme of the standard work on U.S. business history is that "modern business enterprise took the place of market mechanisms in coordinating the activities of the economy and allocating its resources," handling many transactions internally, another large departure from market principles.[27] There are many others. Consider, for example, the fate of Adam Smith's principle that the free movement of people—across borders, for example—is an essential component of free trade. When we move on to the world of transnational corporations, with strategic alliances and critical support from powerful states, the gap between doctrine and reality becomes substantial.

Public statements have to be interpreted in the light of these realities, among them Clinton's call for trade-not-aid for Africa, with a series of provisions that just happen to benefit U.S. investors and uplifting rhetoric that manages to avoid such matters as the long record of such approaches and the fact that the United States already had the most miserly aid program of any developed country even before the grand innovation. Or to take the obvious model, consider Chester Crocker's outline of Reagan Administration plans for Africa in 1981. "We support open market opportunities, access to key resources, and expanding African and American economics," he said, and want to bring African countries "into the mainstream of the free market economy."[28] The statement may seem to surpass cynicism, coming from the leaders of the "sustained assault" against the "free market economy." But Crocker's rendition is fair enough, when it is passed through the prism of really existing market doctrine. The market opportunities and access to resources are for foreign investors and their local associates, and the economies are to expand in a specific way, protecting "the minority of the opulent against the majority." The opulent, meanwhile, merit state protection and public subsidy. How else can they flourish, for the benefit of all?

Of course, the United States is not alone in its conceptions of "free trade," even if its ideologues often lead the cynical chorus. The gap between rich and poor countries from 1960 is substantially attributable to protectionist measures of the rich, a UN development report concluded in 1992. The 1994 report concluded that "the industrial countries, by violating the principles of free trade, are costing the developing countries an estimated $50 billion a year—nearly equal to the total flow of foreign assistance"—much of it publicly subsidized export promotion.[29] The 1996 *Global Report* of the UN Industrial Development Organization estimates that the disparity between the richest and poorest 20 percent of the world population increased by over 50 percent from 1960 to 1989, and predicts "growing world inequality resulting from the globalization process." That growing disparity holds within the rich societies as well, the United States leading the way, Britain not far behind. The business press exults in "spectacular" and "stunning" profit growth, applauding the extraordinary concentration of wealth among the top few percent of the population, while for the majority, conditions continue to stagnate or decline.

The corporate media, the Clinton Administration, and the cheerleaders for the American Way proudly offer themselves as a model for the rest of the world; buried in the chorus of self-acclaim are the results of deliberate social policy of recent years, for example, the "basic indicators" just published by UNICEF,[30] revealing that the United States has the worst record among the industrial countries, ranking alongside Cuba—a poor third world country under unremitting attack by the hemispheric superpower for almost forty years—by such standards as mortality for children under five. It also holds records for hunger, child poverty, and other basic social indicators.

All of this takes place in the richest country in the world, with unparalleled advantages and stable democratic institutions, but also under business rule, to an unusual extent. These are further auguries for the future, if the "dramatic shift away from a pluralist, participatory ideal of politics and towards an authoritarian and technocratic ideal" proceeds on course, worldwide.

It is worth noting that in secret, intentions are often spelled out honestly. For example, in the early post-World War II period, George Kennan, one of the most influential planners and considered a leading humanist, assigned each sector of the world its "function": Africa's function was to be "exploited" by Europe for its reconstruction, he observed, the United States having little interest in it. A year earlier, a high-level planning study had urged "that cooperative development of the cheap foodstuffs and raw materials of northern Africa could help forge European unity and create an economic base for continental recovery," an interesting concept of "cooperation."[31] There is no record of a suggestion that Africa might "exploit" the West for its recovery from the "global meliorism" of the past centuries.

In this review, I have tried to follow a reasonable methodological principle: to evaluate the praise for the "political and economic principles" of the world dominant power by keeping primarily to illustrations selected by the advocates themselves, as their strongest cases. The review is brief and partial, and deals with matters that are obscure and not well understood. My own judgment, for what it is worth, is that the sample is fair enough, and that it yields a sobering picture of the operative principles as well as of the likely "wave of the future" if they prevail unchallenged.

Even if accurate, the picture is seriously misleading, precisely because it is so partial: missing entirely are the achievements of those who really are committed to the fine principles proclaimed, and to principles of justice and freedom that reach far beyond. This is primarily a record of popular struggle seeking to erode and dismantle forms of oppression and domination, which sometimes are all too apparent but are often so deeply entrenched as to be virtually invisible, even to their victims. The record is rich and encouraging, and we have every reason to suppose that it can be carried forward. To do so requires a realistic assessment of existing circumstances and their historical origins, but that is of course only a bare beginning.

Skeptics who dismiss such hopes as utopian and naive have only to cast their eyes on what has happened right here in South Africa in the last few years, a tribute to what the human spirit can accomplish, and its limitless prospects. The lessons of these remarkable achievements should be an inspiration to people everywhere, and should guide the next steps in the continuing struggle here too, as the people of South Africa, fresh from one great victory, turn to the still more difficult challenges that lie ahead.

NOTES

1. UNICEF, *The State of the World's Children 1997* (Oxford University Press, 1997); UNICEF, *The Progress of Nations 1996* (UNICEF House, 1996).

2. Thomas Friedman, *New York Times,* June 2, 1992; National Security Adviser Anthony Lake, *New York Times,* September 26, 1993; historian David Fromkin, *New York Times Book Review,* May 4, 1997, summarizing recent work.

3. On the general picture and its historical origins, see, inter alia, Frederic Clairmont's classic study, *The Rise and Fall of Economic Liberalism* (Asia Publishing House, 1960), reprinted and updated (Penang and Goa: Third World Network, 1996); and Michel Chossudovsky, *The Globalization of Poverty* (Penang: Third World Network, 1997). Clairmont was an UNCTAD economist for many years; Chossudovsky is professor of economics at the University of Ottawa.

4. John Cassidy, *New Yorker,* October 16, 1995. . . . [For quotes that follow, see Harvey Cox, *World Policy Review,* Spring 1997; Martin Nolan, *Boston Globe,* March 5, 1997; John Buell, *Progressive,* March 1997.] The sample is liberal-to-left, in some cases quite critical. The analysis is similar across the rest of the spectrum, but generally euphoric.

5. John Liscio, *Barron's,* April 15, 1996.

6. [Chomsky here cites an earlier reference in *Profit Over People,* 53 f.]

7. Richard Cockett, "The Party, Publicity, and the Media," in Anthony Seldon and Stuart Ball, eds., *Conservative Century: The Conservative Party since 1900* (Oxford University Press, 1994); Harold Lasswell, "Propaganda," in *Encyclopaedia of the Social Sciences,* vol. 12 (Macmillan, 1933). For quotes and discussion, see "Intellectuals and the State" (1977), reprinted in Noam Chomsky, *Towards a New Cold War* (Pantheon, 1982). Also at last available is some of the pioneering work on these topics by Alex Carey, collected in his *Taking the Risk out of Democracy* (University of New South Wales Press, 1995, and University of Illinois Press, 1997).

8. *Ibid.*, and Elizabeth Fones-Wolf, *Selling Free Enterprise: the Business Assault on Labor and Liberalism, 1945–1960* (University of Illinois Press, 1995). Also Stuart Ewen, *PR!: A Social History of SPIN* (Basic Books, 1996). On the broader context, see Noam Chomsky, "Intellectuals and the State" and "Force and Opinion," reprinted in *Deterring Democracy* (Verso, 1991).

9. Editorial, *New Republic,* March 19, 1990.

10. Sanford Lakoff, *Democracy: History, Theory, Practice* (Westview, 1996), 262 f.

11. J. Toye, J. Harrigan, and P. Mosley, *Aid and Power* (Routledge, 1991), vol. 1, 16. On the Leninist comparison, see my essays ["Intellectuals and the State" and "Force and Opinion," reprinted in *Deterring Democracy* (Verso, 1991) and cited earlier] and *For Reasons of State* (Pantheon, 1973), Introduction.

12. Carothers, "The Reagan Years," in Abraham Lowenthal, ed., *Exporting Democracy* (Johns Hopkins University Press, 1991). See also his *In the Name of Democracy* (University of California Press, 1991).

13. See Chapter 2 ["Consent Without Consent: Regimenting the Public Mind" in Chomsky, *Profit Over People*], and for further discussion and sources, Noam Chomsky, *Powers and Prospects* (South End, 1996), "'Consent Without Consent': Reflections on the Theory and Practice of Democracy," *Cleveland State Law Review* 44.4, 1996.

14. *Survey of Current Business,* U.S. Dept. of Commerce, Vol. 76, no. 12 (December 1966).

15. Morton Horwitz, *The Transformation of American Law, 1870–1960* (Harvard University Press, 1992), Chapter 3. See also Charles Sellers, *The Market Revolution* (Oxford University Press, 1991).

16. Michael Sandel, *Democracy's Discontent* (Harvard University Press, 1996), Chapter 6. His interpretation in terms of republicanism and civic virtue is too narrow, in my opinion, overlooking deeper roots in the Enlightenment

and before. For some discussion, see among others Noam Chomsky, *Problems of Knowledge and Freedom* (Pantheon, 1971), Chapter 1; several essays reprinted in James Peck, ed., *The Chomsky Reader* (Pantheon, 1987); and Noam Chomsky, *Powers and Prospects,* Chapter 4.

17. For details, see Noam Chomsky, *Turning the Tide* (Boston: South End, 1985), Chapter 6.3; and Noam Chomsky, *The Culture of Terrorism* (South End, 1988), Chapter 11 (and sources cited), including quotes from Figueres, whose exclusion from the media took considerable dedication. See my *Letters from Lexington* (Common Courage, 1993), Chapter 6, on the record, including the long obituary in the *New York Times* by its Central America specialist and the effusive accompanying editorial, which again succeeded in completely banning his views on Washington's "crusade for democracy." On media coverage of Nicaraguan and Salvadoran elections, see Edward Herman and Noam Chomsky, *Manufacturing Consent* (Pantheon, 1988), Chapter 3. Even Carothers, who is careful with the facts, writes that the Sandinistas "refused to agree to elections" until 1990 (in Lowenthal, *op. cit.*).

18. Another standard falsification is that the long-planned elections took place only because of Washington's military and economic pressures, which are therefore retroactively justified.

19. On the elections and the reaction in Latin America and the United States, including sources for what follows, see Noam Chomsky, *Deterring Democracy,* Chapter 10. For a detailed review of the very successful subversion of diplomacy, hailed generally as a triumph of diplomacy, see Noam Chomsky, *Culture of Terrorism,* Chapter 7; and Noam Chomsky, *Necessary Illusions* (South End, 1989), appendix IV.5.

20. His emphasis, in Lowenthal, *op. cit.*

21. For details, see, inter alia, Richard Garfield, "Desocializing Health Care in a Developing Country," *Journal of the American Medical Association,* 270, no. 8, August 25, 1993, and Noam Chomsky, *World Orders, Old and New* (Columbia University Press, 1994), 131 f.

22. Michael Kinsley, *Wall Street Journal,* March 26, 1987; *New Republic,* editorials, April 2, 1984; March 19, 1990. For more on these and many similar examples, see Noam Chomsky, *Culture of Terrorism,* Chapter 5; Chomsky, *Deterring Democracy,* Chapters 10, 12.

23. H.D.S. Greenway, *Boston Globe,* July 29, 1993.

24. *New York Times,* May 2, 1985.

25. Vincent Cable, *Daedalus* (Spring 1995), citing UN World Investment Report 1993 (which, however, gives quite different figures, noting also

that "relatively little data are available" 164 f.). For more detailed discussion, estimating intra-TNC trade at 40 percent, see Peter Cowhey and Jonathan Aronson, *Managing the World Economy* (New York, Council on Foreign Relations, 1993). On U.S.-Mexico, see David Barkin and Fred Rosen, "Why the Recovery is Not a Recovery," *NACLA Report on the Americas,* January/February 1997; Leslie Crawford, "Legacy of Shock Therapy," *Financial Times,* February 12, 1997 (subtitled "Mexico: A Healthier Outlook," the article reviews the increasing misery of the vast majority of the population, apart from "the very rich"). Post-NAFTA intrafirm transactions: William Greider, *One World, Ready or Not* (Simon & Schuster, 1997), 273, citing Mexican economist Carlos Heredia. Pre-NAFTA estimates of intrafirm U.S. exports never entering Mexican markets passed 50 percent. Senator Ernest Hollings, *Foreign Policy,* Winter 1993–94.

26. 1992 OECD study cited by Clinton's former chief economic adviser Laura Tyson in *Who's Bashing Whom?* (Institute for International Economics, 1992).

27. Alfred Chandler, *The Visible Hand* (Belknap Press, 1977).

28. Speech delivered by C. A. Crocker, Assistant Secretary of State for African Affairs, in Honolulu before the National Security Committee of the American Legion, August 1981. Cited by Hans Abrahamsson, *Hegemony, Region and Nation State: The Case of Mozambique* (Padrigu Peace and Development Research Institute, Gothenburg University, January 1996).

29. For discussion, see Eric Toussaint and Peter Drucker, eds., *IMF/World Bank/WTO, Notebooks for Study and Research* (Amsterdam: International Institute for Research and Education, 1995), 24/5.

30. UNICEF, *State of the World's Children 1997.*

31. George Kennan, PPS 23, February 24, 1948 (*Foreign Relations of the United States,* vol. 1, 1948), 511. Michael Hogan, *The Marshall Plan* (Cambridge University Press, 1987), 41, paraphrasing the May 1947 Bonesteel Memorandum.

10

LAW AND JUSTICE

Howard Zinn

The Modern Era of Law

WE TAKE MUCH PRIDE in that phrase of John Adams, second president of the United States, when he spoke of the "rule of law" replacing the "rule of men." In ancient societies, in feudal society, there were no clear rules, written in statute books, accompanied by constitutions. Everyone was subject to the whims of powerful men, whether the feudal lord, the tribal chief, or the king.

But as societies evolved modern times brought big cities, international trade, widespread literacy, and parliamentary government. With all that came the rule of law, no longer personal and arbitrary, but written down. It claimed to be impersonal, neutral, apply equally to all, and, therefore, democratic.

We profess great reverence for certain symbols of the modern rule of law: the Magna Carta, which set forth what are men's rights as against the king; the American Constitution, which is supposed to limit the powers of government and provide a Bill of Rights; the Napoleonic Code, which introduced uniformity into the French legal system. But we might get uneasy about the connection between law and democracy when we read the comment of two historians (Robert Palmer and Joel Colton) on Napoleon: "Man on horseback though he was, he believed firmly in the rule of law."[1]

I don't want to deny the benefits of the modern era: the advance of science, the improvements in health, the spread of literacy and art beyond tiny elites, and the value of even an imperfect representative system over a monarchy. But those advantages lead us to overlook the fact that the modern era, replacing the arbitrary rule of men with the impartial rule of law, has not brought any fundamental change in the facts of unequal wealth and unequal power. What was done before—exploiting the poor, sending the young to war, and putting troublesome people in dungeons—is still done, except that this no longer seems to be the arbitrary action of the feudal lord or the king; it now has the authority of neutral, impersonal law.

The law appears impersonal. It is on paper, and who can trace it back to what men? And because it has the look of neutrality, its injustices are made legitimate. It was not easy to hold onto the "divine right" of kings—everyone could see that kings and queens were human beings. A code of law is more easily deified than a flesh-and-blood ruler.

Under the rule of men, the oppressor was identifiable, and so peasant rebels hunted down the lords, slaves killed plantation owners, and revolutionaries assassinated monarchs. In the era of the corporate bureaucracies, representative assemblies, and the rule of law, the enemy is elusive and unidentifiable. In John Steinbeck's depression-era novel *The Grapes of Wrath* a farmer having his land taken away from him confronts the tractor driver who is knocking down his house. He aims a gun at him, but is confused when the driver tells him that he takes his orders from a banker in Oklahoma City, who takes his orders from a banker in New York. The farmer cries out: "Then who can I shoot?"

The rule of law does not do away with the unequal distribution of wealth and power, but reinforces that inequality with the authority of law. It allocates wealth and poverty (through taxes and appropriations) but in such complicated and indirect ways as to leave the victim bewildered.

Exploitation was obvious when the peasant gave half his produce to the lord. It still exists, but inside the complexity of a market society and enforced by a library of statutes. A mine owner in Appalachia was asked, some years ago, why the coal companies paid so little taxes and kept so much of the wealth from the coal fields, while local people starved. The owner replied: "I pay exactly what the law asks me to pay."

There is a huge interest in the United States in crime and corruption as ways of acquiring wealth. But the greatest wealth, the largest fortunes, are acquired legally, aided by the laws of contract and property, enforced in the courts by friendly judges, handled by shrewd corporation lawyers, figured out by well-paid accountants. When our history books get to the 1920s, they dwell on the Teapot Dome scandals of the Harding administration, while ignoring the far greater reallocations of wealth that took place legally, through the tax laws proposed by Secretary of the Treasury

Andrew Mellon (a very rich man, through oil and aluminum), and passed by Congress in the Coolidge Administration.

How can this be? Didn't the modern era bring us democracy? Who drew up the Constitution? Wasn't it all of us, getting together to draw up the rules by which we would live, a "social contract"? Doesn't the Preamble to the Constitution start with the words: "We the People, in order to . . . etc., etc."?

In fact, while the Constitution was certainly an improvement over the royal charters of England, it was still a document drawn up by rich men, merchants, and slaveowners who wanted a bit of political democracy, but had no sympathy for economic democracy. It was designed to set up a "rule of law," which would efficiently prevent rebellion by dissatisfied elements in the population. As the Founding Fathers assembled in Philadelphia, they still had in mind farmers who had recently taken up arms in western Massachusetts (Shays' Rebellion) against unjust treatment by the wealth-controlled legislature.[2]

It is a deception of the citizenry to claim that the "rule of law" has replaced the "rule of men." It is still men (women are mostly kept out of the process) who enact the laws, who sit on the bench and interpret them, who occupy the White House or the Governor's mansion, and have the job of enforcing them.

These men have enormous powers of discretion. The legislators decide which laws to put on the books. The president and his attorney-general decide which laws to enforce. The judges decide who has a right to sue in court, what instructions to give to juries, what rules of law apply, and what evidence should not be allowed in the courtroom.

The lawyers, to whom ordinary people must turn for help in making their way through the court system, are trained and selected in such a way as to ensure their conservatism. The exceptions, when they appear, are noble and welcome, but too many lawyers are more concerned about being "good professionals" than achieving justice. As one student of the world of lawyers put it: "it is of the essence of the professionalization process to divorce law from politics, to elevate technique and craft over power, to search for 'neutral principles,' and to deny ideological purpose."[3]

Equal Justice Under Law is the slogan one sees on the marble pillars of the courthouse. And there is nothing in the words of the Constitution or the laws to indicate that anyone gets special treatment. They look as if they apply to everyone. But in the actual administration of the laws are rich and poor treated equally? Blacks and whites? Foreign born and natives? Conservatives and radicals? Private citizens and government officials?

There is a mountain of evidence on this: a CIA official (Richard Helms) commits perjury and gets off with a fine (Alger Hiss spent four years in jail for perjury), a president (Nixon) is pardoned in advance of prosecution for acts against the law, and Oliver North and other Reagan administration officials are found guilty of violating the law in the Iran-Contra affair, but none go to prison.

Still, the system of laws, to maintain its standing in the eyes of the citizenry and to provide safety valves by which the discontented can let off steam, must keep up the appearance of fairness. And so the law itself provides for change. When the pressure of discontentment becomes great, laws are passed to satisfy some part of the grievance. Presidents, when pushed by social movements, may enforce good laws. Judges, observing a changing temper in the society, may come forth with humane decisions.

Thus we have alternating currents of progress and paralysis. Periods of war alternate with periods of peace. There are times of witch-hunts for dissenters and times of apologies for the witch-hunts. We have "conservative" presidents giving way to liberal presidents and back again. The Supreme Court makes decisions one week on behalf of civil liberties and the next week curtails them. No one can get a clear fix on the system that way.

The modern system of the rule of law is something like roulette. Sometimes you win and sometimes you lose. No one can predict in any one instance whether the little ball will fall into the red or the black, and no one is really responsible. You win, you lose. But as in roulette, in the end you almost always lose. In roulette the results are fixed by the structure of the wheel, the laws of mathematical probability, and the rules of "the house." In society, the rich and strong get what they want by the law of contract, the rules of the market, and the power of the authorities to change the rules or violate them at will.

What is the structure of society's roulette wheel that ensures you will, in the end, lose? It is, first of all, the great disparities in wealth that give a tremendous advantage to those who can buy and sell industries, buy and sell people's labor and services, buy and sell the means of communication, subsidize the educational system, and buy and sell the political candidates themselves. Second, it is the system of "checks and balances," in which bold new reforms (try free medical care for all or sweeping protections of the environment) can be buried in committee, vetoed by one legislative chamber or by the president, interpreted to death by the Supreme Court, or passed by Congress and unenforced by the president.

In this system, the occasional victories may ease some of the pain of economic injustice. They also reveal the usefulness of protest and pressure, suggest even greater possibilities for the future. And they keep you in the game, giving you the feeling of fairness, preventing you from getting angry and upsetting the wheel. It is a system ingeniously devised for maintaining things as they are, while allowing for limited reform.

Obligation to the State

Despite all I have said about the gap between law and justice and despite the fact that this gap is visible to many people in the society, the idea of obligation to law, obligation to government, remains powerful. President Jimmy Carter reinstated the draft of young men for military service in 1979, and when television reporters asked the men why they were complying with the law (about 10 percent were not), the most common answer was "I owe it to my country."

The obligation that people feel to one another goes back to the very beginning of human history, as a natural, spontaneous act in human relations.[4] Obligation to government, however, is not natural. It must be taught to every generation.

Who can teach this lesson of obligation with more authority than the great Plato? Plato has long been one of the gods of modern culture, his reputation that of an awesome mind and a brilliant writer of dialogue, his work the greatest of the Great Books. Shrewdly, Plato puts his ideas about obligation in the mouth of Socrates. Socrates left no writings that we know of, so he can be used to say whatever Plato wants. And Plato could have no better spokesman than a wise, gentle old man who was put to death by the government of Athens in 399 B.C. for speaking his mind. Any words coming from such a man will be especially persuasive.

But they are Plato's words, Plato's ideas. All we know of Socrates is what Plato tells us. Or, what we read in the recollections of another contemporary, Xenophon. Or what we can believe about him from reading Aristophanes's spoof on his friend Socrates, in his play *The Clouds*.

So we can't know for sure what Socrates really said to his friend Crito, who visited him in jail, after he had been condemned to death. But we do know what Plato has him say in the dialogue *Crito*[5] (written many years after Socrates's execution), which has been impressed on the minds of countless generations, down to the present day, with deadly effect. Plato's ideas have become part of the orthodoxy of the nation, absorbed into the national bloodstream and reproduced in ordinary conversations and on bumper stickers. ("Love it or leave it"—summing up Plato's idea of obligation.)

Plato's message is presented appealingly by a man calmly facing death, whose courage disarms any possible skepticism. It is made even more appealing by the fact that it follows another dialogue, the *Apology*, in which (according to Plato), Socrates addresses the jury in an eloquent defense of free speech, saying those famous words: "The unexamined life is not worth living."

Plato then unashamedly (lesson one in intellectual bullying: speak with utter confidence) presents us with some unexamined ideas. Having established Socrates's credentials as a martyr for independent thought, he proceeds in the *Crito* to put on Socrates's tongue an argument for blind obedience to government.

It is hardly a dialogue, although Plato is famous for dialogue and the "Socratic method" is based on teaching through dialogue. Poor Crito, who visits Socrates in prison to persuade him to let his friends plan his escape, is virtually tongue-tied. He is reduced to saying, to every one of Socrates's little speeches: "Yes . . . of course . . . clearly . . . I agree. . . . Yes . . . I think that you are right. . . . True." And Socrates is going on and on, like the good trouper that he is, saying Plato's lines, making Plato's argument. We know the ideas are Plato's because in his well-known and much bigger dialogue the *Republic* he makes an even more extended case for a totalitarian state.

To Crito's offer of escape, Socrates replies: I must obey the law. True, he says, Athens has committed an injustice by ordering him to die for speaking his mind (he seems slightly annoyed at this!), but if he complained about this injustice, Athens could rightly say: "We brought you into the world, we raised you, we educated you, we gave you and every other citizen a share of all the good things we could."

Socrates accepts this argument of the state. He tells Crito that by not leaving Athens he agreed to obey its laws. So he must go to his death. Yes, it is Plato's own bumper sticker: "Love it or leave it."

If Plato had lived another 2,000 years or so he would have encountered the argument of Henry David Thoreau, the quiet hermit of Walden Pond who wrote a famous essay on civil disobedience. Thoreau said that whatever good things we have were not given us by the state, but by the energies and talents of the people of the country. And he would be damned if he would pay taxes to support a war against Mexico based on such a paltry argument.

Plato, the Western world's star intellectual, makes a number of paltry arguments in this so-called dialogue. He has Socrates imagining the authorities addressing him: "What complaint have you against us and the state, that you are trying to destroy us? Are we not, first of all, your parents? Through us your father took your mother and brought you into the world."[6]

What complaint? Only that they are putting him to death! The state as parents? Now we understand those words: the Motherland, the Fatherland, the Founding Fathers, Uncle Sam. What neat spades for planting the idea of obligation. It's not some little junta of military men and politicians who are sending you to die in some muddy field in Asia or Central America, it's your mother, your father, or your father's favorite brother. How can you say no? "Through us your father took your mother and brought you into the world." What stately arrogance! To give the state credit for marriage and children, as if without government men and women would remain apart and celibate. Socrates listens meekly to the words of the law:

> Are you too wise to see your country is worthier, more to be revered, more sacred, and held in higher honor both by the gods and by all men of understanding, than your father and your mother and all your other ancestors; that you ought to reverence it and to submit to it . . . and to obey in silence if it orders you to endure flogging or imprisonment or if it sends you to battle to be wounded or to die?[7]

In the face of this seductive argument, Crito is virtually mute, a sad sack of a debater. You would think that Plato, just to maintain his reputation for good dialogue, would give Crito some better lines. But he took no chances.

Plato says (again, through Socrates bullying Crito): "In war, and in the court of justice, and everywhere, you must do whatever your state and your country tell you to do, or you must persuade them that their commands are unjust."

Why not insist that the *state* persuade *us* to do its bidding? There is no equality in Plato's scheme: the citizen may use persuasion, but no more; the state may use force.

It is curious that Socrates (according to Plato) was willing to disobey the authorities by preaching as he chose, by telling the young what he saw as the truth, even if that meant going against the laws of Athens. Yet, when he was sentenced to death, and by a divided jury (the vote was 281 to 220), he meekly accepted the verdict, saying he owed Athens obedience to its laws, giving that puny 56 percent majority vote an absolute right to take his life.

And so it is that the admirable obligation human beings feel to one's neighbors, one's loved ones, even to a stranger needing water or shelter, becomes confused with blind obedience to that deadly artifact called government. And in that confusion, young men, going off to war in some part of the world they never heard of, for some cause that cannot be rationally explained, then say: "I owe it to my country."

It seems that the idea of *owing*, of obligation, is strongly felt by almost everyone. But what does one owe the government? Granted, the government may do useful things for its citizens: help farmers, administer old-age pensions and health benefits, regulate the use of drugs, apprehend criminals, etc. But because the government administers these programs (for which the citizens pay taxes, and for which the government officials draw salaries), does this mean that you owe the government your life?

Plato is enticing us to confuse the *country* with the *government*. The Declaration of Independence tried to make clear that the people of the country *set up* the government, to achieve the aims of equality and justice, and when a government no longer pursues those aims it loses its legitimacy, it has violated *its* obligation to the citizens, and deserves no more respect or obedience.

We are intimidated by the word *patriotism*, afraid to be called unpatriotic. Early in the twentieth century, the Russian-American anarchist and feminist Emma Goldman lectured on patriotism. She said,

> Conceit, arrogance and egotism are the essentials of patriotism. . . . Patriotism assumes that our globe is divided into little spots, each one surrounded by an iron gate. Those who had the fortune of being born on some particular spot, consider themselves better, nobler, grander, more intelligent than the living beings inhabiting any other spot. It is, therefore, the duty of everyone living on that chosen spot to fight, kill, and die in the attempt to impose his superiority upon all the others.[8]

Even the symbols of patriotism—the flag, the national anthem—become objects of worship, and those who refuse to worship are treated as heretics. When in 1989 the U.S. Supreme Court decided that a citizen has a right to express himself or herself by burning the American flag, there was an uproar in the White House and in Congress. President Bush, almost in tears, began speaking of a Constitutional amendment to make flag burning a crime. Congress, with its customary sheepishness, rushed to pass a law providing a year in prison for anyone hurting the flag.

The humorist Garrison Keillor responded to the president with some seriousness:

> Flag-burning is a minor insult compared to George Bush's cynical use of the flag for political advantage. Any decent law to protect the flag ought to prohibit politicians from wrapping it around themselves! Flag-burning is an impulsive act by a powerless individual—but the cool pinstripe demagoguery of this powerful preppie is a real and present threat to freedom.[9]

If patriotism were defined, not as blind obedience to government, not as submissive worship to flags and anthems, but rather as love of one's country, one's fellow citizens (all over the world), as loyalty to the principles of justice and democracy, then patriotism would require us to disobey our government, when it violated those principles. . . .

Thoreau, Jefferson, and Tolstoy

The great artists and writers of the world, from Sophocles in the fifth century B.C. to Tolstoy in the modern era, have understood the difference between law and justice. They have known that, just as imagination is necessary to go outside the traditional boundaries to find and to create beauty and to touch human sensibility, so it is necessary to go outside the rules and regulations of the state to achieve happiness for oneself and others.

Henry David Thoreau, in his famous essay "Civil Disobedience," wrote,

> A common and natural result of an undue respect for law is, that you may see a file of soldiers, colonels, captains, corporals, privates, powder-monkeys, and all, marching in admirable order over hill and dale to the wars, against their wills, ay, against their common sense and consciences, which makes it very steep marching indeed, and produces a palpitation of the heart.

When farmers rebelled in western Massachusetts in 1786 (Shays' Rebellion), Thomas Jefferson was not sympathetic to their action. But he hoped the government would pardon them. He wrote to Abigail Adams:

> The spirit of resistance to government is so valuable on certain occasions that I wish it to be always kept alive. It will often be exercised when wrong, but better so than not to be exercised at all. I like a little rebellion now and then. It is like a storm in the atmosphere.[10]

What kind of person can we admire, can we ask young people of the next generation to emulate—the strict follower of law or the dissident who struggles, sometimes within, sometimes outside, sometimes against the law, but always for justice? What life is best worth living—the life of the proper, obedient, dutiful follower of law and order or the life of the independent thinker, the rebel?

Leo Tolstoy, in his story "The Death of Ivan Ilyich," tells of a proper, successful magistrate, who on his deathbed wonders why he suddenly feels that his life has been horrible and senseless. "'Maybe I did not live as I ought to have done. . . . But how can that be, when I did everything properly?' . . . and he remembered all the legality, correctitude and propriety of his life."

NOTES

1. Palmer and Colton, *A History of the Modern World* (Knopf, 1984).

2. It was distinguished historian Charles Beard, in *An Economic Interpretation of the Constitution* (Macmillan, 1935), who broke through the romanticization of the Founding Fathers with his exploration of their economic interests and their political ideas. Other scholars have claimed to refute him, but I believe his fundamental thesis remains untouched: the relationship between wealth and political power.

3. Jerold S. Auerbach, *Unequal Justice* (Oxford University Press, 1976).

4. Political theorist Michael Walzer writes about "the obligation to disobey." He talks about people having the "obligation to honor the engagements they have explicitly made, to defend the groups and uphold the ideals to which they have committed themselves, even against the state, so long as their disobedience of laws or legally authorized commands does not threaten the very existence of the larger society or endanger the lives of its citizens. Sometimes it is disobedience to the state, when one has a duty to disobey, that must be justified." Michael Walzer, *Obligations* (Harvard University Press, 1970).

5. *Euthyphro, Apology, Crito* (Bobbs-Merrill, 1956).

6. Ibid.

7. Ibid.

8. Emma Goldman, *Anarchism and Other Essays* (Dover, 1969), 128–129.

9. Op-ed page, *New York Times,* July 2, 1989.

10. Dumas Malone, *Jefferson and the Rights of Man* (Little, Brown, 1951).

JEFFERSON, MORRILL, AND THE UPPER CRUST

Wendell Berry

The Land-Grant Colleges

TO UNDERSTAND what eventually became of the land-grant college complex, it will be worthwhile to consider certain significant differences between the thinking of [Thomas] Jefferson and that of [Justin Smith] Morrill [representative and later Senator from Vermont, for whom the Morrill Act, the first of the land-grant college acts to become law, was named]. The most important of these is the apparent absence from Morrill's mind of Jefferson's complex sense of the dependence of democratic citizenship upon education. For Jefferson, the ideals and aims of education appear to have been defined directly by the requirements of political liberty. He envisioned a local system of education with a double purpose: to foster in the general population the critical alertness necessary to good citizenship and to seek out and prepare a "natural aristocracy" of "virtue and talents" for the duties and trusts of leadership. His plan of education for Virginia did not include any form of specialized or vocational training. He apparently assumed that if communities could be stabilized and preserved by the virtues of citizenship and leadership, then the "practical arts" would be improved as a matter of course by local example, reading, etc. Morrill, on the other hand, looked at education from a strictly practical or utilitarian viewpoint. He believed that the primary aims of education were to correct the work of farmers and mechanics and "exalt their usefulness." His wish to break the educational monopoly of the professional class was Jeffersonian only in a very limited sense: he wished to open the professional class to the children of laborers. In distinguishing among the levels of education, he did not distinguish, as Jefferson did, among "degrees of genius."

Again, whereas Jefferson regarded farmers as "the most valuable citizens," Morrill looked upon the professions as "places of higher consideration." We are thus faced with a difficulty in understanding Morrill's wish to "exalt the usefulness" of "those who must win their bread by labor." Would education exalt their usefulness by raising the quality of their work or by making them eligible for promotion to "places of higher consideration"?

Those differences and difficulties notwithstanding, the apparent intention in regard to agriculture remains the same from Jefferson to Morrill to the land-grant college acts. That intention was to promote the stabilization of farming populations and communities and to establish in that way a "permanent" agriculture, enabled by better education to preserve both the land and the people.

The failure of this intention, and the promotion by the land-grant colleges of an *impermanent* agriculture destructive of land and people, was caused in part by the lowering of the educational standard from Jefferson's ideal of public or community responsibility to the utilitarianism of Morrill, insofar as this difference in the aims of the two men represented a shift of public value. The land-grant colleges have, in fact, been very little—and have been less and less—concerned "to promote the liberal and practical education of the industrial classes" or of any other classes. Their history has been largely that of the whittling down of this aim—from education in the broad, "liberal" sense to "practical" preparation for earning a living to various "programs" for certification. They first reduced "liberal and practical" to "practical," and then for "practical" they substituted "specialized." And the standard of their purpose has shifted from usefulness to careerism. And if this has not been caused by, it has certainly accompanied a degeneration of faculty standards, by which professors and teachers of disciplines become first upholders of "professional standards" and then careerists in pursuit of power, money, and prestige.

The land-grant college legislation obviously calls for a system of local institutions responding to local needs and local problems. What we have instead is a system of institutions which more and more resemble one another, like airports and motels, made increasingly uniform by the transience or rootlessness of their career-oriented faculties and the consequent inability to respond to local conditions. The professor lives in his career, in a ghetto of career-oriented fellow professors. Where he may be geographically is of little interest to him. One's career is a vehicle, not a dwelling; one is concerned less for where it is than for where it will go.

The careerist professor is by definition a specialist professor. Utterly dependent upon his institution, he blunts his critical intelligence and blurs his language so as to exist "harmoniously" within it—and so serves his school with an emasculated and fragmentary intelligence, deferring "realistically" to the redundant procedures and meaningless demands of an inflated administrative bureaucracy whose educational purpose is written on its paychecks.

But just as he is dependent on his institution, the specialist professor is also dependent on his students. In order to earn a living, he must teach; in order to teach, he must have students. And so the tendency is to make a commodity of education: to package it attractively, reduce requirements, reduce homework, inflate grades, lower standards, and deal expensively in "public relations."

As self-interest, laziness, and lack of conviction augment the general confusion about what an education is or ought to be, and as standards of excellence are replaced by sliding scales of adequacy, these schools begin to depend upon, and so to institutionalize, the local problems that they were founded to solve. They begin to need, and so to promote, the mobility, careerism, and moral confusion that are victimizing the local population and destroying the local communities. The stock in trade of the "man of learning" comes to be ignorance.

The colleges of agriculture are focused somewhat more upon their whereabouts than, say, the colleges of arts and sciences because of the local exigencies of climate, soils, and crop varieties; but like the rest they tend to orient themselves within the university rather than within the communities they were intended to serve. The impression is unavoidable that the academic specialists of agriculture tend to validate their work experimentally rather than practically, that they would rather be professionally reputable than locally effective, and that they pay little attention, if any, to the social, cultural, and political consequences of their work. Indeed, it sometimes appears that they pay very little attention to its economic consequences. There is nothing more characteristic of modern agricultural research than its divorcement from the sense of consequence and from all issues of value.

This is facilitated on the one hand by the academic ideal of "objectivity" and on the other by a strange doctrine of the "inevitability" of undisciplined technological growth and change. "Objectivity" has come to be simply the academic uniform of moral cowardice: one who is "objective" never takes a stand. And in the fashionable "realism" of technological determinism, one is shed of the embarrassment of moral and intellectual standards and of any need to define what is excellent or desirable. Education is relieved of its concern for truth in order to prepare students to live in "a changing world." As soon as educational standards begin to be dictated by "a changing world" (changing, of course, to a tune called by the governmental-military-academic-industrial complex), then one is justified in teaching virtually anything in any way—for, after all, one never knows for sure what "a changing world" is going to become. The way is thus opened to run a university as a business, the main purpose of which is to sell diplomas—after a complicated but undemanding four-year ritual—and thereby give employment to professors.

Colleges of "Agribusiness" and Unsettlement

That the land-grant college complex has fulfilled its obligation "to assure agriculture a position in research equal to that of industry" simply by failing to distinguish between the two is acknowledged in the term "agribusiness." The word does not denote any real identity either of function or interest, but only an expedient confusion by which the interests of industry have subjugated those of agriculture. This confusion of agriculture with industry has utterly perverted the intent of the land-grant college acts. The case has been persuasively documented by a task force of the Agribusiness Accountability Project. In the following paragraphs, Jim Hightower and Susan DeMarco give the task force's central argument:

"Who is helped and who is hurt by this research?

"It is the largest-scale growers, the farm machinery and chemicals input companies and the processors who are the primary beneficiaries. Machinery companies such as John Deere, International Harvester, Massey-Ferguson, Allis-Chalmer, and J. I. Case almost continually engage in cooperative research efforts at land grant colleges. These corporations contribute money and some of their own research personnel to help land grant scientists develop machinery. In return, they are able to incorporate technological advances in their own products. In some cases they actually receive exclusive licenses to manufacture and sell the products of tax-paid research.

"If mechanization has been a boon to agribusiness, it has been a bane to millions of rural Americans. Farmworkers have been the earliest victims. There were 4.3 million hired farm workers in 1950. Twenty years later that number had fallen to 3.5 million . . .

"Farmworkers have not been compensated for jobs lost to mechanized research. They were not consulted when that work was designed, and their needs were not a part of the research that resulted. They simply were left to fend on their own—no re-training, no unemployment compensation, no research to help them adjust to the changes that came out of the land grant colleges.

"Independent family farmers also have been largely ignored by the land grant colleges. Mechanization research by land grant colleges is either irrelevant or only incidentally adaptable to the needs of 87 to 99 percent of America's farmers. The public subsidy for mechanization actually has weakened the competitive position of the family farmer. Taxpayers, through the land grant college complex, have given corporate producers a technological arsenal specifically suited to their scale of operation and designed to increase their efficiency and profits. The independent family farmer is left to strain his private resources to the breaking point in a desperate effort to clamber aboard the technological treadmill."

The task force also raised the issue of academic featherbedding—irrelevant or frivolous research or instruction carried on by colleges of agriculture, experiment stations, and extension services. Evidently, people in many states may expect to be "served" by such studies as one at Cornell that discovered that "employed homemakers have less time for housekeeping tasks than non-employed homemakers." An article in the *Louisville Courier-Journal* lately revealed, for example, that "a 20-year-old waitress . . . recently attended a class where she learned 'how to set a real good table.'

"She got some tips on how to save steps and give faster service by 'carrying quite a few things' on the same tray. And she learned most of the highway numbers in the area, so she could give better directions to confused tourists.

"She learned all of that from the University of Kentucky College of Agriculture. Specialists in restaurant management left the Lexington campus to give the training to waitresses . . .

"The UK College of Agriculture promotes tourism.

"The college also helps to plan highways, housing projects, sewer systems and industrial developments throughout the state.

"It offers training in babysitting, 'family living' . . . "

This sort of "agricultural" service is justified under the Smith-Lever Act, Section 347a, inserted by amendment in 1955, and by Representative Lever's "charge" to the Extension Service in 1913. Both contain language that requires some looking at.

Section 347a is based mainly upon the following congressional insight: that "in certain agricultural areas," "there is concentration of farm families on farms either too small or too unproductive or both . . . " For these "disadvantaged farms" the following remedies were provided: "(1) Intensive on-the-farm educational assistance to the farm family in appraising and resolving its problems; (2) assistance and counseling to local groups in appraising resources for capability of improvement in agriculture or introduction of industry designed to supplement farm income; (3) cooperation with other agencies and groups in furnishing all possible information as to existing employment opportunities, particularly to farm families having underemployed workers; and (4) in cases where the farm family, after analysis of its opportunities and existing resources, finds it advisable to seek a new farming venture, the providing of information, advice, and counsel in connection with making such change."

The pertinent language of Representative Lever's "charge," which is apparently regarded as having the force of law, at least by the University of Kentucky Cooperative Extension Service, places upon extension agents the responsibility "to assume leadership in every movement, whatever it may be, the aim of which is better farming, better living, more happiness, more education and better citizenship."

If Section 347a is an example—as it certainly is—of special-interest legislation, its special interest is only ostensibly and vaguely in the welfare of small ("disadvantaged") farmers. To begin with, it introduces into law and into land-grant philosophy the startling concept that a farm can be "too small" or "too unproductive." The only standard for this judgment is implied in the clauses that follow it: the farmers of such farms "are unable to make adjustments and investments required to establish profitable operations"; such a farm "does not permit profitable employment of available labor"; and—most revealing—"many of these farm families are not able to make full use of current extension programs . . . "

The first two of these definitions of a "too small" or "too unproductive" farm are not agricultural but economic: the farm must provide, not a living, but a profit. And it must be profitable, moreover, in an economy that—in 1955, as now—favors "agribusiness." (Section 347a is a product of the era in which then Assistant Secretary of Agriculture John Davis and Earl Butz were advocating "corporate control to 'rationalize' agriculture production"; in which Mr. Davis himself invented the term "agribusiness"; in which then Secretary of Agriculture Ezra Taft Benson told farmers to "Get big or get out.") Profitability may be a standard of a sort, but a most relative sort and by no means sufficient. It leaves out of consideration, for instance, the possibility that a family might farm a small acreage, take excellent care of it, make a decent, honorable, and independent living from it, and yet fail to make what the authors of Section 347a would consider a profit.

But the third definition is, if possible, even more insidious: a farm is "too small" or "too unproductive" if it cannot "make full use of current extension programs." The farm is not to be the measure of the service; the service is to be the measure of the farm.

It will be argued that Section 347a was passed in response to real conditions of economic hardship on the farm and that the aim of the law was to permit the development of *new* extension programs as remedies. But that is at best only half true. There certainly were economic hardships on the farm in 1955; we have proof of that in the drastic decline in the number of farms and farmers since then. But there was plenty of land-grant legislation at that time to permit the extension service to devise any program necessary to deal with agricultural problems *as such*. What is remarkable about Section 347a is that it permitted the land-grant colleges to abandon these problems as such, to accept the "agribusiness" revolution as inevitable, and to undertake non-agricultural solutions to agricultural problems. And the assistances provided for in Section 347a are so general and vague as to allow the colleges to be most inventive. After 1955, the agricultural academicians would have a vested interest, not in the welfare of farmers, but in virtually anything at all that might happen to ex-farmers, their families, and their descendants forevermore. They have, in other words, a vested interest in their own failure—foolproof job security.

But it is hard to see how the language of Section 347a, loose as it is, justifies the teaching of highway numbers to waitresses, the promotion of tourism, and the planning of industrial developments, sewer systems, and housing projects. For justification of these programs we apparently must look to the language of Representative Lever's "charge," which in effect tells the extension agents to do anything they can think of.

These new "services" seem little more than desperate maneuvers on the part of the land-grant colleges to deal with the drastic reduction in the last thirty years of their lawful clientele—a reduction for which the colleges themselves are in large part responsible because of their eager collaboration with "agribusiness." As the conversion of farming into agribusiness has depopulated the farmland, it has become necessary for the agriculture specialists to develop "programs" with which to follow their erstwhile beneficiaries into the cities—either that or lose their meal ticket in the colleges. If the colleges of agriculture have so assiduously promoted the industrialization of farming and the urbanization of farmers that now "96 percent

of America's manpower is freed from food production," then the necessary trick of survival is to become colleges of industrialization and urbanization—that is, colleges of "agribusiness"—which, in fact, is what they
have been for a long time. Their success has been stupendous: as the number of farmers has decreased, the colleges of agriculture have grown larger.

The bad faith of the program-mongering under Section 347a may be
suggested by several questions:

Why did land-grant colleges not address themselves to the *agricultural*
problems of small or "disadvantaged" farmers?

Why did they not undertake the development of small-scale technologies and methods appropriate to the small farm?

Why have they assumed that the turn to "agribusiness" and big technology was "inevitable"?

Why, if they can promote tourism and plan sewer systems, have they
not promoted cooperatives to give small farmers some measure of protection against corporate suppliers and purchasers?

Why have they watched in silence the destruction of the markets of the
small producers of poultry, eggs, butter, cream, and milk—once the main-
stays of the small-farm economy?

Why have they never studied or questioned the necessity or the justice
of the sanitation laws that have been used to destroy such markets?

Why have they not tried to calculate the real (urban and rural) costs of
the migration from farm to city?

Why have they raised no questions of social, political, or cultural value?

That the colleges of agriculture should have become colleges of
"agribusiness"—working, in effect, *against* the interests of the small farmers, the farm communities, and the farmland—can only be explained by
the isolation of specialization.

First we have the division of the study of agriculture into specialties.
And then, within the structure of the university, we have the separation
of these specialties from specialties of other kinds. This problem is outlined with forceful insight by Andre Mayer and Jean Mayer in an article
entitled "Agriculture, the Island Empire," published in the summer 1974
issue of *Daedalus*. Like other academic professions, agriculture has gone
its separate way and aggrandized itself in its own fashion: "As it developed into an intellectual discipline in the nineteenth century, it did so in
academic divisions which were isolated from the liberal arts center of the
university . . ." It "produced ancillary disciplines parallel to those in the
arts and sciences . . ." And it "developed its own scientific organizations;
its own professional, trade, and social organizations; its own technical

and popular magazines; and its own public. It even has a separate political system . . ."

The founding fathers, these authors point out, "placed agriculture at the center of an Enlightenment concept of science broad enough to include society, politics, and sometimes even theology." But the modern academic structure has alienated agriculture from such concerns. The result is an absurd "independence" which has produced genetic research "without attention to nutritional values," which has undertaken the so-called Green Revolution without concern for its genetic oversimplification or its social, political, and cultural dangers, and which keeps agriculture in a separate "field" from ecology.

A Betrayal of Trust

The educational *ideal* that concerns us here was held clearly in the mind of Thomas Jefferson, was somewhat diminished or obscured in the mind of Justin Morrill, but survived indisputably in the original language of the land-grant college acts. We see it in the intention that education should be "liberal" as well as "practical," in the wish to foster "a sound and prosperous agriculture and rural life," in the distinction between agriculture and industry, in the purpose of establishing and maintaining a "permanent" agriculture, in the implied perception that this permanence would depend on the stability of "the rural home and rural life." This ideal is simply that farmers should be educated, liberally and practically, *as farmers*; education should be given and acquired with the understanding that those so educated would return to their home communities, not merely to be farmers, corrected and improved by their learning, but also to assume the trusts and obligations of community leadership, the highest form of that "vigilant and distrustful superintendence" without which the communities could not preserve themselves. This leadership, moreover, would tend to safeguard agriculture's distinction from and competitiveness with industry. Conceivably, had it existed, this leadership might have resulted in community-imposed restraints upon technology, such as those practiced by the Amish.

Having stated the ideal, it becomes possible not merely to perceive the degeneracy and incoherence of the land-grant colleges within themselves, but to understand their degenerative influence on the farming communities. It becomes possible to see that their failure goes beyond the disintegration of intellectual and educational standards; it is the betrayal of a trust.

The land-grant acts gave to the colleges not just government funds and a commission to teach and to do research, but also a purpose which may be generally stated as the preservation of agriculture and rural life. That this purpose is a practical one is obvious from the language of the acts; no one, I dare say, would deny that this is so. It is equally clear, though far less acknowledged, that the purpose is also moral, insofar as it raises issues of value and of feeling. It may be that pure practicality can deal with agriculture so long as agriculture is defined as a set of problems that are purely technological (though such a definition is in itself a gross falsification), but it inevitably falters at the meanings of "liberal," "sound and prosperous," "permanent and effective," "development and improvement"; and it fails altogether to address the concepts of "the rural home and rural life." When the Hatch Act, for instance, imposed upon the colleges the goals of "a permanent and effective agricultural industry" and "the development and improvement of the rural home and rural life," it implicitly required of them an allegiance to the agrarian values that have constituted one of the dominant themes of American history and thought.

The tragedy of the land-grant acts is that their moral imperative came finally to have nowhere to rest except on the careers of specialists whose standards and operating procedures were amoral: the "objective" practitioners of the "science" of agriculture, whose minds have no direction other than that laid out by career necessity and the logic of experimentation. They have no apparent moral allegiances or bearings or limits. Their work thus inevitably serves whatever power is greatest. That power at present is the industrial economy, of which "agribusiness" is a part. Lacking any moral force or vision of its own, the "objective" expertise of the agriculture specialist points like a compass needle toward the greater good of the "agribusiness" corporations. The objectivity of the laboratory functions in the world as indifference; knowledge without responsibility is merchandise, and greed provides its applications. Far from developing and improving the rural home and rural life, the land-grant colleges have blindly followed the drift of virtually the whole population away from home, blindly documenting or "serving" the consequent disorder and blindly rationalizing this disorder as "progress" or "miraculous development."

At this point one can begin to understand the violence that has been done to the Morrill Act's provision for a "liberal and practical education." One imagines that Jefferson might have objected to the inclusion of the phrase "and practical," and indeed in retrospect the danger in it is clearly visible. Nevertheless, the law evidently sees "liberal and practical" as a description of *one* education, not two. And as long as the two terms are thus associated, the combination remains thinkable: the "liberal" side, for instance, might offer necessary restraints of value to the "practical"; the "practical" interest might direct the "liberal" to crucial issues of use and effect.

In practice, however, the Morrill Act's formula has been neatly bisected and carried out as if it read "a liberal *or* a practical education." But though these two kinds of education may theoretically be divided and given equal importance, in fact they are no sooner divided than they are opposed. They enter into competition with one another, and by a kind of educational Gresham's Law the practical curriculum drives out the liberal.

This happens because the *standards* of the two kinds of education are fundamentally different and fundamentally opposed. The standard of liberal education is based upon definitions of excellence in the various disciplines. These definitions are in turn based upon example. One learns to order one's thoughts and to speak and write coherently by studying exemplary thinkers, speakers, and writers of the past. One studies *The Divine Comedy* and the Pythagorean theorem not to acquire something to be exchanged for something else, but to understand the orders and the kinds of thought and to furnish the mind with subjects and examples. Because the standards are rooted in examples, they do not change.

The standard of practical education, on the other hand, is based upon the question of what will work, and because the practical is by definition of the curriculum set aside from issues of value, the question tends to be resolved in the most shallow and immediate fashion: what is practical is what makes money; what is most practical is what makes the most money. Practical education is an "investment," something acquired to be exchanged for something else—a "good" job, money, prestige. It is oriented entirely toward the future, toward what *will* work in the "changing world" in which the student is supposedly being prepared to "compete." The standard of practicality, as used, is inherently a degenerative standard. There is nothing to correct it except suppositions about what the world will be like and what the student will therefore need to know. Because the future is by definition unknown, one person's supposition about the future tends to be as good, or as forceful, as another's. And so the standard of practicality tends to revise itself downward to meet, not the needs, but the desires of the student who, for instance, does not want to learn a science because he *intends* to pursue a career in which he does not *think* a knowledge of science will be necessary.

It could be said that a liberal education has the nature of a bequest, in that it looks upon the student as the potential heir of a cultural birthright, whereas a practical education has the nature of a commodity to be

exchanged for position, status, wealth, etc., *in the future.* A liberal education rests on the assumption that nature and human nature do not
change very much or very fast and that one therefore needs to understand
the past. The practical educators assume that human society itself is the
only significant context, that change is therefore fundamental, constant,
and necessary, that the future will be wholly unlike the past, that the past
is outmoded, irrelevant, and an encumbrance upon the future—the present being only a time for dividing past from future, for getting ready.

But these definitions, based on division and opposition, are too simple.
It is easy, accepting the viewpoint of either side, to find fault with the
other. But the wrong is on neither side; it is in their division. . . . The practical, divorced from the discipline of value, tends to be defined by the
immediate interests of the practitioner, and so becomes destructive of
value, practical and otherwise. But it must not be forgotten that, divorced
from the practical, the liberal disciplines lose their sense of use and influence and become attenuated and aimless. The purity of "pure" science is
then ritualized as a highly competitive intellectual game without awareness of use, responsibility, or consequence, such as that described in *The
Double Helix,* James D. Watson's book about the discovery of the structure of DNA. And the so-called humanities become a world of their own,
a collection of "professional" sub-languages, complicated circuitries of
abstruse interpretation, feckless exercises of sensibility. Without the balance of historic value, practical education gives us that most absurd of
standards: "relevance," based upon the suppositional needs of a theoretical future. But liberal education, divorced from practicality, gives something no less absurd: the specialist professor of one or another of the
liberal arts, the custodian of an inheritance he has learned much about,
but nothing from.

And in the face of competition from the practical curriculum, the liberal has found it impossible to maintain its own standards and so has
become practical—that is, career-oriented—also. It is now widely assumed
that the only good reason to study literature or philosophy is to become
a teacher of literature or philosophy—in order, that is, to get an income
from it. I recently received in the mail a textbook of rhetoric in which the
author stated that "there is no need for anyone except a professional lin-
guist to be able to explain language operations specifically and accurately." Maybe so, but how does one escape the implicit absurdity that
linguists should study the language only to teach aspiring linguists?

The education of the student of agriculture is almost as absurd, and it
is more dangerous: he is taught a course of practical knowledge and procedures for which uses do indeed exist, but these uses lie outside the

purview and interest of the school. The colleges of agriculture produce agriculture specialists and "agribusinessmen" as readily as farmers, and they are producing far more of them. Public funds originally voted to provide for "the liberal and practical education" of farmers thus become, by moral default, an educational subsidy given to the farmers' competitors.

The Vagrant Aristocracy

But in order to complete an understanding of the modern disconnection between work and value, it is necessary to see how certain "aristocratic" ideas of status and leisure have been institutionalized in this system of education. This is one of the liabilities of the social and political origins not only of our own nation, but of most of the "advanced" nations of the world. Democracy has involved more than the enfranchisement of the lower classes; it has meant also the popularization of the more superficial upper-class values: leisure, etiquette (as opposed to good manners), fashion, everyday dressing up, and a kind of dietary persnicketiness. We have given a highly inflated value to "days off" and to the wearing of a necktie; we pay an exorbitant price for the *looks* of our automobiles; we pay dearly, in both money and health, for our predilection for white bread. We attach much the same values to kinds of profession and levels of income that were once attached to hereditary classes.

It is extremely difficult to exalt the usefulness of any productive discipline *as such* in a society that is at once highly stratified and highly mobile. Both the stratification and the mobility are based upon notions of prestige, which are in turn based upon these reliquary social fashions. Thus doctors are given higher status than farmers, not because they are more necessary, more useful, more able, more talented, or more virtuous, but because they are *thought* to be "better"—one assumes because they talk a learned jargon, wear good clothes all the time, and make a lot of money. And this is true generally of "office people" as opposed to those who work with their hands. Thus an industrial worker does not aspire to become a master craftsman, but rather a foreman or manager. Thus a farmer's son does not usually think to "better" himself by becoming a better farmer than his father, but by becoming, professionally, a better *kind* of man than his father.

It is characteristic of our present society that one does not think to improve oneself by becoming better at what one is doing or by assuming some measure of public responsibility in order to improve local conditions; one thinks to improve oneself by becoming different, by "moving up" to a "place of higher consideration." Thinkable changes, in other words, tend to be quantitative rather than qualitative, and they tend to involve movement that is both social and geographic. The unsettlement at once of population and of values is virtually required by the only generally acceptable forms of aspiration. The typical American "success story" moves from a modest rural beginning to urban affluence, from manual labor to office work.

We must ask, then, what must be the educational effect, the influence, of a farmer's son who believes, with the absolute authorization of his society, that he has mightily improved himself by becoming a professor of agriculture. Has he not improved himself by an "upward" motivation which by its nature avoids the issue of quality—which assumes simply that an agriculture specialist is better than a farmer? And does he not exemplify to his students the proposition that "the way up" leads away from home? How could he, who has "succeeded" by earning a Ph.D. and a nice place in town, advise his best students to go home and farm, or even assume that they might find good reasons for doing so?

I am suggesting that our university-based structures of success, as they have come to be formed upon quantitative measures, virtually require the degeneration of qualitative measures and the disintegration of culture. The university accumulates information at a rate that is literally inconceivable, yet its structure and its self-esteem institutionalize the likelihood that not much of this information will ever be taken *home*. We do not work where we live, and if we are to hold up our heads in the presence of our teachers and classmates, we must not live where we come from. . . .

Experience and Experiment

The expert knowledge of agriculture developed in the universities, like other such knowledges, is typical of the alien order imposed on a conquered land. We can never produce a native economy, much less a native culture, with this knowledge. It can only make us the imperialist invaders of our own country.

The reason is that this knowledge has no cultural depth or complexity whatever. It is concerned only with the most immediate practical (that is, economic and *sometimes* political) results. It has, for instance, never mastered the crucial distinction between experiment and experience. Experience, which is the basis of culture, tends always toward wholeness because it is interested in the *meaning* of what has happened; it is necessarily as interested in what does not work as in what does. It cannot hope or desire without remembering. Its approach to possibility is always conditioned by its remembrance of failure. It is therefore not an "objective" voice, but at once personal and communal. The experimental intelligence, on the other hand, is only interested in what works; what doesn't work is ruled out of consideration. This sort of intelligence tends to be shallow in that it tends to impose upon experience the metaphor of experiment. It invariably sees innovation, not as adding to, but as replacing what existed or was used before. Thus machine technology is seen as a *substitute* for human or animal labor, requiring the "old way" to be looked upon henceforth with contempt. In technology, as in genetics, the experimental intelligence tends toward radical oversimplification, reducing the number of possibilities. Whereas the voice of experience, of culture, counsels, "Don't put all your eggs in one basket," the experimental intelligence, which behaves strangely like the intelligence of imperialists and religious fanatics, says, "This is the *only* true way."

And this intelligence protects itself from the disruptive memories and questions of experience by building around itself the compartmental structure of the modern university, in which effects and causes need never meet. The experimental intelligence is a tyrant that is saved from the necessity of killing bearers of bad news because it lives at the center of a maze in which the bearers of bad news are lost before they can arrive.

But it is imperative to understand that this sort of intelligence is tyrannical. It is at least potentially totalitarian. To think or act without cultural value, and the restraints invariably implicit in cultural value, is simply to wait upon force. This sort of behavior is founded in the cultural disintegration and despair which are also the foundation of political totalitarianism. Whether recognized or not, there is in the workings of agricultural specialization an implicit waiting for the total state power that will permit experimentally derived, technologically pure solutions to be imposed by force.

PART FIVE

THE PUBLIC AND THE PERSONAL

IN PART FOUR we explored some of the larger political, social, legal, and economic issues that come into play when we begin to think seriously about education and democracy. Before we focus on the purpose of education and schools in a democratic society, as we will in Part Six, other issues require some attention. The chapters in this section thus serve as a bridge between the issues raised in the preceding section and the more focused treatment that follows.

We begin in Chapter Twelve with John Dewey's "Democracy and Human Nature." Dewey, one of America's most prolific and best-known philosophers, observes that many of us are inclined to believe that various social issues are somehow predetermined by "human nature." It is an assumption, he declares, that "is the source of serious social ills." For example, when left to itself, human nature does not automatically result in democracy. "We have to see that democracy means the belief that humanistic culture *should* prevail," Dewey explains; "we should be frank and open in our recognition that the proposition is a moral one—like any idea that concerns what *should* be." Warning that dispositions formed under conditions that are inconsistent with democratic ideals may, in a crisis, be "aroused to act in positively anti-democratic ways for anti-democratic ends,"

Dewey argues that, although we may "have advanced far enough to say that democracy is a way of life," we have yet to realize, as we must, "that it is [also] a way of personal life and one which provides a moral standard for personal conduct."

This connection between the public and the personal aspects of democracy, between democracy and human nature, is also a focus of Chapter Thirteen, by Philip Green, which deals with the politics of equality. Green, a professor emeritus of government at Smith College, suggests that it is impossible to think seriously about a proposition like the one that argues that a humanistic culture should prevail, without confronting the issue of equality. "Egalitarian solidarity," Green writes, "is not merely a particular cultural expression like any other; nor is it a 'perspective' reducible to some unique and 'different' social position. It is an ineradicable and universal aspect of being human. The politics of equality proceeds from, and can only proceed from, that understanding."

In Chapter Fourteen, the concluding chapter in this section, Mark Johnson, chair of the department of philosophy at the University of Oregon, takes up this theme on yet a more personal level by introducing the notion of "moral imagination." As C. Douglas Lummis declared in Chapter Two, "Human beings cannot arrive at moral certainty on their own." Martin Buber, in Chapter Eight, suggested that the "great character can be conceived neither as a system of maxims nor as a system of habits. It is peculiar to him to act from the whole of his substance. That is, it is peculiar to him to react in accordance with the uniqueness of every situation which challenges him as an active person." Johnson further pursues these ideas when he asserts that the "envisioning of possibilities for fruitful, meaningful, and constructive action requires moral imagination." By this he means that "no person can be moral in a suitably reflective way who cannot imagine alternative viewpoints as a means of understanding and transforming the limits of his own convictions and commitments." It is "moral imagination that gives us the modest, but absolutely necessary, freedom we have to grow and develop morally and socially."

12

DEMOCRACY AND HUMAN NATURE

John Dewey

IT IS NOT ACCIDENTAL that the rise of interest in human nature coincided in time with the assertion in political matters of the rights of the people as a whole, over against the rights of a class supposedly ordained by God or Nature to exercise rule. The full scope and depth of the connection between assertion of democracy in government and new consciousness of human nature cannot be presented without going into an opposite historic background, in which social arrangements and political forms were taken to be an expression of Nature—but most decidedly not of *human* nature. There would be involved an account, upon the side of theory, of the long history of the idea of *Laws of Nature* from the time of Aristotle and the Stoics to the formulators of modern jurisprudence in the sixteenth and seventeenth centuries.

The story of this development and of the shift, in the eighteenth century, from Natural Law to Natural Rights is one of the most important chapters in the intellectual and moral history of mankind. But to delve into it would here take us too far away from the immediate theme. I must content myself then with emphatic reassertion of the statement that regard for *human* nature as the source of legitimate political arrangements is comparatively late in European history; that when it arose it marked an almost revolutionary departure from previous theories about the basis of political rule and citizenship and subjection—so much so that the fundamental difference between even ancient republican and modern democratic governments has its source in the substitution of human nature for cosmic nature as the foundation of politics. Finally changes and the need for further change in democratic theory are connected with an inadequate theory of the constitution of human nature and its component elements in their relation to social phenomena.

The subject matter which follows is that of a drama in three acts, of which the last is the unfinished one now being enacted in which we, now living, are the participants. The first act, as far as it is possible to tell its condensed story, is that of a one-sided simplification of human nature which was used to promote and justify the new political movement. The second act is that of the reaction against the theory and the practices connected with it, on the ground that it was the forerunner of moral and social anarchy, the cause of dissolution of the ties of cohesion that bind human beings together in organic union. The third act, now playing, is that of recovery of the moral significance of the connection of human nature and democracy, now stated in concrete terms of existing conditions and freed from the one-sided exaggerations of the earlier statement. I give this summary first because in what follows I have been compelled to go in some detail into matters that if pursued further are technically theoretical.

I begin by saying that the type of theory which isolated the "external" factor of interactions that produce social phenomena is paralleled by one which isolated the "internal" or human factor. Indeed, if I had followed the historic order the latter type of theory would have been discussed first. And this type of theory is still more widely and influentially held than we might suppose. For its vogue is not now adequately represented by those professional psychologists and sociologists who claim that all social phenomena are to be understood in terms of the mental operations of individuals, since society consists in the last analysis only of individual persons. The practically effective statement of the point of view is found in economic theory, where it furnished the backbone of laissez-faire economics; and in the British political liberalism which developed in combination with this economic doctrine. A particular view of human motives in relation to social events, as explanations of them and as the basis of all sound social policy, has not come to us labeled psychology. But as a theory about human nature it is essentially psychological. We still find a view put forth as to an intrinsic and necessary connection between democracy and capitalism which has a psychological foundation and temper. For it is only because of belief in a certain theory of human nature that the two are said to be Siamese twins, so that attack upon one is a threat directed at the life of the other.

The classic expression of the point of view which would explain social phenomena by means of psychological phenomena is that of John Stuart Mill in his *Logic*—a statement that probably appeared almost axiomatic when it was put forth. "All phenomena of society are phenomena of human nature . . . and if therefore the phenomena of human thought, feeling and action are subject to fixed laws, the phenomena of society cannot but conform to law." And again, "The laws of the phenomena of society are and can be nothing but the laws of the actions and passions of human beings united in the social state." And then, as if to state conclusively that being "united in the social state" makes no difference as to the laws of individuals and hence none in those of society, he adds, "Human beings in society have no properties but those which are derived from and may be resolved into the laws of the nature of individual man."

This reference to "individual man" discloses the nature of the particular simplification which controlled the views and the policies of this particular school. The men who expressed and entertained the type of philosophy whose method was summed up by Mill were in their time revolutionaries. They wished to liberate a certain group of individuals, those concerned in new forms of industry, commerce and finance, from shackles inherited from feudalism which were endeared by custom and interest to a powerful landed aristocracy. If they do not appear now to be revolutionary (operating to bring about social change by change in men's opinions not by force), it is because their views are now the philosophy of conservatives in every highly industrialized country.

They essayed an intellectual formulation of principles which would justify the success of the tendencies which present day revolutionaries call the bourgeois capitalism they are trying to overthrow. The psychology in question is not that of present textbooks. But it expressed the individualistic ideas that animated the economic and political theories of the radicals of the time. Its "individualism" supplied the background of a great deal of even the technical psychology of the present day—pretty much all of it, save that which has started on a new tack because of biological and anthropological considerations. At the time of its origin, it was not a bookish doctrine even when written down in books. The books were elaborations of ideas that were propounded in electoral campaigns and offered as laws to be adopted by parliament.

Before engaging in any detailed statements, I want to recall a statement made earlier; namely, that the popular view of the constitution of human nature at any given time is a reflex of social movements which have either become institutionalized or else are showing themselves against opposing social odds and hence need intellectual and moral formulation to increase their power. I may seem to be going far afield if I refer to Plato's statement of the way by which to determine the constituents of human nature. The proper method, he said, was to look at the version of human nature written in large and legible letters in the organization of classes in society, before trying to make it out in the dim petty edition found in individuals. And so on the basis of the social organization with which he was acquainted he found that since in society there was a laboring class toiling to find the means of satisfying the appetites, a citizen soldiery class loyal even to death to the laws of the state, and a legislative class, so the human soul must be composed of appetite at the base—in both significations of "base"—of generous spirited impulses which looked beyond personal enjoyment, while appetite was engaged only in taking in and absorbing for its own satisfaction, and finally reason, the legislative power.

Having found these three things in the composition of human nature, he had no difficulty in going back to social organization and proving that there was one class which had to be kept in order by rules and laws imposed from above, since otherwise its action was without limits, and would in the name of liberty destroy harmony and order; another class, whose inclinations were all towards obedience and loyalty to law, towards right beliefs, although itself incapable of discovering the ends from which laws are derived; and at the apex, in any well-ordered organization, the rule of those whose predominant natural qualities were reason, after that faculty had been suitably formed by education.

It would be hard to find a better illustration of the fact that any movement purporting to discover the psychological causes and sources of social phenomena is in fact a reverse movement, in which current social tendencies are read back into the structure of human nature; and are then used to explain the very things from which they are deduced. It was then "natural" for the men who reflected the new movement of industry and commerce to erect the appetites, treated by Plato as a kind of necessary evil, into the cornerstone of social well-being and progress. Something of the same kind exists at present when love of power is put forward to play the role taken a century ago by self-interest as the dominant "motive"—and if I put the word motive in quotation marks, it is for the reason just given. What are called motives turn out upon critical examination to be complex attitudes patterned under cultural conditions, rather than simple elements in human nature.

Even when we refer to tendencies and impulses that actually are genuine elements in human nature we find, unless we swallow whole some current opinion, that of themselves they explain nothing about social phenomena. For they produce consequences only as they are shaped into acquired dispositions by interaction with environing cultural conditions. Hobbes, who was the first of the moderns to identify the "state of nature" and its laws—the classic background of all political theories—with the raw uneducated state of human nature, may be called as witness. According to Hobbes, "In the nature of man we find three principal causes of quarrel. First competition, secondly diffidence, thirdly glory. The first maketh men invade for gain; the second for safety; and the third for reputation. The first use violence to make themselves the masters of other persons; the second to defend them; the third for trifles as a word, a smile, a different opinion or any other sign of undervalue, either direct in their persons or by reflection in their kindred, their friends, their nation."

That the qualities mentioned by Hobbes actually exist in human nature and that they may generate "quarrel," that is, conflict and war between states and civil war within a nation—the chronic state of affairs when Hobbes lived—is not denied. Insofar, Hobbes' account of the natural psychology which prevents the state of security which is a prerequisite for civilized communities shows more insight than many attempts made today to list the traits of raw human nature that are supposed to cause social phenomena. Hobbes thought that the entire natural state of men in their relations to one another was a war of all against all, man being naturally to man "as a wolf." The intent of Hobbes was thus a glorification of deliberately instituted relations, authoritative laws and regulations which should rule not just overt actions, but the impulses and ideas which cause men to hold up certain things as ends or goods. Hobbes himself thought of this authority as a political sovereign. But it would be in the spirit of his treatment to regard it as glorification of culture over against raw human nature, and more than one writer has pointed out the likeness between his Leviathan and the Nazi totalitarian state.

There are more than one instructive parallelisms that may be drawn between the period in which Hobbes lived and the present time, especially as to insecurity and conflict between nations and classes. The point here pertinent, however, is that the qualities Hobbes selected as the causes of disorders making the life of mankind "brutish and nasty," are the very "motives" that have been selected by others as the cause of *beneficent* social effects; namely, harmony, prosperity, and indefinite progress. The position taken by Hobbes about competition as love of gain was completely reversed in the British social philosophy of the nineteenth century. Instead of being a source of war, it was taken to be the means by which individuals found the occupation for which they were best fitted; by which needed goods reached the consumer at least cost, and by which a state of ultimate harmonious interdependence would be produced—provided only competition were allowed to operate without "artificial" restriction. Even today one reads articles and hears speeches in which the cause of our present economic troubles is laid to political interference with the beneficent workings of private competitive effort for gain.

The object of alluding to these two very different conceptions of this component in human nature is not to decide or discuss which is right. The point is that both are guilty of the same fallacy. In itself, the impulse (or whatever name be given it) is neither socially maleficent nor beneficent. Its significance depends upon consequences actually produced; and these depend upon the conditions under which it operates and with which it interacts. The conditions are set by tradition, by custom, by law, by the kind of public approvals and disapprovals; by all conditions constituting the environment. These conditions are so pluralized even in one and the same country at the same period that love of gain (regarded as a trait of human nature) may be both socially useful and socially harmful. And, in spite of the tendency to set up cooperative impulses as thoroughly beneficial, the same thing is true of them—regarded simply as components of human nature. Neither competition nor cooperation can be judged as traits of human nature. They are names for certain relations among the actions of individuals as the relations actually obtain in a community.

This would be true even if there were tendencies in human nature so definitely marked off from one another as to merit the names given them and even if human nature were as fixed as it is sometimes said to be. For even in that case, human nature operates in a multitude of different environing conditions, and it is interaction with the latter that determines the consequences and the social significance and value, positive or negative, of the tendencies. The alleged fixity of the structure of human nature does not explain in the least the differences that mark off one tribe, family, people, from another—which is to say that in and of itself it explains no state of society whatever. It issues no advice as to what policies it is advantageous to follow. It does not even justify conservatism as against radicalism.

But the alleged unchangeableness of human nature cannot be admitted. For while certain needs in human nature are constant, the consequences they produce (because of the existing state of culture—of science, morals, religion, art, industry, legal rules) react back into the original components of human nature to shape them into new forms. The total pattern is thereby modified. The futility of exclusive appeal to psychological factors both to explain what takes place and to form policies as to what *should* take place, would be evident to everybody—had it not proved to be a convenient device for "rationalizing" policies that are urged on other grounds by some group or faction. While the case of "competition" urging men both to war and to beneficent social progress is most obviously instructive in this respect, examination of the other elements of Hobbes supports the same conclusion.

There have been communities, for example, in which regard for the honor of one's self, one's family, one's class, has been the chief conservator of all worthwhile social values. It has always been the chief virtue of an aristocratic class, civil or military. While its value has often been exaggerated, it is folly to deny that in interaction with certain cultural conditions, it has had valuable consequences. "Diffidence" or fear as a motive is an even more ambiguous and meaningless term as far as its consequences are concerned. It takes any form, from craven cowardice to prudence, caution, and the circumspection without which no intelligent foresight is possible. It may become reverence—which has been exaggerated in the abstract at times but which may be attached to the kind of objects which render it supremely desirable. "Love of power," to which it is now fashionable to appeal, has a meaning only when it applies to everything in general and hence explains nothing in particular.

Discussion up to this point has been intended to elicit two principles. One of them is that the views about human nature that are popular at a given time are usually derived from contemporary social currents; currents so conspicuous as to stand out or else less marked and less effective social movements which a special group believes *should* become dominant:—as for example, in the case of the legislative reason with Plato, and of competitive love of gain with classical economists. The other principle is that reference to components of original human nature, even if they actually exist, explains no social occurrence whatever and gives no advice or direction as to what policies it is better to adopt. This does not mean that reference to them must necessarily be of a "rationalizing" concealed apologetic type. It means that whenever it occurs with practical significance it has *moral* not psychological import. For, whether brought forward from the side of conserving what already exists or from that of producing change, it is an expression of valuation, and of purpose determined by estimate of values. When a trait of human nature is put forward on this basis, it is in its proper context and is subject to intelligent examination.

The prevailing habit, however, is to assume that a social issue does not concern values to be preferred and striven for, but rather something predetermined by the constitution of human nature. This assumption is the source of serious social ills. Intellectually it is a reversion to the type of explanation that governed physical science until say, the seventeenth century: a method now seen to have been the chief source of the long-continued retardation of natural science. For this type of theory consists of appeal to general forces to "explain" what happens.

Natural science began to progress steadily only when general forces were banished and inquiry was directed instead to ascertaining correlations that exist between observed changes. Popular appeal to, say, electricity, light or heat, etc., as a force to account for some particular event still exists, as to electricity to explain storms attended by thunder and lightning. Scientific men themselves often talk in similar words. But such general terms are in their case shorthand expressions. They stand for uniform relations between events that are observed to occur; they do not mark appeal to something behind what happens and which is supposed to produce it. If we take the case of the lightning flash and electricity, Franklin's identification of the former as of the electrical kind brought it into connection with things from which it had been formerly isolated, and knowledge about them was available in dealing with it. But instead of electricity being an explanatory force, knowledge that lightning is an electrical phenomenon opened a number of special problems, some of which are still unsolved.

If the analogy between the relatively sterile condition of natural science when this method prevailed and the present state of the social "sciences" is not convincing, the misdirection of inquiry that results may be cited in evidence. There is an illusion of understanding, when in reality there is only a general word that conceals lack of understanding. Social ideas are kept in the domain of glittering generalities. Opinion as distinct from knowledge breeds controversy. Since what is regarded as a cause is that which is used as an agency or instrumentality of production, there is no controlled method of bringing anything into existence and of preventing the occurrence of that not wanted, save as there is knowledge of the conditions of its occurrence. When men knew that a certain kind of friction produced fire, they had at command at least one means, rubbing of sticks together, for producing fire when they wanted it. And it goes without saying that greater acquaintance with causal conditions has multiplied men's practical ability to have fire when needed, and to use it for an increased number of ends. The principle applies to the relation of social theory and social action.

Finally theories supposed to explain the course of events are used to urge and justify certain practical policies. Marxism is, of course, a striking instance. But it is so far from being the only instance that non-Marxian and anti-Marxian social theories often exemplify the principle. Utilitarianism used the idea that pleasure and pain are the sole determinants of human action to advance a sweeping theory of legislation, judicial and penal procedure; namely, that they be directed to secure the greatest happiness of the greatest number. Explanation of events on the basis of free, unimpeded manifestation of wants was used on the practical side as active propaganda for an open-market economic regime with all political and legal measures adapted to it. Belief in the general character of the alleged "force" rendered it unnecessary to keep track of actual events so as to check the theory. If things happened that obviously went contrary to the creed, the inconsistency was not taken as a reason for examining it, but as the cue for alleging special reasons for the failure, so that the truth of the principle could be kept intact.

Mere general ideas can be argued for and against without the necessity of recourse to observation. The arguments are saved from being a mere matter of words only because there are certain emotional attitudes involved. When general ideas are not capable of being continuously checked and revised by observation of what actually takes place, they are, as a mere truism, in the field of opinion. Clash of opinions is in that case the occasion for controversy, not, as is now the case in natural science, a location of a problem and an occasion for making further observations. If any generalization can be safely laid down about intellectual matters and their consequences, it is that the reign of opinion, and of controversial conflicts, is a function of absence of methods of inquiry which bring new facts to light and by so doing establish the basis for consensus of beliefs.

Social events are sufficiently complex in any case so that the development of effective methods of observation, yielding generalization about correlation of events, is difficult. The prevailing type of theory adds the further handicap of making such observation unnecessary—save as this and that arbitrarily selected event is used in argumentative controversy. The prime necessity is to frame general ideas, first, to promote search for problems—as against the assumption of a ready-made solution in view of which there are no problems; and, secondly, to solve these problems by generalizations that state interactions between analytically observed events.

I return to the particular social philosophy which associates the economic regime actuated by effort to make private profit with the essential conditions of free and democratic institutions. It is not necessary to go back to the theory in its early English formulation at the hands of laissez-faire liberals. For in spite of the discrediting of the philosophy by events, efforts put forth in this country to establish so-called social control of business have led at present to its revival in an extremely naked form. One does not need to endorse the measures for control that are used to be aware of the fallacy of the theory upon which current objections to them are based. The theory is that capitalism, interpreted as the maximum range of free personal opportunity for production and exchange of goods and services is the Siamese twin of democracy. For the former is identical, so it is claimed, with the personal qualities of initiative, independence, vigor, that are the basic conditions of free political institutions. Hence, so it is argued, the check given to the operation of these personal qualities by governmental regulation of business activities is at the same time an attack upon the practical and moral conditions for the existence of political democracy.

I am not concerned here with the merits of the special arguments put forth in behalf of and against the measures employed. The point is that appeal to certain alleged human motivations in a wholesale way, such as "initiative, independence, enterprise" at large, obscures the need for observation of events in the concrete. If and when special events are observed, interpretation of them is predestined instead of growing out of what is observed. By keeping the issues in the realm of opinion, appeal to equally general wholesale views on the other side is promoted. Then we get a kind of head-on conflict between something called "individualism" on one side and "socialism" on the other. Examination of concrete conditions might disclose certain specifiable conditions under which both of the methods vaguely pointed at by these words would operate to advantage.

The current use of the word *enterprise* as an honorific term is especially instructive with regard to the attempt to draw support for policies from a reference to general inherent traits of human nature. For the only legitimate signification of "enterprise" is a neutral one, an *undertaking* the desirability of which is a matter of actual results produced, which accordingly need to be studied in the concrete. But *enterprise* is given the significance of a certain desirable trait of human nature, so that the issue is taken out of the field of observation into that of opinion plus a eulogistic emotion. "Enterprise" like "initiative" and like "industry" can be exerted in behalf of an indefinite number of objects; the words may designate the activities of an Al Capone or a racketeering labor union as well as a socially useful industrial undertaking.

The case is cited in some detail because it provides a striking example, first, of the conversion of an existing mode of social behavior into a psychological property of human nature; and, secondly, conversion of an alleged matter of psychological fact into a principle of value—a moral matter. Social problems that are set by conditions having definite spatial and temporal boundaries—which have to be determined by observation— are made into matters capable of absolute determination without reference to conditions of place and date. Hence they become matters of opinion and controversial argument—and as the latter decides nothing, the final tendency is to appeal to force as the ultimate arbiter.

The theory of the components of human nature used by the intellectual radicals of Great Britain to justify popular government and freedom included more than the self-interest motivation. It was officially held that sympathy with the gains and losses, the pleasures and pains of others, is a native part of the human endowment. The two components, self-interest and sympathy, opposite in quality, were ingeniously linked together in the complete doctrine—occasionally with explicit reference to the supposedly analogous centripetal and centrifugal components of Newtonian celestial mechanics. The self-interest phase supplied the foundation of the theory of public and governmental action; the sympathetic phase took care of the relations of individuals to one another in their private capacities. The doctrine taught that if political institutions were reformed to do away with special privileges and unfair favoritisms, the sympathetic motive would have a vastly enlarged field of effective and successful operation, since bad institutions were the chief cause that led men to find their personal advantage in acts injurious to others.

The theory was even more important in the reaction it called out than in itself. For "organic idealistic" philosophies developed in Germany during the nineteenth century, and now form the theoretical background and justification of totalitarianism. They took their clew and point of departure from the weaknesses of the theories that based politics and morals, in theory and in practice, upon alleged components of human nature. An adequate account of the form and substance of the reaction would take us into matters which cannot be set forth without going into technicalities. But its basis is simple.

The attempt to locate the source of authority of politics and morals in human nature was regarded as the source of anarchy, disorder, and conflict;—an attempt to build social institutions and personal relationships upon the most unstable of shifting quicksands. At the same time, the philosophers who formulated the new view were Protestants and Northerners. Hence their reaction did not move them to urge acceptance of the doctrines of the Roman Church as the bulwark against the dissolving tendencies of ultra-individualistic ideas and policies.

The French Revolution, with its excesses, was uniformly regarded in German thought as the logical outcome of the attempt to locate authority where nothing binding could be found. It was thus taken to be a practical large scale demonstration of the weakness inherent in the position. The most that could be said for the doctrine was what could be said in defense of the French Revolution—it helped to get rid of abuses that had grown up. As a positive and constructive principle, it was a tragic delusion. The statement of the Rights of Man setting forth the official creed of the Revolution was said to be a summary of the false doctrines that had produced all the characteristic evils of the age. The protest, as just said, refused to accept the doctrines of the Church as the basis for its criticisms and for the constructive measures it proposed. It was itself too deeply influenced by the conditions which had produced the individualism against which it revolted. The extent of this influence is why the movement is criticized by representatives of the Hellenic-medieval ideas as itself intensely "subjectivistic." It found the way to "reconcile" freedom and authority, individuality and law, by setting up an Absolute Self, Mind, Spirit, of which human beings are individually partial manifestations, a "truer" and fuller manifestation being found in social institutions, the state and the course of history. Since history is the final court of judgment and since it represents the movement of absolute Spirit, appeal to force to settle issues between nations is not "really" an appeal to force, but rather to the ultimate logic of absolute reason. The individualistic movement was a necessary transitional movement to bring men to recognition of the primacy and ultimacy of Spirit and Personality in the constitution of nature, man, and society. German organic idealism was to save all that is true in the movement, while eliminating its errors and dangers by lifting it up to the plane of absolute Self and Spirit. There is much that is technical in the movement; much of its detail can be explained only on the ground of special intellectual events. But its heart and core is found in its attempt to find a "higher" justification for individuality and freedom where the latter are merged with law and authority, which *must* be rational since they are manifestations of Absolute Reason. Contemporary totalitarianism has no difficulty in discovering that the Germanic racial spirit embodied in the German state is an adequate substitute, for all practical purposes, for the Hegelian Absolute Spirit.

Rousseau is usually, and in many respects properly, regarded as the prophet and intellectual progenitor of the French Revolution. But by one of those ironies with which history abounds he was also a step-father of the theory that came to full expression in Germany. He served in this capacity partly indirectly by his attack on culture which, as previously said, was the challenge that resulted in glorification of culture over against human nature. But he also acted positively and directly. For in his political writings he advanced the idea that a Common Will is the source of legitimate political institutions; that freedom and law are one and the same thing in the operations of the Common Will, for it must act for the Common Good and hence for the "real" or true Good of every individual.

If the latter set up their purely personal desires against the General Will, it was accordingly legitimate (indeed necessary) to "*force* them to be free." Rousseau intended his theory to state the foundation of self-governing institutions and majority rule. But his premise was employed to prove that the Common—or Universal—Will and Reason was embodied in the national state. Its most adequate incarnation was in those states in which the authority of law, order, and discipline had not been weakened by democratic heresies:—a view which was used in Germany after the Napoleonic conquest to create an aggressive national spirit in that country, one which provided the basis for systematic depreciation of French "materialistic" civilization as over against German *Kultur*—a depreciation later extended to condemnation of democratic institutions in any country.

While this brief exposition of the reaction against the individualistic theory of human nature suggests the ground pattern of National Socialism, it also throws some light upon the predicament in which democratic countries find themselves. The fact that the individualistic theory was used a century and more ago to justify political self-government and then aided promotion of its cause does not constitute the theory a present trustworthy guide of democratic action. It is profitable to read today the bitterly vivid denunciations of Carlyle on the theory as it was originally put forth. He denounced with equal fierceness the attempt to erect political authority upon the basis of self-interest and private morals upon the exercise of sympathy. The latter was sentimentalism run riot and the former was "Anarchy plus the Constable"—the latter being needed to preserve even a semblance of outward order. His plea for discipline and order included even a plea for leadership by select persons.

The present predicament may be stated as follows: Democracy does involve a belief that political institutions and law be such as to take fundamental account of human nature. They must give it freer play than any non-democratic institutions. At the same time, the theory, legalistic and moralistic, about human nature that has been used to expound and justify this reliance upon human nature has proved inadequate. Upon the legal and political side, during the nineteenth century it was progressively overloaded with ideas and practices which have more to do with business carried on for profit than with democracy. On the moralistic side, it has tended to substitute emotional exhortation to act in accord with the Golden Rule for the discipline and the control afforded by incorporation of democratic ideals into *all* the relations of life. Because of lack of an adequate theory of human nature in its relations to democracy, attachment to democratic ends and methods has tended to become a matter of tradition and habit—an excellent thing as far as it goes, but when it becomes routine is easily undermined when change of conditions changes other habits.

Were I to say that democracy needs a new psychology of human nature, one adequate to the heavy demands put upon it by foreign and domestic conditions, I might be taken to utter an academic irrelevancy. But if the remark is understood to mean that democracy has always been allied with humanism, with faith in the potentialities of human nature, and that the present need is vigorous reassertion of this faith, developed in relevant ideas and manifested in practical attitudes, it but continues the American tradition. For belief in the "common man" has no significance save as an expression of belief in the intimate and vital connection of democracy and human nature.

We cannot continue the idea that human nature when left to itself, when freed from external arbitrary restrictions, will tend to the production of democratic institutions that work successfully. We have now to state the issue from the other side. We have to see that democracy means the belief that humanistic culture *should* prevail; we should be frank and open in our recognition that the proposition is a moral one—like any idea that concerns what *should* be.

Strange as it seems to us, democracy is challenged by totalitarian states of the Fascist variety on moral grounds just as it is challenged by totalitarianisms of the left on economic grounds. We may be able to defend democracy on the latter score, as far as comparative conditions are involved, since up to the present at least the Union of Soviet Socialist Republics has not "caught up" with us, much less "surpassed" us, in material affairs. But defense against the other type of totalitarianism (and perhaps in the end against also the Marxist type) requires a positive and courageous constructive awakening to the significance of faith in human nature for development of every phase of our culture:—science, art, education, morals and religion, as well as politics and economics. No matter how uniform and constant human nature is in the abstract, the conditions within which and upon which it operates have changed so greatly since political democracy was established among us, that democracy cannot now depend upon or be expressed in political institutions alone. We cannot even be certain that they and their legal accompaniments are actually democratic at the present time—for democracy is expressed in the attitudes of human beings and is measured by consequences produced in their lives.

The impact of the humanist view of democracy upon all forms of culture, upon education, science and art, morals and religion, as well as upon industry and politics, saves it from the criticism passed upon moralistic exhortation. For it tells us that we need to examine every one of the phases of human activity to ascertain what effects it has in release, maturing and fruition of the potentialities of human nature. It does not tell us to "re-arm morally" and all social problems will be solved. It says, Find out how all the constituents of our existing culture are operating and then see to it that whenever and wherever needed they be modified in order that their workings may release and fulfill the possibilities of human nature.

It used to be said (and the statement has not gone completely out of fashion) that democracy is a by-product of Christianity, since the latter teaches the infinite worth of the individual human soul. We are now told by some persons that since belief in the soul has been discredited by science, the moral basis for democracy supposed to exist must go into the discard. We are told that if there are reasons for preferring it to other arrangements of the relations of human beings to one another, they must be found in specialized external advantages which outweigh the advantages of other social forms. From a very different quarter, we are told that weakening of the older theological doctrine of the soul is one of the reasons for the eclipse of faith in democracy. These two views at opposite poles give depth and urgency to the question whether there are adequate grounds for faith in the potentialities of human nature and whether they can be accompanied by the intensity and ardor once awakened by religious ideas upon a theological basis. Is human nature intrinsically such a poor thing that the idea is *absurd*? I do not attempt to give any answer, but the word *faith* is intentionally used. For in the long run democracy will stand or fall with the possibility of maintaining the faith and justifying it by works.

Take, for example, the question of intolerance. Systematic hatred and suspicion of any human group, "racial," sectarian, political, denotes deep-seated scepticism about the qualities of human nature. From the standpoint of a faith in the possibilities of human nature possessing religious quality it is blasphemous. It may start by being directed at a particular group, and be supported in name by assigning special reasons why that group is not worthy of confidence, respect, and decent human treatment. But the underlying attitude is one of fundamental distrust of human nature. Hence it spreads from distrust and hatred of a particular group until it may undermine the conviction that any group of persons has any intrinsic right for esteem or recognition—which, then, if it be given, is for some special and external grounds, such as usefulness to our particular interests and ambitions. There is no physical acid which has the corrosive power possessed by intolerance directed against persons because they belong to a group that bears a certain name. Its corrosive potency gains with what it feeds on. An anti-humanist attitude is the essence of every form of intolerance. Movements that begin by stirring up hostility against a group of people end by denying to them all human qualities.

The case of intolerance is used as an illustration of the intrinsic connection between the prospects of democracy and belief in the potentialities of human nature—not for its own sake, important as it is on its own account. How much of our past tolerance was positive and how much of it a toleration equivalent to "standing" something we do not like, "putting up" with something because it involves too much trouble to try to change it? For a good deal of the present reaction against democracy is probably simply the disclosure of a weakness that was there before; one that was covered up or did not appear in its true light. Certainly racial prejudice against Negroes, Catholics, and Jews is no new thing in our life. Its presence among us is an intrinsic weakness and a handle for the accusation that we do not act differently from Nazi Germany.

The greatest practical inconsistency that would be revealed by searching our own habitual attitudes is probably one between the democratic method of forming opinions in political matters and the methods in common use in forming beliefs in other subjects. In theory, the democratic method is persuasion through public discussion carried on not only in legislative halls but in the press, private conversations and public assemblies. The substitution of ballots for bullets, of the right to vote for the lash, is an expression of the will to substitute the method of discussion for the method of coercion. With all its defects and partialities in determination of political decisions, it has worked to keep factional disputes within bounds, to an extent that was incredible a century or more ago. While Carlyle could bring his gift of satire into play in ridiculing the notion that men by talking to and at each other in an assembly hall can settle what is true in social affairs any more than they can settle what is true in the multiplication table, he failed to see that if men had been using clubs to maim and kill one another to decide the product of 7 times 7, there would have been sound reasons for appealing to discussion and persuasion even in the latter case. The fundamental reply is that social "truths" are so unlike mathematical truths that unanimity of uniform belief is possible in respect to the former only when a dictator has the power to tell others what they must believe—or profess they believe. The adjustment of interests demands that diverse interests have a chance to articulate themselves.

The real trouble is that there is an intrinsic split in our habitual attitudes when we profess to depend upon discussion and persuasion in politics and then systematically depend upon other methods in reaching conclusions in matters of morals and religion, or in anything where we depend upon a person or group possessed of "authority." We do not have to go to theological matters to find examples. In homes and in schools, the places where the essentials of character are supposed to be formed, the usual procedure is settlement of issues, intellectual and moral, by appeal to the "authority" of parent, teacher, or textbook. Dispositions formed under such conditions are so inconsistent with the democratic method that in a crisis they may be aroused to act in positively anti-democratic ways for anti-democratic ends; just as resort to coercive force and suppression of civil liberties are readily palliated in nominally democratic communities when the cry is raised that "law and order" are threatened.

It is no easy matter to find adequate authority for action in the demand, characteristic of democracy, that conditions be such as will enable the potentialities of human nature to reach fruition. Because it is not easy the democratic road is the hard one to take. It is the road which places the greatest burden of responsibility upon the greatest number of human beings. Backsets and deviations occur and will continue to occur. But that which is its weakness at particular times is its strength in the long course of human history. Just because the cause of democratic freedom is the cause of the fullest possible realization of human potentialities, the latter when they are suppressed and oppressed will in time rebel and demand an opportunity for manifestation. With the founders of American democracy, the claims of democracy were inherently one with the demands of a just and equal morality. We cannot now well use their vocabulary. Changes in knowledge have outlawed the significations of the words they commonly used. But in spite of the unsuitability of much of their language for present use, what they asserted was that self-governing institutions are the means by which human nature can secure its fullest realization in the greatest number of persons. The question of what is involved in self-governing methods is now much more complex. But for this very reason, the task of those who retain belief in democracy is to revive and maintain in full vigor the original conviction of the intrinsic moral nature of democracy, now stated in ways congruous with present conditions of culture. We have advanced far enough to say that democracy is a way of life. We have yet to realize that it is a way of personal life and one which provides a moral standard for personal conduct.

EGALITARIAN SOLIDARITY

Philip Green

WHAT THEORY CAN TELL US, if not *how* to forge common bonds, is *what* kind of sentiment would have to undergird them. I say "sentiment" because it is essential to understand that a transformative egalitarian politics can never be based merely on strategic considerations: "you and I must form a coalition, because neither of us can separately gain our desired ends." If the parties to a coalition are simply using each other, it will break up in fairly short order. Only some kind of mutual recognition, of equality and in equality, can make an egalitarian coalition work. What kind of mutual recognition must that be?

To begin with, it is crucial to distinguish the egalitarian sentiment from some others that look like it, and are often mistaken for it, but are actually far from being the same thing. Egalitarian politics is motivated, always, by outrage at the disparity between the lives of those who possess an immense superfluity and of those many millions more who lack even a bare sufficiency. It is a moral outrage generated, as I have remarked, by the fact that the disparity can be justified neither by any apparent social necessity nor by any apparent difference in deservingness among the groups who benefit and suffer from it. But this mobilizing sense of outrage, when it is truly general, is based not so much on my envy of he who has more than I do, as on my sorrow for she who has less. Solidarity is not mass envy. It is the sentiment behind Franklin Roosevelt's declaration . . . that "a civilization is judged not by how much it gives to those who already have a lot, but by how much it gives to those who have little"; behind Eugene Debs's famous assertion that "while there is a lower class,

I am in it; while there is a criminal element, I am of it; while there is a soul in prison, I am not free"; and behind the political theorist Christian Bay's simple statement that "a society is as free as its underdogs are."[1] The Swedish welfare state, again, worked so well for so long because it was concretely rooted in this kind of sentiment: the L.O., the national labor organization, struck a comprehensive collective bargaining agreement with Swedish industry, the essence of which was that the first goal of all wage settlements—the "wage solidarity policy" as it has been called—was to narrow the gap between the best paid and the worst paid.[2]

Thus we see that this kind of solidarity is also not merely collective economic interest. Class interests certainly do exist everywhere, and they cause trouble for social cohesion (from the standpoint of those who benefit unreservedly from it). But the solidarity that grows out of expressed or activated interests, such as those mobilized by a strike, is usually localized; and if more than that, rarely lasts very long beyond the occasion. Only where massed workers have implemented some version of the general strike, as in Sweden in 1931 or the United States in 1936–37, has the result of labor action been system-challenging legislation.[3] Still, the enveloping sense of a general interest soon dissolves into the fragmentary interests that momentarily came together.

In contrast, egalitarian solidarity, which exists much more rarely, does not depend on short-term and occasional mobilizations. As we learn from the Swedish example, this kind of solidarity requires what we might call a certain disposition.[4] It is the disposition to ally oneself with others not because they are similar to oneself in social background or agree with one's own tastes and values but precisely because they are different *and yet* have permanently common human interests. It is the mutual recognition of *these* interests, not the mere recognition of being in the same economic or social position, that defines solidarity among equals.

Without this sense of mutual recognition, as well as the sentiment of empathy that underlies it, a mass politics of resentment is possible but egalitarian politics is not. These are not, of course, attitudes addressed toward humanity at large, in some vague generalities that lead to a politically demobilizing inability to distinguish between allies and enemies. Equality, even when defined narrowly, has numerous and important enemies; these cannot be wished out of existence and they are owed no more respect or civility than the forcefulness of their own enmity and opposition suggests.

The solidarity required of egalitarian politics is instead *solidarity with all one's potential allies*. These allies, it ought to go without saying, have to be numerous enough to form a substantial majority when an egalitarian movement has reached its full potential. Otherwise it can't be an egalitarian movement, for the basic decision-making procedure of equality is majority rule, in that no other decision-making procedure treats all those putatively subject to its decisions as formally equal. As I have noted earlier, whereas minority *right* is fundamental to equality, minority *rule* in the name of equality is a contradiction in terms, since at the very least it rules out the achievement of *political* equality.[5]

What then ought we to mean by these constituent terms, mutual recognition and empathy? We can approach an answer to that question by thinking about so-called identity politics, and the effort to forge alliances out of groups that experience oppression or injustice in different ways.[6]

On the one hand, identity politics seems to be a destructive solvent of all efforts to achieve political solidarity; even the famous universal solvent. This is the argument made by, for example, Todd Gitlin, in his recent *Twilight of Common Dreams*.[7] The "common dream" Gitlin's most concerned with is the Left's dream of democratic socialism (a term that as amended by feminist understandings might easily be attached to the philosophy I've outlined . . .). His contention is that the dream has become unrealizable, chiefly because the social groups that might be its constituents are too narcissistically focused on their own oppressions to form effective political alliances with each other; and especially with, he clearly implies, those white men (and often white women) without whose support there can be no effective mass movement. In the spring and summer of 1997 Gitlin's fears achieved the status of journalistic recognition when the white "Left" representative in the New York City mayoral race, Ruth Messinger, was forced to choose between two would-be candidates (among others) for Manhattan borough president on the Democratic ticket, one a black woman and the other a gay woman; and the supporters of each made it perfectly clear that there would be no forgiveness once she made, as she inevitably had to make, the "wrong" endorsement.

Clearly Gitlin is correct that a mass egalitarian movement is unattainable in the face of this kind of identity politics. It is equally clear, although here Gitlin is reluctant to acknowledge the obvious, that identity politics is a historically generated movement (or series of movements) that responds quite accurately, *in the short run,* to the circumstances of a fractured polity. The working class has decomposed (not just in the United States but in almost all contemporary capitalist societies) in the face of rapid technological change and the internationalization of competition. Consequently even reformist (let alone revolutionary) labor movement politics has clearly become the politics of considerably less than half the people as well as being ill-attuned to the real problems of globalization.

In these circumstances, those persons who understand themselves as oppressed by the majority in a democratic society, if they seek formal political relief at all, often turn to liberal institutions of constitutional protection rather than to mass democratic institutions of political party mobilization. If they are too oppressed or alienated even to see the legal system as a possible protector, they turn back on themselves—the only group they can trust.

In the United States, however, where the politics of group self-defense has advanced farther than almost anywhere else (the former Yugoslavia, India, and Rwanda being signal exceptions to that generalization), the official ideology of liberal constitutionalism *demands* the assertion of identity in order to merit its protection.[8] For example, the American Supreme Court has ruled that "race" is a suspect category, in that anything that looks like racial discrimination must pass the highest level of judicial scrutiny. For those who practice discrimination, judicial scrutiny is also a lot more threatening than its always reluctant legislative counterpart; it is hard for the victims of discrimination not to be aware of this.[9]

In order for a particular *individual* in the United States to merit this judicial protection, however, he or she must be seen as belonging to the protected category; and this becomes yet one more compelling reason to embrace what may already be strongly felt group identities. Just as, in Sartre's famous phrase, a Jew is anyone society treats as a Jew, so an African American, for example, becomes anyone society treats as such; both for worse and for better. So "race," the most destructively divisive category in human social history and one of the most conceptually and scientifically fraudulent, first becomes hypostatized as though it were a concrete reality, and then, disastrously, actually becomes a concrete reality.

As with race, so with ethnic origin or nationality, sexuality, gender: not through some conspiracy of liberal elites or the irrational stubbornness of the excluded and marginalized but through the normal, expectable operations of political institutions. The condition of minorities asserting their identities is simply that they do not have, or reasonably do not think they have, any other chance of obtaining fair treatment from a majority that has never treated them as equals. In the absence of a mass movement such as Roosevelt's New Deal coalition or the European Communist and Socialist parties, a movement able to persuade its constituent parts that it represents the historical needs of everyone, they have no other alternative. The most successful of these and the model for all mass reformist movements, Swedish social democracy in its heyday, was rooted in a national labor federation (the L.O.) that represented almost the entire nonrural work force. This now seems to belong in a distant, almost utopian, past (even in relatively homogeneous Sweden).

Identity politics, in other words, is not the *cause* of the disappearance of mass mobilizing politics, but is rather one of its most devastating effects. The dilemma of the Left—Ruth Messinger's dilemma—is insoluble because it has no mass constituency for its would-be elements to be a part of. The solution to that dilemma is simple in principle, but impossible to will into existence in practice. A movement must come into being that is founded on egalitarian solidarity, a movement that mobilizes as equal members all those constituent elements. And yet, it can only come into being if they are prepared to be mobilized by it. Which must happen first, however, is a question that cannot be answered. Instead, egalitarians wherever they find themselves have to ask themselves what it means to practice solidarity in the search for more equality without worrying about how to generate it by probably impossible acts of will. If we can't or won't do that much, then the search will be fruitless.

What ought mutual recognition and empathy to mean, then, from the standpoint either of those who like Gitlin (and myself) still adhere to universalistic principles of political action, or of those practitioners of identity politics whom he criticizes? The answer to this question is two-sided.

On the one hand, universalistic principles ("justice," "fairness," "equality," etc.) are empty verbiage until and unless they find concrete application in an understanding of the different kinds of lives that people live and the different ways in which personality can manifest itself. If I can't recognize particular forms of injustice to others, then I cannot claim to be able to recognize it at all. [For example,] the law of "self-defense" is *not* truly universal when stated as an invariant requirement that the defender who invokes it must have been in immediate danger of her life, must not have been able to escape, and must have had no other recourse to save her life except to kill the person against whom she was defending herself. Here, because of the historical and cultural conditioning as well as, for many, the biological reality that makes women's resort to violence so much more of a last resort than men's; and because not only for that reason but for many others women very often find it extremely difficult to simply leave the men with whom they live (which, for example, might also require leaving children at their mercy), the invocation of formal legal rules is a travesty of fairness and equal treatment. But it is a proper understanding of those universal principles, not repudiation of them, that exposes the travesty and compels us to try to change the law itself.

The true task of the self-styled universalist is to listen to accounts of the history with which he or she is unfamiliar and, *more crucially,* to enlarge his or her previous vision of what constitutes the bedrock issues of egalitarian politics. The male leftists who throw up their hands in despair when a female colleague announces uncompromisingly that the right to abortion is the bedrock issue for egalitarians are doing much more damage to any putative egalitarian movement than she is.[10] It's not that she's necessarily right about her priority (only history will decide that) or that one can't claim to be both opposed to abortion rights and a "real" egalitarian. What is unquestionable, rather, is that her statement stems from a reasoned, historically informed assessment linking gendered conditions and practices (e.g., men don't get pregnant and find it much easier to escape the various consequences of child-bearing) to the real prospects of equal opportunity for concrete female persons. This is a theory of linkage that many feminists have been elaborating for more than two decades and that millions of women have been "voting for" with their bodies. Not to know this, not to understand the linkage at least well enough to be able politely to argue with it on its own terms, is not to have been listening.

In the same way, it requires an extraordinary failure of attention not to know that much of the time urban police forces in the United States appear to many African Americans, quite reasonably, as a sometimes brutal and often uncaring occupying army; and that this relationship is again less the consequence of the "law and order" problem than its continuing cause. How can there be a commitment to "law and order" when its official representatives are constantly observed to be unlawful and disorderly? Or, to revert to a previous example, when middle class African Americans, male or female, know that they can not walk through department stores without being trailed by store detectives or floorwalkers; and when in large cities even African American detectives walk in fear of being "mistaken" for criminals by their colleagues? To be always and everywhere one of the usual suspects marks one's entire life; it is a different life, and apparently self-centered theories of "difference" become, whatever else they are, no less than accurately descriptive of that life.

This is even more evident when we encounter the justifications for discriminatory treatment, which is that some unspecified but particularly large proportion of African Americans in fact does commit crimes of street violence, or shoplift in department stores. The truth or falsity of these justifications doesn't matter. To treat individuals as though they are nothing but representatives of stereotypes is what we mean by "discrimination." What this does is to reinscribe the practices of racial discrimination that were and to this extent still are the daily face of white supremacism. As a practice of self-defense—the maintenance of a threatened privilege—white supremacism can of course be justified. But not as a practice of egalitarianism.[11] It is the politics of force rather than of equality.

This particular understanding is thus based on the kind of recognition of another's circumstances that we call "empathy." We who have never been in this particular instance of what feels to the person in it like an inescapable trap, imaginatively put ourselves in that person's place and try to appreciate her situation from her point of view. Men, for example, have to *recognize* the femaleness of being female; recognize it not as a "condition" in the sense of a dread disease but as a structured social condition that is fundamentally different and in some instances fundamentally more dangerous than their own. At the same time, however, these same reflective men have to recognize that there are different ways of being male, some of which—being gay, for example—may be every bit as "different" and dangerous as being anatomically and socially "female." This particular process of understanding leads to the recognition that there is such a thing as, say, a socially meaningful class of gay men in general, distinct from women in general but similar to each other in being also distinct from men in general taken as normatively "masculine."

In this way the putative process of coalition formation advances; the number of people who understand themselves as having what I've called permanently common but in some way endangered human interests and who are thus prepared to demand equal opportunity in concert with other people's similar demands grows decisively. Unfortunately, it is precisely this kind of empathy that is missing from the approach that many universalistic white leftists, such as Gitlin in *The Twilight of Common Dreams*, consistently take toward those who respond to a different history in a different voice. When "difference" visibly comes to mean "other," empathy disappears; and dialogue stops.

Obviously dialogue cannot always end in agreement; that would have no credibility and would be a waste of everyone's time. But however dialogue is to proceed, there is a serious problem with traditional, universalistic appeals to solidarity such as Gitlin's. The problem is evident in Gitlin's title, "The Twilight of *Common Dreams* [Green's emphasis]." To speak, whether in mourning or in celebration, the language of commonality, is to imply that one knows what the common language is, and what "dreams" (including presumably moral and political dreams) it entails. But this is precisely what we don't know and can't imply. If I think back to the "common dreams" of the socialist movement at its height, for example, these are among the many "dreams" that its leaders did *not* consider part of its common moral language: the dream that every woman has the right to control her own body; the dream that choice of sexual partners is a rightfully important aspect of one's human identity; even the fully racially integrative "dream" of Martin Luther King Jr.

What is even more problematic than overstating the commonality of the common is what usually follows the correction of that overstatement; that is, an amendment of the speaker's notion of solidarity to include those who were previously excluded. The amendment process unfortunately is even more problematic, in that by virtue of those previous exclusions the common language was not truly common. To think that we can best proceed by amending it is still to privilege its authors (traditional Marxists and liberals, usually) as authoritative. "We" begin where "they" benignly left off; their vision was incomplete but otherwise unobjectionable. As Jodi Dean writes in her book *Solidarity of Strangers,* "liberal tolerance seems to adopt a just-add-it-on perspective toward inclusion . . . " One typical outcome of this approach, for example, is that "by denying our responsibility to displace those crystallizations of meaning constructing women and homosexuals as 'other,' it fails to examine the oppositional and exclusionary interpretations of rights as they have become embedded in our legal system."[12] As long as our own claims to authority and our own failures of self-examination go unnoticed by spokespersons for an egalitarian movement yet to be, there will be no such movement.

Thus on the one hand, after reading not only Gitlin's critical account of the Oakland school board's debate about adopting "Ebonics" as a primary language skill (the account with which he begins his critique of "identity politics") as well as the contrary accounts of those who support the board's decision to do so, I have come to the considered judgment that he has a good point. The kind of cultural nationalism lying behind the board's decision-making process, even though it responded to a real need, was a pedagogical and political disaster in the making. However, this is not because it represented a separatist, segregationist deviation from a universalistic standard of liberal tolerance that once was and is now being betrayed.[13] Rather, the fight for "Ebonics" represented a separatist, segregationist, obstacle to creating a universalist standard of solidarity in mutual recognition *that is yet to be.*[14]

The italicized phrase tells us where we must begin the search for a workable universalism. The essential first step in generating the universalistic spirit of solidarity consists in a twofold recognition on the part of its *soi-disant* spokespersons. First, no one ever had or yet does have a legitimate monopoly in knowing how to separate true universality from its impersonations; classical philosophies of solidarity—*fraternité,* for example—were always only partial at best.[15] Second, the universalistic spirit of solidarity in its next incarnation, whatever it may turn out to be, will only come into existence out of the experiences of those people who have been excluded from its earlier representations; who have been positioned as "other" and thus have had to struggle against the weight of structured inequality.

. . . These include feminists who, drawing upon their unique experience of being oppressed and yet necessarily living in intimacy with the oppressor, understand both the necessity of female solidarity and the equal necessity of transcending it.[16] In the United States they include also African American theorists, Latino American theorists, "queer theorists," and others who can argue powerfully for a transnational solidarity. This is so precisely because these theorists have experienced the ambiguous but real attractions of the nationalist sentiment and of unforgiving rage at being constantly an object of exclusion, oppression, or contempt. Unlike most members of the white left, they understand not only the necessity of transcending cultural particularism, but also why it is genuinely unavoidable in the first place.[17]

The universalistic spirit of solidarity, in other words, has to emanate from a truly universalist community, whether of activists or intellectuals. The inadequacy of Gitlin's, and my own, response to "Ebonics" is that we have never *needed* to speak another language; we have never felt *excluded* from the one we are supposed to speak; we have never felt *rage* at the depths of the need and the coldness of the exclusion. The understanding of that position is part of any allegedly universal ideal in action.

To be sure, this is so far the description only of a one-way process, consisting of nothing but the recognition by some people that others' lives are worse than theirs. It's the essential first step, but not the only one. No egalitarian politics ever was or ever will be constructed out of such a one-way process, which however necessary to it is not sufficient for it. Respect for others means treating them as equals, and equal treatment is always necessarily a *two-way* process. It is at this point that the requirements of a politics of solidarity, properly understood, do become incompatible with a certain kind of contemporary identity politics.

The root problem of the kinds of identity politics that are incompatible with the spirit of solidarity is that . . . they take on the character of the politics of discrimination that inspired them in the first place. *What both deny is respect for individuals as such.* Egalitarianism does not demand the repudiation of felt group identities, but it does demand the repudiation of their moral primacy.

For example, "black power" as a slogan may have been a necessary inspiration to effectual political activity for some people; in the short run, the expulsion of non-black people from civil rights organizations it mandated may even have been an organizational necessity. In the same way, the slogan "black is beautiful" may have begun life as a necessary component of personality formation for many people in the United States. However, eventually and ineluctably, the two slogans taken together, and copied by many other marginalized or oppressed peoples as well—and, fatefully, even by people who can't be described in any such manner—have come to justify the resegregation of civil life.

At this point, "blackness" and "whiteness" take on the character of a willed opposition that denies the reality of the lives of millions of people who are neither "black" nor "white" in this prescriptive sense. "Black power," as a response to the implicit whiteness of legitimate power and authority, was historically the first moment of this movement; but the same thing happens, and is happening today, with all such polarities. Today American society is full of similar obstacles to the realization of a larger solidarity. Although hardly as central a support of inequality as the white complacency that gives it its sense of validity, black nationalism is one of these.

This is always the outcome of ethnic or cultural nationalism and of a politics based on them, whatever psychic benefits they might incidentally confer. This type of politics does call attention to experiences of injustice that others may not have previously recognized, and to that extent it performs a necessary function. But it does so at a heavy cost. Denying the full range of respect to others who are superficially not like the nationalist's self-image, and [forgoing] any impulse to empathize with *their* lives, it imposes stereotypes on individuals who were once not necessarily in opposition, but now are and must be; because they are no longer individuals with their own feelings, their own beliefs. Adopting the defining slogan of white racism as his own, the cultural nationalist asks plaintively, "How can you not want to be with your own people?"—a "people" thus reduced to nothing but the shading of a skin color, the intonation of a voice, or an anatomical description. That life is fuller for all of us when we live it among *different* people, all respecting and identifying with each other in that difference, becomes the thought that no one ever thinks. That is the life of multiculturalism properly understood; of cultural and social diversity; of a genuine pluralism.

That life, of cooperation with others of different experiences in seeking common goals, is also the only kind of life that will create the institutions of equal opportunity. In this context, the problem of group nationalism is not the difficulty it creates for excluded peoples in making common cause with persons such as myself or Todd Gitlin; to understand it in that way would be to trivialize it. The real difficulty with group nationalism—especially exclusivist group nationalism—is the obstacles it puts in the way of the excluded and oppressed who wish to build bridges *to each other*. To take one exemplary instance: in one Northeastern city with a large proportion of Spanish-speaking residents, the representatives of an organization devoted to improving the living condition of poor Latinos refuse to attend any conference with like-minded people unless the conference is held in Spanish. They don't want simultaneous translation from the English (the working language of most of the other likely participants in any coalition); they want Spanish to be the official language. But rather than putting up effective opposition to "English First" nativist intolerance, they have merely replicated its social divisiveness, for the conference has many African American representatives attending it as well, and their first language is English.

For many African Americans too[,] linguistic exclusion has been a problem, but only in the more general sense that language has always been used by the privileged to separate themselves from those who lack privilege. Indeed, it has been a class and gendered phenomenon at least as much as a racial one. Failure to recognize what is held in common, as in this case, means that we can emphasize only that which divides us. Starting from a collection of such exclusivist nationalisms and nonnegotiable demands, the politics of equality quickly runs into the ground. Fighting each other replaces fighting together, and the already existing clash of material economic interests (for example, as we've seen, residents against immigrants) is accelerated.

Here then we have to distinguish between two kinds of "identity," only one of which leads in the direction of solidarity. In the most common contemporary usage, "identity" has come to mean the assertion of some special noteworthiness. "We" (and the "we" tends to be coercively inclusive) are meritorious because *some* of us are especially good at something, not because we all participate in a common humanity. Sandy Koufax was a great pitcher—and a Jew; Ralph Ellison is a great novelist—and black; Michelangelo was a great artist—and gay; Virginia Woolf was a great novelist—and a woman. This can all too unfortunately come to sound like its own version of the language of "Americanism": the exclusivist language of the Immigration Act of 1996, which divides the world into "us" and "them," the virtuous few and the alien others.

The antinomian version of identity plays itself out disastrously. It produces the stereotype of the person as always being one thing rather than another, as reducible to an identity constructed not by the struggles of achieving personhood but by some self-contradictory combination of biology and coercive social processes. It also easily produces a politics of victimization in which there is no sympathy for suffering in general, but only sympathy for the suffering of people who are exactly like oneself. At the same time it also produces the stereotype that all whites are "white" (or all men "male"), that as such they all benefit from a certain kind of privilege, and that none of them can understand what it is to be nonwhite (or female, etc.). Every one of those stereotypes is demonstrably false.

Much more insidious from an egalitarian perspective is the separatist solidarity that often follows from invocations of *fundamental* and ineradicable "difference." This version of solidarity can lead us into a moral and political cul-de-sac. Are gay men really more worthy of respect because Michelangelo was one of them? Does "black is beautiful" mean that the homeless black vet huddled in a doorway deserves a place to live because he is "beautiful"? If he was of what we consider mixed racial ancestry and did not call himself "black," would he be less deserving? On the contrary, he deserves whatever he deserves because he is a human being in need.

The dangerous temptation here is to confuse the strategic and political uses of nationalism, its capacity to inspire people to resist oppression and to demand self-government, with a moral theory that tells us who we are and why we deserve what we deserve. Nationalism cannot do that, and exclusivist nationalisms—the nationalisms of "identity"—least of all. Instead, when substituted for a moral theory of humanness, they tend to internalize the politics of contempt and then defiantly return it as a proclamation of the self. But the sole long-term result of this transaction is that contempt is further entrenched as the currency of political life. I must be something special, I must *belong*, to be deserving; and if I am not something special, if I do not belong, then I deserve nothing. The white liberals whose liberalism has turned to racial scorn . . . now have more company than they deserve. . . .

Whatever their short-term historical justifications, exclusivist nationalisms ask the wrong question: who will respect my different way of life, or beliefs, or culture, instead of who will respect my equal human rights?[18] That latter question leads to the second way of asserting "identity." This, the politics of what I've called a genuine multiculturalism, or pluralism, is totally different. It demands not so much that we discard stereotypes (after all, most of them would not have been developed if their distortions were not predicated on some observable condition), as that we recognize their irrelevance to reasoned or ethical behavior. They are irrelevant because I am whoever I am regardless of my social background; my identity is nothing more nor less than how I behave to others. If, as may be necessary on occasion, I assert pride in my identity, it is on the one hand because of my differences from you; but at the same time because of our fundamental similarity: we are both human.

The identity ascribed to a person and which that person may choose to embrace—her ethnicity, her religion, his language, his sexuality—is legitimately a source of pride only in this sense. First, it describes one way among many of being fully human. Second, it represents what for some people has been the special experience of struggle necessary to make others recognize that common humanity, which they have denied. But what makes all of us fully human is the fact that *they* are wrong. My full humanity, or yours, or anyone's, exists *regardless* of any particular identity. It inheres in the equal possibility we all have of living an ethical life: of being willing to work cooperatively for the benefit of others as well as one's own; of neither oppressing the weak nor toadying to the strong; and being always ready to recognize the common but differently inflected experiences of injustice.

The political salience of this kind of "identity," in contrast to that of identity politics, is indeed egalitarian. We empathize with the person who has been unjustly deprived of rights because that person is an individual and no individual should be unjustly deprived of rights; not because that person has one cultural identity rather than another. As to that, the real but limited usefulness of cultural group identities precisely depends on the extent to which they are reliable indicators that a person who claims to have suffered some deprivation probably has actually suffered it.

More concretely, to return to where we began this discussion, when a *multitude* of persons with a shared social identity tell a common story about the frequency with which they experience deprivation or injustice, that story demands everyone else's attention. But the story is not worth any more than its truth value in the light of reasoned discussion. The supposed deprivation may not in fact exist. Neonazis are not, as they claim they are, white people suffering from racial oppression; white people as white people have never suffered from racial oppression. They are merely white people who have, because of various resentments, allowed themselves to become sociopaths. Alternatively, the supposed injustice may be entirely spurious. It is not unjust or unfair for the children of biblical literalists to be exposed to the theory of evolution, for otherwise they would be deprived of the chance every human being ought to have: to encounter and perhaps pursue scientific reasoning. In a democracy, educators should not willingly allow anyone to be so deprived.[19]

Thus the practitioners of an egalitarian politics of solidarity can never and should never promise that concrete *demands* consequent to the assertion of a group identity (e.g., adoption or rejection of a particular school curriculum; specifications of priorities in a political program; communal or educational segregation) will always be made good. If that promise is kept, then the next step in this dance is that, as in the United States, certain groups of whites who feel themselves to be culturally outcast, will demand rejection of a "multicultural" curriculum, insist on the teaching of creationism in place of biological science, and so forth. The politics of oppressive censorship and coercive separatism is firmly in place, and we are back in 1895—as though a century of egalitarianism had never happened.

What is missing in this movement is precisely what its exemplars sometimes purport to stand for: a notion of *equality as a form of the good*. For a politics of equal opportunity the good is equal opportunity. As I've argued, mutual recognition is essential to the pursuit of this good. But mutual recognition is only a means to that good, and then only if the terms of mutual recognition are themselves egalitarian. Although mutual recognition is an absolute historical necessity, in its own terms it is valueless. It is compatible with any politics, even any oppression (some Nazis were at first more "Zionist" than most German Jews). Contrarily, egalitarianism is incompatible with many sincerely held political positions and certainly with any that justify oppression. For an egalitarian to be asked to give full respect to a "legitimate" cultural expression that is "incidentally" homophobic, misogynistic, separatist (and therefore segregationist), or contemptuous of others for stereotypical or meretricious reasons, is to be asked to do the impossible. Violent resistance to oppression is always in principle justifiable, even though it may or may not be justifiable in any particular instance. The oppression of others is *never* justifiable in any circumstances.

The problem with an unmitigated politics of identity, therefore, is that it turns a necessary and valid pride in oneself for being one kind of human being among many, into an excuse for behaviors that, in addition to being in no way justifiable, are in no way egalitarian. That those who are oppressive to others—say, men who abuse women—may themselves be oppressed in some other way, is an interesting fact for psychologists to theorize about, but no more than that. An explanation is not an excuse. The ultimate trajectory of this development is a self-defeating withdrawal from the only kind of collaborative politics that makes the pursuit of greater equality possible.

In sum, the sentiment of egalitarian solidarity is not merely a particular cultural expression like any other; nor is it a "perspective" reducible to some unique and "different" social position. It is an ineradicable and universal aspect of being human. The politics of equality proceeds from, and can only proceed from, that understanding.

NOTES

1. Roosevelt's words are emblazoned on one of the walls of the FDR Memorial in Washington, D.C. Bay's remark, from *The Structure of Freedom,* is the culmination of an argument that begins on p. 3 of that book and climaxes on p. 7.

2. ... Swedish egalitarianism had the limits of coexisting with a capitalist economic structure. Collective bargaining could not narrow the wealth gap between Swedish workers—well or poorly paid—and Swedish industrialists.

3. Of course there was no "general strike" in the United States in that period, but there were various municipal general strikes (Seattle, Tacoma, Minneapolis, San Francisco) that led up to the great occupations and sit-downs at the major auto works. These in turn resonated throughout the nation, so that, for example, the women of Woolworth's department stores joined the men of Flint Number One in "sitting down." The National Labor Relations Act of 1937 was framed and debated in direct response to this movement. See Jeremy Brecher, *Strike!* (Boston: South End Press, 1972). For the more common experience of labor action, see Rick Fantasia, *Cultures of Solidarity: Consciousness, Action, and Contemporary American Workers* (Berkeley: University of California Press, 1988). The ordinary strike is real and inspiring, and often culturally transformative. But politically it is evanescent. As to why this is so, the best account is probably Mike Davis's *Prisoners of the American Dream: Politics and Economy in the History of the U.S. Working Class* (London: Verso Books, 1986); and Gary Gerstle's *Working-Class Americanism: The Politics of Labor in a Textile City, 1914–1960* (New York: Cambridge University Press, 1989). These studies describe the difficulty of mobilizing Americans en masse but do not question the necessity of it.

4. See [Henry] Milner, [*Sweden: Social Democracy in Practice* (New York: Oxford University Press, 1990)], for his discussion of the "wage solidarity policy."

5. In order to avoid confusion, it's important to stipulate that majority rule is necessary but not sufficient for political equality. Minority right is also necessary (but not sufficient). Minority rule, unlike majority rule, is neither

necessary nor sufficient for political equality. A federation of associated polities, each armed with a discretionary veto power, might in some cases seem to be a preferable alternative to a unitary state. However, this alternative does not dispense with majority rule but merely relocates it to within each of the associated polities. Moreover, I would strongly dispute whether any federation could exist for long if the federated peoples felt only internal solidarity with each other and none toward those others with whom they were "federated." This would be the United Nations, or the European Economic Union, as polities: and as now constituted they aren't polities, egalitarian or otherwise.

6. See, for example, Iris Marion Young's *Justice and the Politics of Difference* (Princeton: Princeton University Press, 1990), especially chapters 2 and 5.

7. Gitlin, *The Twilight of Common Dreams: Why America Is Wracked by Culture Wars* (New York: Henry Holt and Company, 1995).

8. Liberal constitutionalism is not the only American ideology. But it is overwhelmingly dominant, as can be seen in the way it is paid homage by its *soi-disant* enemies. When D'nesh D'Souza, e.g., decries the alleged triumphs of "illiberal education," he is invoking what he savages from the other side of his mouth. The word "liberal" has the same historical etymology in the two apparently disparate contexts. In each case, especially, institutional neutrality among competing values is a *sine qua non*. The attack on "political correctness" is a demand that institutions of higher education "return" to that alleged state of political neutrality (they never practiced it, in fact). In the same way, the development of "race" as a protected category is a direct development from Harlan's ideal of "color blindness."

9. This remains true even as the Rehnquist Court leads a retreat from affirmative action. Its retreat is a lot more orderly and slightly more nuanced than that mandated by, for example, the people and governor of California.

10. In my hearing a prominent leader of the New Democratic Party of Canada once referred to feminist demands on that party as "destructive" and "obscene." At that moment one could confidently have removed the NDP from the roster of candidates for the future leadership of Canadian egalitarianism.

11. It might seem odd to speak of freedom from fear of crime as a "privilege." But that's exactly what it is. What whites who move to suburbs or call for more toughness on crime want is precisely to be free of the threat that ghettoized urban black people live with because the same concatenation of private and public lending and building practices that created the white suburbs also forced blacks into urban ghettos.

12. Jodi Dean, *Solidarity of Strangers: Feminism after Identity Politics* (Berkeley: University of California Press, 1996), p. 178. See also the discussion of inclusion and exclusion by bell hooks, *Feminist Theory: From Margin to Center* (Boston: South End Press, 1984), pp. 43–65.

13. This is the whining litany of D'Souza and similar opponents of "political correctness," who are actually themselves about as faithful supporters of liberal tolerance as the average slaveholder was. D'Souza came to fame as part of a movement of viciously bigoted Dartmouth students who among their other "politically incorrect" behaviors actually set out deliberately to destroy the career of a black member of the music department, publicly using the vilest racist (and other) slurs imaginable to drive him from the classroom. Next, I suppose, David Duke will be complaining about the illiberal treatment of Nazis.

14. This is not meant as a judgment in principle. There are certainly coherent and intelligent defenses of the idea of putting more emphasis on local dialects or languages than is currently the case in American public education; the politics of the Oakland debate made it less than that, however.

15. Public discussion on the question of universals versus relativism is often confused by the fact that it's quite possible, indeed frequent, for a person to argue correctly on behalf of universally valid standards and yet be quite wrongheaded about what they are in particular. This is an argument not against the existence of universal moral truths but against such a person's politics, morality, or philosophy.

16. [This statement is drawing upon Green's argument in chapter 7, "Why Not Equality?" in *Equality and Democracy*, pp. 159–184.]

17. For an articulation of the principle of solidarity from the outside looking in, see Bernice Johnson Reagon, "Coalition Politics: Turning the Century," in Barbara Smith, ed., *Homegirls: A Black Feminist Anthology* (New York: Kitchen Table—Women of Color Press, 1983). A black woman addressing an audience of mostly white women at a women's music festival, Reagon (a member of the singing group Sweet Honey in the Rock) says, "That is often what it feels like if you're really doing coalition work. Most of the time you feel threatened to the core and if you don't, you're not really doing no coalescing" (p. 356). The principle of mutual recognition has serious costs for everyone; it is the ineluctability of these costs that Gitlin, for one, fails to grasp.

18. Understanding the difference, we see how supposedly troubling institutions such as nonconsensual female genital "circumcision" are actually non-issues. Far from being a defense of a human right by an oppressed people

for whom it is culturally a human right, it is actually an attack on the human rights of some of those people. It doesn't matter what "culture" one lives in; "no" always means "no."

19. Conversely, the children of secularists are not unfairly deprived of anything by not being taught "creation science," because there is no such thing.

MORAL IMAGINATION

Mark Johnson

. . .

What Difference Does Moral Imagination Make?

A THEORY OF MORALITY should be a theory of moral understanding. Moral understanding is in large measure imaginatively structured. The primary forms of moral imagination are concepts with prototype structure, semantic frames, conceptual metaphors, and narratives. To be morally insightful and sensitive thus requires of us two things: (1) We must have knowledge of the imaginative nature of human conceptual systems and reasoning. This means that we must know what those imaginative structures are, how they work, and what they entail about the nature of our moral understanding. (2) We must cultivate moral imagination by sharpening our powers of discrimination, exercising our capacity for envisioning new possibilities, and imaginatively tracing out the implications of our metaphors, prototypes, and narratives.

The first requirement above, gaining knowledge of our moral understanding, entails that we will give up the illusions both of absolute moral values and of radical moral subjectivism. It requires us to give up the idea that moral reasoning is finding prearticulated rules and fitting them to situations. It demands that we study in detail the metaphoric structure of our morality, asking what it highlights and what it hides. Finally, it gives us a way to determine what might be changeable in our understanding and what such changes would entail for who we are and how we affect others.

The second requirement, that of developing our moral imagination, changes our conception of moral development. It sees our primary task as less a matter of learning how to apply moral laws and more a task of refining our perception of character and situations and of developing empathetic imagination to take up the part of others.

These, then, are some of the senses in which an experientialist view of moral theory can still give us some of the kinds of guidance we desire from a moral theory. It can't tell us what to do in given situations, but then neither could traditional Moral Law theories. Rather, it gives the kind of general guidance that comes from enhanced moral understanding and self-knowledge.

Empathetic Imagination

Traditional moral theories have almost entirely ignored one of our most important moral capacities—the capacity for empathy. Hume's treatment of what he called "sympathy" or "fellow-feeling"[1] touches on this issue, but it does not go to the heart of imaginative empathetic projection into the experience of other people.[2] As a limiting case, it requires the ability to imagine *ourselves* in different situations and conditions at past and future times. Unless we can put ourselves in the place of another, unless we can enlarge our own perspective through an imaginative encounter with the experience of others, unless we can let our own values and ideals be called into question from various points of view, we cannot be morally sensitive.

Hume was therefore at least partially correct in recognizing a general sympathy as the basis for morality: "Utility is only a tendency to a certain end; and were the end totally indifferent to us, we should feel the same indifference towards the means. It is requisite a *sentiment* should here display itself, in order to give a preference to the useful above the pernicious tendencies. This sentiment can be no other than a feeling for the happiness of mankind, and a resentment of their misery."[3]

What Hume misses is that, beyond a feeling for the well-being of others, we need also to imaginatively take up their experience. According to the traditional interpretation of Hume's moral theory, he misses this aspect because of his rigid separation of reason and feeling, which forces him to deny reason a central role in morality. But Annette Baier has argued that Hume is actually criticizing this strict separation of reason and feeling. She suggests that Hume's entire project gradually builds up a rich and subtle account of rational sentiment as underlying our ability to imaginatively take up the part of another person.[4] In any case, the most charitable way to consume Hume's sentiment for the welfare of others is as a blending of feeling, imagination, and reason.

This "taking up the place of another" is an act of imaginative experience and dramatic rehearsal of the sort described by Nussbaum and Eldridge in their accounts of narrative moral explorations. It is perhaps the most important imaginative exploration we can perform. It is not sufficient merely to manipulate a cool, detached "objective" reason toward the situation of others. We must, instead, go out toward people to inhabit their worlds, not just by rational calculations, but also in imagination, feeling, and expression.

Reflecting in this way involves an *imaginative rationality* through which we can participate empathetically in another's experience: their suffering, pain, humiliation, and frustrations, as well as their joy, fulfillment, plans, and hopes. Morally sensitive people are capable of living out, in and through such an experiential imagination, the reality of others with whom they are interacting, or whom their actions might affect.

I would describe this imaginative rationality as *passionate,* if that word were not so laden with subjectivist connotations. Roberto Unger describes as passionate "the whole range of interpersonal encounters in which people do not treat one another as means to one another's ends."[5] Passion is the basis of our noninstrumental relations to others, and it takes us beyond fixed character, social roles, and institutional arrangements.

. . . Kant's categorical imperative requires imaginative (metaphoric) interpretation[;] we can now see that the Kantian imperative always to treat others (and oneself) as ends-in-themselves has no practical meaning independent of our imaginatively taking up the place of the other. Contrary to Kant's explicit claims, we cannot know what it means to treat someone as an end-in-himself, in any concrete way, unless we can imagine his experience, feelings, plans, goals, and hopes. We cannot know what respect for others demands of us, unless we participate imaginatively in their experience of the world.

We need this same reflective attitude toward, and imaginative knowledge of, ourselves, if we hope ever to rise above the level of creatures driven by immediate needs, desires, and whims. For we must be able to imagine how we might feel and think and act in various hypothetical situations.

It is extremely important to understand that the kind of empathetic imaginative understanding involved here is not merely personal or subjective. Such a romantic view of empathy, as a kind of flowing-into-the-other by giving oneself up to strong fellow-feeling, is an artifact of an erroneous traditional separation of reason, imagination, and feeling. However, even the romantic poets understood the shared, communal character of imagination and feeling. The poetry of both Wordsworth and Coleridge, for example, often involves meditations directed toward revivifying strong human feelings that bind us together in community. Both the *Lyrical Ballads* and the *Biographia Literaria* explore the communal and transformative character of an imagination that makes it possible for us to understand each other, to share a world, and to reach out to others in a caring way. . . .

Moral imagination is public and shared.[6] It has the same public character as do our social relations, practices, and institutions, for all of these are defined by metaphors and other imaginative structures. Imagination, as I have described it, is the primary means by which social relations are constituted. Consider, for example, the imaginative dimensions of all sexual relations that have a truly social dimension. A sexual act can be meaningful only if it is more than a sequence of passive reactions to stimulation. Each person must imaginatively grasp the other's acts as responses to one's own intentions and acts. I must experience your touching of me as both expressing your desire and as directed toward me and my desire. I must take up and carry forward your desire in my active response to you. In happy cases the result is a reciprocal play between partners, a kind of erotic dialectic in which we share in each other's experience. Joseph Kupfer explains the nature of this reciprocity as

> sharing in each other's ends, each taking risks in respect to the same things and with regard to one another at the same time. . . . Sexual reciprocity is also responding to another's physical response: moving to the other's movement, stroking the caressing hand, embracing the embracer. It includes acting on the needs and desires which we perceive the other to have. At the same time, our partner is responding in like fashion to us. Furthermore, reciprocity includes responding both for our own sake and for the sake of the other, independent of our personal stake.[7]

Meaningful sexual relations are, in this way, social and deeply imaginative. As such, they are representative of human relations generally, which rest on the ability to take up the part of the other and to let one's ongoing interactions and relations be guided by one's imaginative grasp of the experience and intentions of other people. It is this kind of empathetic understanding that underlies the possibility of any morality that is more than mere rule-following.

The Imaginative Envisionment of Possibilities for Acting

Beyond knowledge of our own and others' cognitive and moral capacities and perspectives, beyond an abiding fellow-feeling, beyond the ability to inhabit imaginatively the world of another, something more is yet required. That "something more" is an ability to imaginatively discern various possibilities for acting within a given situation and to envision the potential help and harm that are likely to result from a given action.

Care, concern, and good intentions are not enough. We are social creatures who live in communities, whose material and emotional well-being require social relationships and interactions, and whose individual and joint projects require actions directed toward goals, such as satisfying our material, interpersonal, and cultural needs. We need, not just to will purely, but rather to act in ways that promote the well-being of ourselves and others.

Kant is famous for denying that purposive activity is or ever could be definitive of the morality of our willing. He sought to remind us that a good will stands forth as morally praiseworthy in its own right, without regard to any ends it might or might not achieve: "Even if it should happen that, by a particularly unfortunate fate or by the niggardly provision of a stepmotherly nature, this will should be wholly lacking in power to accomplish its purpose, and if even the greatest effort should not avail it to achieve anything of its end, and if there remained only the good will (not as a mere wish but as the summoning of all the means in our power), it would sparkle like a jewel in its own right, as something that had its full worth in itself."

Kant was right in observing that uncontrollable contingencies ought not to detract from the merit of good willing. However, moral action requires us to realize ends, both immediate (e.g., to assist an accident victim) and long-range (e.g., to educate the young), both narrow (e.g., to help someone find shelter) and comprehensive (e.g., to realize an overarching pattern of social relations). Good willing doesn't exist in itself, locked up in inner mental space and isolated from our actions. Will is not an entity separated from its directedness toward the realization of various ends, purposes, and plans, most of which require joint actions and projects. Our will is thus spread out in the activity of our ongoing lives, though it is not reducible to that activity.

The envisioning of possibilities for fruitful, meaningful, and constructive action requires moral imagination. Our ability to criticize a moral view depends on our capacity for imagining alternative viewpoints on, and solutions to, a particular moral problem. In order to adapt and grow, we must be able to see beyond our present vantage point and to grow beyond our present selves. We must be able to imagine new dimensions for our character, new directions for our relationships with others, and even new forms of social organization. Roberto Unger has articulated both the need and the conditions of possibility for imaginative transformation of this sort.

> So you know . . . that, though it is your fate to live within conditional worlds, you also have the power to break outside them. When you do that, however, you do not reach the unconditional: the thought beyond limiting method and language, the society beyond limiting practical and imaginative structure, the personality beyond limiting character. You can, nevertheless, work toward a situation that keeps alive the power to break the limits: to think thoughts that shatter the available canon of reason and discourse, to experiment with forms of collective life that the established practical and imaginative order of society locks out or puts down, to reach out toward the person beyond the character.[8]

It is precisely by recognizing the always partial nature of our metaphors, schemas, and narratives that we can keep ourselves alerted to the constant necessity of stretching ourselves beyond our present identity and context. No person can be moral in a suitably reflective way who cannot imagine alternative viewpoints as a means of understanding and transforming the limits of his own convictions and commitments. This is an activity of moral imagination.

Imaginative Moral Reasoning

The metaphors and other imaginative structures that make us aware of our conditioned state and the need to seek out alternative viewpoints turn out to give us the means we need to do this. The very character of metaphorical understanding that undermines absolutist pretensions—its relative indeterminacy and multiplicity of meanings—also supplies us with a range of possible meanings and directions that we might previously have overlooked. On the one hand, our imaginative understanding creates certain problems for us, since it introduces a multivalence and open-endedness into our understanding and reasoning. On the other hand, it does not leave us without resources for dealing with indeterminacies in our experience. It opens up a range of constrained alternatives that might help us solve our problem or accomplish our general goal.

As an example of the way this kind of imaginative transformation of our moral understanding operates in an open-ended, yet highly constrained, manner, I want to consider Steven Winter's analysis of the imaginative basis of a landmark case of legal reasoning.[9] The case examined by Winter is *legal*, but because his analysis focuses on imaginative structures present in conceptualization and reasoning generally, it can stand as an example of what typically goes on in the creative use of *moral* imagination, too.

The case, *NLRB* v. *Jones and Laughlin Steel Corp.*, concerns the issue of whether the federal government should have the power to regulate labor relations in manufacturing. The outcome established an important precedent for greater government regulation in this and many other areas as well. The steel company wanted to preserve its power to restrict union activities. Relying on well-established nineteenth-century precedent, the steel manufacturers argued that we must distinguish manufacturing from commerce. Manufacturing is *local* and thus subject only to the laws of the state in which the goods are made. Commerce, to the extent that it extends across state boundaries, would be subject to federal regulation. So construed, the federal government would have no jurisdiction over the steel company's handling of labor problems arising at the level of manufacturing.

The drafters of the National Labor Relations Act argued differently, building their argument on the metaphor of a STREAM OF COMMERCE. Taking that metaphor as fundamental, they reasoned that a corporation's interfering with labor's collective bargaining has "the necessary effect of burdening and obstructing commerce by (a) impairing the efficiency, safety, or operation of the instrumentalities of commerce; (b) *occurring in the current of commerce*; (c) materially affecting, *restricting, or controlling the flow* of raw materials or manufactured or processed goods from or *into the channels of commerce* . . . or (d) causing diminution of employment and wages in such *volume* as substantially to impair or disrupt the market for goods *flowing from or into the channels of commerce.*"[10]

What Justice Hughes discerned in this argument was not only the STREAM OF COMMERCE metaphor, but also the SOURCE-PATH-GOAL schema that underlies it. He used this schema as the basis for an alternative metaphorical understanding that would justify even greater governmental control over business. Arguing that the STREAM OF COMMERCE metaphor covers only a limited range of cases, Hughes then elaborates his alternative metaphoric frame: "The congressional authority to protect interstate commerce from burdens and obstructions is not limited to transactions which can be deemed to be an essential part of a 'flow' of interstate or foreign commerce. *Burdens and obstructions* may be due to *injurious action springing from other sources.* The fundamental principle is that the power to regulate commerce is the power to enact 'all appropriate legislation' for its '*protection and advancement*' . . . and it is primarily for Congress to consider and decide the *fact of the danger* and to *meet it.*"[11]

Hughes is transforming the logic of the argument here from one of avoiding obstructions to the free flow of commerce (STREAM OF COMMERCE metaphor) to one of actively meeting potential dangers that might limit the *advancement* of commerce. A much more aggressive role for the government is being sanctioned. The basis for this expanded role is the emergence of a new metaphoric conception of COMMERCE AS JOURNEY. As Hughes says, what if we regard commerce as "*a great movement* of iron ore, coal and limestone *along well-defined paths.*"[12] Commerce, personified as a traveler, must then be supported and protected as it moves along its journey (following a SOURCE-PATH-GOAL schema). A much more active role of protector is justified for the federal government, in which anticipated dangers or obstructions must be directly confronted. That would mean that the government could intervene at any point in the commerce journey, even at the "start" of the journey in the manufacturing plants.

Winter summarizes Hughes's imaginative transformation of the underlying metaphors and their basic image schema:

> The older model was premised on a *stream* metaphor that entailed a quite limited congressional role: If commerce is a stream, then Congress's job is to *regulate* its flow and protect it from *obstructions*. Hughes' model, premised on the much richer *journey* metaphor, yields more wide ranging entailments. If commerce is a traveler on a journey, then the potential sources of interference are much more widespread. The focus now becomes not mere obstructions, but harms of many sorts such as *throttling, danger, injurious actions springing from other sources.* The correlative congressional power shifts from *regulation* to *protection and advancement.* Congress is now the interstate police protecting the always vulnerable traveler and expediting her journey.[13]

Hughes goes on to explore the entailments of his new metaphor, including the key notion that "*stoppage* of those [manufacturing] operations by *industrial strife* would have a most serious effect on interstate commerce,"[14] so that the federal government may find it necessary to interfere with labor relations, insofar as they might pose a threat to the ability of commerce to make its journey.

The critical move, as we have seen, has already been accomplished—the shift of metaphors carried off by discerning their underlying shared SOURCE-PATH-GOAL schema. This is an important part of what I mean by the imaginative exploration of possibilities for action that lies at the heart of moral reasoning. What is crucial in such cases of reasoning is that we can employ metaphoric and other imaginative materials that are already operating in our present understanding of a situation to transform that situation by discovering novel alternatives for evaluation and action.

Justice Hughes's reasoning in *Jones and Laughlin* is imaginative in that it utilizes metaphoric resources available to all members of our culture, and it carries us, via an underlying image schema, from one systematic metaphor for commerce to a novel one that has very different entailments concerning the extent of government control in business. We have seen that Hughes's exercise of moral imagination is, although highly constrained by preexisting frames and values, nevertheless not altogether determined by them. He is able to reason creatively from one metaphorical conception to another by his imaginative elaboration of an image schema shared by both metaphorical mappings.

Hughes's reasoning in this legal case is exemplary of the nature of moral imagination generally. In our moral reasoning we use imaginative structures and contents given to us by our culture and articulated through our personal experience as a basis for imaginatively exploring new possibilities for meaning, relationships, social organizations, and forms of practice.

What is crucial is that our moral reasoning can be *constrained* by the metaphoric and other imaginative structures shared within our culture and moral tradition, yet it can also be *creative* in transforming our moral understanding, our identity, and the course of our lives. Without this kind of imaginative reasoning we would lead dreadfully impoverished lives. We would be reduced to repeating habitual actions, driven by forces and contingencies beyond our control. It is moral imagination that gives us the modest, but absolutely necessary, freedom we have to grow and develop morally and socially.

It is unsettling to some people to realize that there is a certain amount of ineliminable indeterminacy in our experience of situations, and that human moralities cannot escape this indeterminacy. But the fact that there are always multiple framings possible for any situation ought not to generate either despair or cynicism. Rather, we ought to celebrate the multivalence of situations that makes it possible for us to deal creatively and constructively with them, for this means that we are not locked into the same old fixed patterns of behavior and response. We can transform our experience, we can try out new ideas, and we can grow.

NOTES

1. David Hume, *An Enquiry concerning the Principles of Morals,* ed. L. A. Selby-Bigge (1777; Oxford: Oxford University Press, 1902), sec. 5, pt. 2, 181–83, 221–22.

2. I have in mind what Hans Georg Gadamer describes in *Truth and Method* (New York: Crossroad Publishing, 1975) as "horizon fusion," the merging through a dialectical interaction with others, of the horizon of one's own world with that of another, in such a way as to lay one's own prejudgments open to criticism and possible transformation.

3. Hume, *Principles of Morals,* appendix 1.

4. . . . The Hume presented in Annette C. Baier's *A Progress of Sentiments: Reflections on Hume's Treatise* (Cambridge: Harvard University Press, 1991) does seem to recognize the form of empathetic imagination I am describing.

5. Roberto Unger, *Passion: An Essay on Personality* (New York: Free Press, 1984), 105–6.

6. For examples of the role of imagination in the constitution of our shared reality, see my *Body in the Mind* (Chicago: University of Chicago Press, 1987).

7. Joseph Kupfer, *Experience as Art: Aesthetics in Everyday Life* (Albany: State University of New York, 1983), 103–4.

8. Unger, *Passion,* 262–63.

9. Steven Winter, "Transcendental Nonsense, Metaphoric Reasoning, and the Cognitive Stakes for Law," *University of Pennsylvania Law Review* 137, no. 4 (1989).

10. *United States Code* 29 (1982):151 (congressional findings in sec. 1 of the act). Emphasis added by Winter ("Transcendental Nonsense," 1200).

11. *NLRB* v. *Jones and Laughlin Steel Corp.,* in *United States Reports* 301:36–37 (quoting *The Daniel Ball, United States Report* 77 [1870]:557, 564, and *Stafford* v. *Wallace, United States Reports* 258 [1922]:495, 521), as quoted in Winter, "Transcendental Nonsense" 1202, emphasis added.

12. *Jones and Laughlin,* 42 (emphasis added by Winter).

13. Winter, "Transcendental Nonsense," 1204.

14. *Jones and Laughlin,* 42 (emphasis added by Winter).

PART SIX

EDUCATION IN A DEMOCRATIC SOCIETY

THIS SECTION offers three readings concerned with the purposes of education in democratic societies. We begin with Chapter Fifteen, by C. A. Bowers. Recognizing that "the core values and assumptions of modernity are themselves ecologically problematic," Bowers argues that schools need to begin to promote "a sense of moral connectedness to the life forms that constitute the non-human environment." Bowers, who has studied the cultural implications of technology and the ecological crisis while teaching at both the University of Oregon and Portland State University, proposes that educators have a responsibility to coming generations to pass along the kind of wisdom and practical knowledge necessary for all of us to live within the limits of our environment. Focusing on the places where teachers are taught, "How Colleges of Education Package the Myth of Modernity" not only recognizes the connection between education and the public good, it also suggests that there might be similarities between our "moral connectedness" to nonhuman forms of life and our connectedness to one another in a democratic context.

In Chapter Sixteen, "Democratic Education in Difficult Times," Amy Gutmann, dean of the faculty at Princeton

University and founding director of the University Center for Human Values, approaches this issue by noting that the "content of public schooling cannot be neutral among competing conceptions of the good life, and if it could, we would not and should not care to support it." This leads Gutmann to ask which freedoms and virtues deserve to be promoted in our nation's classrooms. Couching her discussion in the context of "democratic professionalism" and the need to prepare citizens to participate equally in the conscious reproduction—not just replication—of their society, Gutmann offers a thoughtful analysis of how educators ought to deal with the tension between our notions of individual freedom and the common good—a tension, it should be noted, that also often surfaces in discussions dealing with ecological responsibilities.

Clearly, education as a public good involves much more than simply preparing students for the workforce. Therefore, it seems only appropriate that this section conclude by asking, What is education for? Chair of the environmental studies program at Oberlin College and education editor for the journal *Conservation Biology*, David W. Orr approaches this topic in Chapter Seventeen with the realization that "the worth of education must now be measured against the standards of decency and human survival—the issues now looming so large before us in the twenty-first century. It is not education, but education of a certain kind, that will save us." Orr identifies six myths that serve to form the contentious foundations for much of contemporary educational praxis. He then offers six guiding principles to help us rethink the public purpose of education as measured against what he calls the "agenda of human survival."

15

HOW COLLEGES OF EDUCATION PACKAGE THE MYTH OF MODERNITY

C. A. Bowers

PROFESSORS OF EDUCATION responsible for providing the professional knowledge that public school teachers will use as a basis for making curricular and pedagogical decisions in the classroom, and for guiding the graduate studies of the next generation of teacher educators, have relatively low status within the academic community. Indeed, they are near the bottom. But their contribution to perpetuating the most extreme expressions of modern consciousness, and thus their contribution to raising the next generation of youth who will carry modernity to an even further extreme (with all its consequences for the environment), surpasses that of the more high-status departments known for their scholarly rigor and accomplishments. The academic status system, however, does not take account of the fact that what is taught in education courses, as well as what is ignored in these courses, will exert a powerful influence on young students during their most formative period of intellectual and moral development. The conceptual and ideological framework that public school students acquire through the content of the curriculum, which can be traced back to what their teachers acquired from their professional education classes, lays the groundwork for their receptivity to the mythic dimensions of Western modernism being further elaborated in the courses they will take in departments of philosophy, economics, psychology, history, and so on.

To put this another way, when students enroll in the university they have already acquired the basic conceptual and ideological categories that their university-level classes will build upon. And for public school students who do not go on to some form of higher education, their limited classroom and enlarged television-based education will leave them with the taken-for-granted patterns of thinking that will make them easily influenced by business and technological elites who face the continual challenge of creating consumer demand for the new products essential to growth-mania. . . . These conceptual and ideological patterns of thinking include the following: the Western myth of an anthropocentric universe; an individually-centered way of understanding intelligence, creativity, and moral judgment; a view of science and technology as both culturally neutral and as the manifestation of human progress; the experience of time as linear and progressive (thus making the judgment of the individual the primary authority for assessing the relevance and worth of traditions—which are understood in astonishingly simplistic ways); the privileging of literacy-based thought and communication over oral-based forms of cultural storage and renewal; and the continual search for what is new and innovative (often based on the emotive expression of a supposedly autonomous individual or driven by the messianic ideology that equates competitive relationships with the discovery of a higher truth and economic growth). These patterns of thinking, which are essential to the organization of knowledge in most university classes, and to sustaining a taken-for-granted attitude toward the economic and technological agenda of modernity, are learned indirectly (that is, largely unconsciously) as students proceed from the elementary grades through high school. When they arrive on the university campus, or at their first low-paying, low-skill job, they bring with them these deeply held and mostly taken-for-granted patterns of thinking. While other university departments gild the lily, provide the credentials that will enable their technologically oriented graduates access to elite professions, and look upon their colleagues in education departments with disdain, it is these low-status professors of education who are ultimately responsible for the sense of mission and narrowness of vision that accounts for the cultural mediation and consciousness-forming process that occurs in most public school classrooms. In fairness, responsibility for the cultural myths reproduced through the curriculum of the public schools should also be borne by the professors who teach the more "academic" classes required as part of the teacher certification process.

These criticisms do not apply to all public school teachers or, for that matter, to all professors of education. In the use of any powerful generalization, the margins are not as accurately represented as the mainstream.

Here we are addressing the modern orthodoxies that serve as the conceptual and ideological framework for the professional educational establishment, which includes graduate schools of education, teacher education programs, professional journals, and the educationally oriented entrepreneurs who promote the latest fads borrowed from scientific research (e.g., brain research) and pop psychology. How some public school teachers resist being swept along in the current of educational fads by quietly and persistently providing the basis for a deep and critical understanding of cultural experience must also be taken into account in any effort to put education on a more ecologically responsive pathway. It is also important to recognize the efforts of the few professors of education who are attempting to introduce into the study of education, and into teacher education programs, an understanding [of] how the classroom can be used to foster understandings and experiences that renew human/environmental relationships. However, working collaboratively with these marginalized educators who are committed to a deep cultural and environmental approach to all areas of education will not bring about changes on the scale that is now required. The basic reality is that their efforts are still marginalized.

To the casual observer, it might appear that teacher education, as well as graduate education programs, are characterized by a diverse number of theoretical frameworks. The increased emphasis on computer-mediated learning appears to be based on a different set of assumptions than approaches to education that promote a more critical and participatory approach to decision-making—such as comes out of the John Dewey and Paulo Freire traditions of educational thought. But an examination of such seemingly diverse approaches as cooperative learning, direct instruction, outcome-based education, assertive discipline, multiple intelligences, and critical literacy, will reveal that the surface diversity is less significant than the deep cultural assumptions shared by all these approaches. That is, each of the approaches, while representing the process of learning as occurring in different ways, reinforces the modern view of the individual. And this modern view ignores . . . how individuals are cultural beings and how cultures are dependent upon natural systems. While differing over how to facilitate change (which they all associate with progress), each approach misrepresents the nature of tradition, and thus the differences in how cultures recognize and value what has been learned and handed down over time, as backward and in need of being modernized. The significance of the differences between educators who associate empowerment with procedural problem-solving, emotive-based judgment, and critical reflection, largely disappear when we realize that all three approaches reinforce the highly experimental approach to cultural life that is the hallmark of modernity.

This experimental orientation, where new ideas, values, and techniques (and technologies) are seen as progressive steps forward, leads to viewing as both irrelevant and obstructionist the forms of transgenerational communication that characterize ecologically centered cultures. Stated more succinctly, none of the current approaches to educational reform (with the possible exception of the Foxfire Curriculum) help to clarify the nature and importance of transgenerational communication—and how youth play a necessary part in this vital cultural renewal and ecologically centering process. Lastly, these seemingly diverse approaches to education, with their equally diverse vocabularies, all reinforce the most extreme expression of Western anthropocentrism—that is, the individual is represented as totally separate from the environment. Even the greening of certain areas of the public school curriculum (which seems further advanced than what can only be described as the culturally reactionary position of university level professional education courses) has not led to the recognition that the core values and assumptions of modernity are themselves ecologically problematic.

Just as professors of education and classroom teachers became aware of gender discrimination in the curriculum and staffing patterns *only* after feminists had made significant gains in focusing public attention on the problem, professors of education and classroom teachers are again repeating this earlier pattern by promoting a taken-for-granted attitude toward the deep cultural assumptions now being questioned by the more thoughtful individuals within the environmental movement. But it is more complex than being trapped in what is now a reactionary pattern of thinking. If the literature that represents the cutting-edge thinking of the technocratically oriented educators is considered, it becomes clear that educational reform is being influenced primarily by powerful economic and technological interest groups. Evidence of this trend can be seen in the number of states and provinces across North America shifting to what is called "outcome-based education." The justification for this approach to educational reform is couched in language that explains the need to contribute directly to the country's economic and technological competitiveness in an increasingly globalized economy.

The following explanation of what is termed "transformational outcome-based education" is important because it clearly suggests that there is a need for a new form of linkage between the content of the curriculum and life experiences—which educational and political reformers are interpreting to mean life experiences in a computer-mediated work environment.

According to William Spady, a leading advocate of educational restructuring,

> transformational OBE (outcome-based education) means that curriculum content is no longer the grounding and defining element of outcomes. Instead, outcomes are seen as culminating Exit role performances that include sometimes complex arrays of knowledge, competencies, and orientations and require learning demonstrations in varying role contexts. . . . The bottom line of Transformational OBE is that students' learning is manifested through their ability to carry out performance roles in contexts that at least simulate life situations and challenges.[1]

Learning to carry out performance roles that simulate "life situations" does not include the small-scale community-oriented economic and technological practices that fulfill local needs. Nor does it involve learning to participate in renewing and carrying forward local traditions not dependent upon consumer and work-oriented relationships. Rather, when educational reformers think of performance outcomes that take account of the challenges that lie ahead, they have in mind the need to contribute to the development and use of the new computer-driven technologies that will keep the economy expanding and the local work force fully employed. What is not being considered is the connection between the globalizing of the technologically based economic system that educational restructuring is helping to further and the ecological crisis. Nor do educational reformers recognize that computer-based thinking and communicating threaten the stability of local economies and help create what Barbara Garson has called the "electronic sweatshop."

The varied concerns of environmentalists are also being ignored by educational reformers who identify themselves with the emancipatory, consciousness-raising tradition of liberal education. These reformers write a great deal about the need to use the classroom to foster critical thinking, to instill in students a sense of social justice that will lead them to work for the elimination of all forms of social oppression, and, in the name of democracy, to celebrate cultural differences while continually renegotiating the basis of relationships that govern everyday life. Using the language of postmodernism that represents every aspect of culture as a text, and critical literacy as the ability to deconstruct the forms of domination encoded in the texts (language systems of a culture), Peter McLaren and Colin Lankshear summarize what is seen by radical educators as the democratic alternative to the direction mainstream educational reform is moving in. As they state it, *critical literacy,* as we are using it here, becomes the interpretation of the social present for the purpose of transforming the cultural life of certain groups, for questioning tacit assumptions and unarticulated presuppositions of current cultural and social formations and the subjectivities and capacities for agenthood that they foster. It aims at understanding the ongoing social struggles over the signs of culture and over the definition of social reality—over what is considered legitimate and preferred meaning at any given historical period.[2]

This statement, which is representative of the thinking of radical educational reformers, also reveals why environmentalists should not be optimistic about finding allies within this group. While borrowing variously from pre-ecological thinkers such as Marx, Dewey, Freire, and now the deconstruction tradition of postmodern European intellectuals, they have retained as the basis of their vision of educational emancipation the most nihilistic elements of the modern mind set. By identifying the critical reflection of the individual as the sole source of authority for all forms of judgments, including moral judgments, their approach to education reinforces all the assumptions of modernity identified earlier: an extreme form of individualism supposedly free of all cultural influence, change as the expression of progress, anthropocentrism, and so forth. If these radical educational theorists were to address specific forms of social injustice, recognize that the modern nihilistic way of thinking they uphold as a universal human need is actually a culturally specific way of thinking, and take seriously the possibility that the conceptual and moral foundations of their view of emancipation have been turned into a reactionary position by the ecological crisis, environmentalists might then be able to establish a working relationship with them. Instead, this group of reformers continues to think in the context-free metaphors of freedom and equality, without considering the fundamental differences that exist between cultures and how these differences represent alternative pathways to living in relative balance with local natural systems.

Recent efforts to think about curriculum reform have also ignored the connections between the cultural patterns reinforced through education and the growing evidence that humans are altering both the micro- and macro-patterns of life in the Earth's ecosystems. Curriculum reform within the educational mainstream is increasingly being influenced by developments in the area of computer-based technologies—with more of the curriculum reflecting the shift from books to interactive software programs. Changes in curriculum are also being influenced by professors of education who promote the modern idea that knowledge is constructed through the creative insight of the individuals, and through participatory decision making within the same age group. Even among the curriculum theorists who see themselves as extrapolating from postmortem thinking, and the principles of quantum physics, the form of curriculum that will enable people to live meaningful lives in the next century cannot escape the problem of using the vocabulary that privileges the reactionary beliefs and values of modernity. But it is a vocabulary that will make sense only to those teachers who already assume that everything is relative, and that what is immediately meaningful to the student should be the primary concern of the educator. Witness the concluding statement by Jacques Daignault, who is described by another leading curriculum theorist as the "major post-structuralist theoretician in curriculum studies":

> Hence learning is relevant to a logic of the signified; and teaching, to a logic of the signifier. And everybody repeats: the teacher, his analogies; the learner, his errors. So that the play of the repetition and the difference digs an abyss in the core of the teaching-learning process. Now, there is a paradoxical instance that circulates in the difference of the teaching-learning process: the "nonsense" of the differential repetition of analogies to themselves. And this *sui-reference* of analogies is itself a function of the differences put forth for the joy of teaching.[3]

And from a philosopher turned curriculum theorist, we learn that quantum physics and chaos theory have revolutionary implications for organizing school knowledge in ways that will foster a form of consciousness more in harmony with the ongoing process of becoming. Wayne B. Hamilton describes this new "holographic curriculum" in the following way:

> By exposing our students to the holographic core curriculum, we may affect their entire thought process. Thought now has totality as its content. As such, it is more like an art form than definite knowledge about how things are; its function, like that of all metaphorical thinking, is to give rise to a *new* perception, to *new* ways of looking at the whole. Knowledge and thinking are thus related to the ever-changing flux, the dynamic character of reality and knowledge.[4]

The thinking of Daignault and Hamilton may appear extreme to readers who are unfamiliar with educational literature. But it is not fundamentally at odds with the "anti-tradition tradition" of thinking that underlies the process-oriented followers of Freire and Dewey. Nor is it at odds with the view of knowledge being promoted by the computer industry. CD-ROMs that enable students to "navigate" through stored images and data in route to constructing their own interpretations and narratives (indeed, their own sense of history), and the prospects of entering virtual realities as a way of escaping the limitations of their cultural embeddedness, are simply a more technologically based expression of the same anthropocentric, change-oriented, individually centered form of modernism. But these expressions of modernism have a particularly ironic consequence: namely, the more extreme the form of individualism, the more the individual is vulnerable to being manipulated by elite groups who have an economic interest in representing "progress" in terms of the latest technological innovations. Alasdair MacIntyre's observation that self-identity is constituted within the context of a particular set of cultural narratives seems particularly relevant here. He notes that the individual

> can only answer the question "What am I to do?" if (she/he) can answer the prior question "Of what story or stories do I find myself a part?" We enter human society, that is, with one or more imputed characters—roles into which we have been drafted—and we have to learn what they are in order to be able to understand how others respond to us and how our responses to them are apt to be understood.[5]

If the stories are about communication over the Internet, the continuous changes in computer technology and navigating through the storehouse of digitalized cultural artifacts, a corresponding form of subjectivity will emerge. Similarly, if the stories are about deconstructing all cultural texts and creating one's own ideas and values, the individual's self-identity and sense of moral responsibility will be equally limited. But these will not be forms of individualism that take for granted a sense of moral connectedness to the life forms that constitute the non-human environment. Nor do they represent forms of individualism that will experience a sense of responsibility to carry forward and renew the culture's wisdom and practical knowledge of how to live within the limits of the environment— which is essential to ensuring that the prospects of future generations are not diminished.

As these brief observations about the modernizing orientation of public schools and universities suggest, radical reform is urgently needed. But it will be difficult to achieve, partly because the culture of modernism is also the basis of progressive thinking so highly valued at all levels of education. The various professional languages, regardless of whether they are technological or emancipatory in orientation, continue to reinforce the educator's natural attitude toward the moral and intellectual certainties of modern consciousness. But the challenge of initiating fundamental reform will be no more difficult (or should we say at least as difficult?) than getting scientists to recognize (and to take responsibility for) changes they introduce into the world's cultures, and in getting humanists and social scientists to recognize the importance of learning from more ecologically centered cultures. . . .

NOTES

1. William Spady, "Outcome-Based Education" in *A Leader's Guide to School Restructuring: A Special Report of the NASSP Commission on Restructuring* (Reston, Va.: National Association of Secondary School Principals, 1992), p. 54.

2. Peter McLaren and Colin Lankshear, "Critical Literacy and the Postmodern Turn" in *Critical Literacy: Politics, Praxis, and the Postmodern*, ed. Colin Lankshear and Peter McLaren (Albany: State University of New York Press, 1993), p. 413.

3. Jacques Daignault, "Traces at Work from Different Places" in *Understanding Curriculum and Phenomenology and Deconstructed Text*, ed. William Pinar and William Reynolds (New York: Teacher's College Press, 1992), pp. 212–213.

4. Wayne B. Hamilton, "The Metaphysics of the Curriculum" in *Holistic Education Review*, 7.2 (Summer 1994): 19, italics added. [Note: Since this writing, *Holistic Education Review* has been renamed *Encounter*.]

5. Alasdair MacIntyre, *After Virtue: A Study in Moral Theory* (Notre Dame, IN: University of Notre Dame Press, 1984 edition), p. 216.

DEMOCRATIC EDUCATION
IN DIFFICULT TIMES

Amy Gutmann

THESE ARE DIFFICULT TIMES because we are difficult people. There are undoubtedly other, less "personal" reasons that make these difficult times and also other, more "structural" reasons that help explain why we are difficult people, but I want to begin by focusing on the fact that we *are*—for whatever simple or complicated reasons—difficult people.

When I say we are difficult people, I have something very simple in mind. Most Americans value freedom of speech and also value protection from falsehood, deceit, and defamation. Yet it is impossible to provide complete freedom of speech and still prevent the widespread dissemination of falsehoods, deceits, and defamations. Most Americans value freedom of religion, and also want governments to shape the social environment so that people are predisposed to believe in "good" religions (or philosophies of life) rather than "bad" ones. Yet a society that grants complete freedom of religion cannot shape an environment resistant to repugnant religions.

Most Americans value living and working where we like, and also value stable, friendly, and familiar places in which to live and work. We value the freedom to choose our sexual partners and rechoose them, and we also place a high value on stable nuclear families. Most Americans want to use their market freedom to secure a standard of living that is staggeringly high by any historical perspective, yet we are also sensitive to the plight of other people's children, which threatens this expectation. Most Americans would like to see our freedoms extended to other people, but we fear that by opening our borders, we decrease the chances of our own (and our children's) educational and economic improvement.

The tension within each set of values—between individual freedom and civic virtue—poses a challenge for educating Americans. It is impossible to educate children to maximize both their freedom and their civic virtue. Yet Americans want both—although some people seem willing to settle for freedom for themselves and civic virtue for others. This formula obviously will not work. Far from obvious, however, is how our educational institutions should come to terms with the tension between individual freedom and civic virtue. Should they try to reconcile these seemingly unreconcilable values? Or give priority to one value over the other? Or find the one, morally best way of coping with each of these tensions? Or should we continue to muddle through much as we have done in the past? Rarely do Americans turn to philosophy for help, except in those rare times when the consequences of muddling through seem unbearable. We then reconcile ourselves to philosophizing; we make a necessity out of a virtue.

While these times are undoubtedly difficult in many ways, philosophy is probably not necessary for getting us through them (and philosophy will certainly not be sufficient). Our nation's political ideals—liberty *and* justice *for all*—remain at risk, but the risks to economically and educationally advantaged Americans are not so great that we have no practical alternative to muddling through. Philosophizing still seems to be a practical luxury. Some of us may be able to withstand the practical risks of politics and education as usual. But, as a society we would do better, both morally and practically, to be more philosophically guided in our educational politics.

By what philosophy should we be guided? The several philosophies that compete for our allegiance suggest radically different ways of dealing with the tensions that make us difficult people. Despite their differences, they all try to dissolve the tension between individual freedom and civic virtue in a potent philosophical solution, and thereby avoid the political problems that flow from the tension. Perhaps the most distinctive feature of a democratic theory of education is its simultaneous refusal to dissolve these tensions philosophically and its insistence on finding a principled, rather than simply a pragmatic, way of living with the tensions. Living with the tensions will never be easy, but the alternatives to democratic education that promise to make us easier people are far worse. One of the strongest arguments for democratic education—as for democracy itself—is that the alternatives are worse. So let us consider the two most philosophically potent and politically influential alternatives to a democratic state of education: a Platonic family state and a liberal state of individuals.

The Family State and the Liberal State

One of the greatest treatises on education ever written, Plato's *Republic*, offers a way of dissolving the tensions between individual freedom and civic virtue: Subsume all that is valuable with regard to individual freedom into civic virtue. The means of subsumption is education: Teach children that they cannot realize their own good except by contributing to the social good. Not just any social good will do: Children must be taught the true good, the one that rightly orders their souls, the one consonant with their varying natures. Unless children learn to associate their own good with the social good, a peaceful and prosperous society will be impossible. Unless the social good that they are taught is consonant with their nature and worthy of their pursuit, they will grow to be unfulfilled and dissatisfied with the society that miseducated them. All education that is not guided by *the* social good and the *truth* in human nature is miseducation. All such societies will degenerate because of internal disharmony.

Peculiarly enough, the Platonic family state provides the philosophical underpinnings of an ongoing American search for "the one best system." The system tries to dissolve the tensions between individual freedom and civic virtue by educating all children to identify their interests with the social good. In practice, the moral costs of dissolving the tension are great: Catholic children were once whipped for refusing to read the ("right") King James version of the Bible; college students today are ridiculed (or dismissed as uneducable) for reading Plato's *Phaedrus* in the wrong way. (So Allan Bloom asks rhetorically: "How does a youngster who sees sublimation where Plato saw divination learn from Plato, let alone think Plato can speak to him?"[1])

Repression of reasonable points of view is half the problem of the family state. The other half is political tyranny justified in the name of educational enlightenment. In the *Republic*, Socrates tells Glaucon that "it's better for all to be ruled by what is divine and prudent, especially when one has it as his own within himself; but, if not, *set over one from outside*, so that insofar as possible all will be alike and friends, piloted by the same thing."[2] Children must not be set free until the right regime—the "divine and prudent" one—is established within their souls.

Who holds the key to the right regime? Not the Socrates who boasts of being the only Athenian wise enough to know his own ignorance. Socrates imagines that there may be someone wiser even than he, someone who has left the cave, and seen the light, someone who therefore knows the right regime for all souls. To create a family state, that philosopher must return to the cave, become "king," and wipe the social slate clean by exiling "all those in the city who happen to be older than ten: and taking over their children . . . rear them—far away from those dispositions they now have from their parents."[3] This is not a small price to pay for dissolving the tensions with which we now live. Socrates himself recoils from the idea on behalf of his imaginary philosopher king, suggesting that he "won't be willing to mind the political things . . . unless some divine chance coincidentally comes to pass."[4]

This problem with the family state is not a purely practical one—pointing to the impossibility of finding someone wiser than Socrates who could educate well-ordered souls in a poorly ordered society. Even if there were someone wiser than Socrates in our midst, he or she still could not claim the right to order the souls of all citizens. A good life must be one that a person recognizes as such, lived from the inside, according to one's own best lights. The neo-Platonic quest for the one best system, which subsumes individual freedom into the social good, denies this insight of individualism. Even if Plato were right about the objectively good life, we would still have to look past the *Republic* for a politically legitimate way of associating individual freedom and civic virtue, through governing.

Radically opposed to the family state is what I call the state of individuals, or the liberal state as it is commonly but misleadingly called. The state of individuals overcomes the tensions between freedom and virtue in a way precisely the opposite of that in the family state: It actively supports only those institutions instrumental to individual freedom of choice. The principled neutrality of the state of individuals aims to maximize the freedom of individuals to pursue their diverse conceptions of the private good. If the Platonic family state strives for the unity of a traditional family, the state of individuals strives for the diversity of a modern shopping mall. To paraphrase John Stuart Mill: All attempts by the state to bias the conclusions of its citizens, including its children, on disputed subjects are evil, as are all unnecessary restrictions on their choices. This is the contemporary liberal credo of neutrality for the sake of opportunity and choice.

Just as the family state provides the philosophical underpinnings for "the one best system," the state of individuals provides philosophical inspiration for "child-centered" education. Of course, proponents of the state of individuals recognize that all educators must limit children's choices, but only for the sake of developing their capacity for rational choice or for the sake of cultural coherence. American schoolchildren are taught English rather than Bengali or Spanish, not by choice but by cultural determination. This culturally determined curriculum, contemporary liberals like Bruce Ackerman tell us, legitimately limits the range of their future choices insofar as such limitation is necessary for cultural coherence. Other limits on children's choices—whether for the sake of moral development or the shaping of democratic character—are unjustified, for these would be based on what Ackerman calls "adult pretensions to moral superiority."[5]

The horticultural imagery so prevalent in Plato—pruning and weeding children's desires, shaping their character—has no place in the state of individuals: "We have no right to look upon future citizens as if we were master gardeners who can tell the difference between a pernicious weed and a beautiful flower."[6] We do have a right, according to Ackerman, perhaps even a duty, to shape the character and bias the choices of children for the sake of cultural coherence. Education in the state of individuals builds on our cultural but not our moral biases. We educate children to be Americans who are free to choose but we do not bias their choices (or shape their character) for the sake of moral goodness. We educate rational shoppers but not good people or virtuous citizens.

Why say that parents and teachers should be free to guide children's choices for the sake of cultural coherence but not for the sake of cultivating good character or choosing a morally good life? After all, sometimes the claim on the part of parents and teachers that they know the difference between morally good and bad, or better and worse, is not a *pretension* to moral superiority, but a reflection of their greater moral understanding. Honesty is better than deceitfulness, industriousness better than sloth, insight better than insensitivity, kindness better than cruelty— and not just because honest, industrious, insightful, and kind people have more freedom of choice. They may have less freedom of choice precisely because they are constrained by these virtues. We nonetheless value these virtues because there is more to a good life and to a good society than freedom; that is one good reason why we are likely to remain difficult people, torn between freedom and other virtues that are not mere means to or byproducts of freedom.

The "neutrality" premise (no authority has a right to act on a belief that one conception of the good life is better than any other) simplifies life for some contemporary liberals, allowing them to defend freedom of choice singlemindedly, but the lameness of the defense is particularly evident in American education. Consumer choice is a reasonable guiding principle for designing a shopping mall, but it is an irresponsible and incomplete principle for designing a high school. Educators must limit students' freedom of choice on some ground; otherwise education simply ceases. Cultural prejudice may seem like the politically safest guide to limiting choice, but it is not a satisfactory substitute for moral principle. Nor is it politically safe: Teaching cultural prejudices is no less politically controversial than teaching moral principles, as recent battles over bilingualism and the content of core curricula indicate.

The family state and the state of individuals offer us the following choice: Either we must educate children so that they are free to choose among the widest range of lives because freedom of choice is the paramount good, or we must educate children so that they will choose *the* life that is best because a rightly ordered soul is the paramount good. Let children define their own identity or define it for them. Give children liberty or give them virtue. This is a morally false choice. Cultivating character and intellect through education constrains children's future choices, but it does not uniquely determine them. There need be nothing illegitimate about such constraints, although some constraints surely are illegitimate. The question we must therefore ask is not whether to maximize freedom or to inculcate virtue, but how to combine freedom with virtue. This creates a new question: which freedoms and what virtues? We must focus not just on the future freedom of children but also the present freedom of parents, not just on the virtues necessary for a good life but also those necessary for a just society.

This reformulation does not resolve but at least it comprehends the problem of associating individual freedom and civic virtue that Americans face today: Citizens of a religiously and ethnically diverse society disagree on the relative value of freedom and virtue; we disagree on the nature of a good life and good character. No political philosophy can authoritatively resolve all our disagreements—not only because no one is smart enough to comprehend a comprehensive good, but because no mortal, no matter how wise, can legitimately impose a good life on people who cannot live that life from the inside. Nor can anyone legitimately impose liberal neutrality on people who value virtue as well as freedom. We stand at a philosophical and political impasse unless we can defend another alternative.

A Democratic Alternative: Public Debate

The alternative I want to defend is democratic in several significant respects. First, it does not tyrannize over common sense, either by subsuming individual freedom into the common social good or by collapsing civic virtue (or social justice) into individual freedom. Second, a democratic theory of education provides principled criticism of all educational authorities (including parents) who tyrannize children in any way, whether by depriving them of an education adequate to citizenship or by repressing reasonable challenges to popular ideas. Third, a democratic theory supports educational institutions that are conducive to democratic deliberation, institutions that make a democratic virtue out of our inevitable disagreements over educational problems. The virtue, too simply stated, is that we can publicly debate educational problems in a way much more likely to increase our understanding of education and each other than if we were to leave the management of schools, as Kant suggested, "to depend entirely upon the judgment of the most enlightened experts."[7] The policies that result from our democratic deliberations will not always be the right ones, but they will be more enlightened—by the values and concerns of the many communities that constitute a democracy—than those that would have been made by unaccountable experts.

This understanding of democratic education is, however, incomplete. The threat of repression and discrimination remains. Democratic processes can be used to destroy democratic education. They can be used to undermine the intellectual foundations of future democratic deliberations by repressing unpopular ways of thinking or excluding some future citizens from an education adequate for participating in democratic politics. A democratic society must not be constrained to legislate what the wisest parent or philosopher wants for his or her child, but it must be constrained not to legislate policies that render democracy repressive or discriminatory. A democratic theory of education recognizes the importance of empowering citizens to make educational policy and also of constraining their choices to a broad range of policies that are nonrepressive and nondiscriminatory, so as to preserve the intellectual and social foundations of democracy. Democracy must be understood not merely (or primarily) as a *process* of majority rule, but rather as an *ideal* of a society whose adult members are, and continue to be, equipped by their education and authorized by political structures to share in ruling. A democratic society must educate all educable children to be capable of participating in collectively shaping their society.

Democracy makes no claim to being an uncontroversial standard. Not all societies or all citizens in our society are committed to democracy (although all, according to this argument, should be). Those who are not committed to democracy are stuck at the impasse I characterized earlier: They assert their commitment to civic virtue or to individual freedom always at the expense of denying the legitimacy of the other value. The practical consequence of this thinking is that basic freedoms are sacrificed to communal virtue or freedom is expanded so far as to forgo the virtues essential to a just society. The legitimating claim of democracy is therefore not that it will be accepted by all citizens (let alone all philosophers)— no political philosophy can sensibly claim such a Panglossian future. Its legitimating claim is one of political morality: A state of democratic education is minimally objectionable insofar as it leaves maximum moral room for citizens deliberately to shape their society, not in their own image, but in an image that they can legitimately identify with their informed, moral choices.

You cannot govern unless you have first been governed. You must govern after you have been governed. These twin maxims, not Platonic but Aristotelian in origin, are at the root of a democratic understanding of both politics and education: being governed and governing in turn, where governing includes the nurturing of children by parents, their formal instruction by professionals, the structuring of public instruction by public officials accountable to citizens, and the shaping of culture by both private and public authorities—constrained or ideally informed by the principles of nonrepression and nondiscrimination.

There are many ways that this democratic understanding (were it more fully elaborated) could make a difference in the way we think about education and practice it. I offer here one small but significant example.

Evolution or Creationism: A Test Case

In October 1986, a federal district court ruled that the public schools of Hawkins County, Tennessee, must exempt the children of a group of fundamentalist Christian parents from basic reading classes. Those classes assigned Holt, Rinehart, & Winston texts, texts that had been unanimously approved by the Hawkins County Board of Education on recommendation of their textbook selection committee. The content of the Holt, Rinehart series offended the religious views of these parents, who had joined together as Citizens Organized for Better Schools (COBS) and unsuccessfully petitioned the school board to have their children taught from unoffensive texts. The parents objected to, among other things: a story depicting a young boy having fun while cooking on grounds that the story "denigrates the differences between the sexes" that the Bible endorses; a story entitled "A Visit to Mars" on grounds that it encourages children to use their imaginations in ways incompatible with fundamentalist faith; a story entitled "Hunchback Madonna," which describes the religious and social practices of an Indian settlement in New Mexico, on grounds that the story teaches Catholicism; and an excerpt from Anne Frank's *Diary of a Young Girl* on grounds that it suggests that nonorthodox belief in God is better than no belief at all. The principal and school board both refused to exempt the children from using the Holt, Rinehart readers. The parents took the Hawkins County Public School District to court.

District Court Judge Thomas Hull found nothing wrong with the Holt, Rinehart series, and said so. Yet he concluded that the children must be exempted from reading the series and therefore from their reading classes because, in his words,

> plaintiffs [the parents of the children] sincerely believe that the affirmation of these philosophical viewpoints is repulsive to their Christian faith, so repulsive that they must not allow their children to be exposed to the Holt series. This is their religious belief. They have drawn a line, and it is not for us to say that the line they drew was an unreasonable one.[8]

Why is it not for us to say?

> Not because the parents of those children should have ultimate authority over their education. If that were the case, it would not be for us (or Judge Hull) to say that they must be educated at all. Yet Judge Hull ruled that the children take standardized tests in reading rather than read standardized texts. If standardized tests are justified, then there must be something that all children should learn independently of what their parents want them to learn.

> Not because democratic education is compatible with the fundamentalist view that forbids exposure to knowledge about religions, cultures, and convictions that differ from their own, on grounds that such knowledge corrupts the soul. The parents in this case claimed that their children would be corrupted by exposure to beliefs and values that contradict their own religious views unless it was explained that the other views are incorrect and that their views are the correct ones. Democratic education is surely incompatible with this fundamentalist view of knowledge and morality.

> Not because democratic education rests on a conception of the good society that threatens the fundamentalist view of a good life and must defer to fundamentalism for the sake of neutrality. Any defensible political understanding of education depends on some conception of a good society, and every conception worth defending threatens some way of life.

It is a sad fact of democracy in the United States that some citizens still hold religious beliefs that reject teaching children the democratic values of mutual respect for reasonable differences of opinion and rational deliberation among differing ways of life. A rejection of democratic values does not, however, constitute a criticism of democracy any more than the rejection by a committed misogynist of the rights of women constitutes a critique of feminism. Both the parents and the misogynists of course have a right to voice their opinions, but in neither case do they have a right to insist that a democratic state teach or sanction their opinions.

Another argument sometimes offered in defense of the claims of fundamentalist parents is that democratic education consists solely of reaching certain facts, not certain values or virtues, to future citizens. This position is superficially similar to John Stuart Mill's conclusion that the state limit its educational authority to probate examinations "confined to facts and positive science exclusively."[9] If this is what we should say about public education, it cannot be because knowing facts is more crucial to a good life or good citizenship than being virtuous. Nor can it be because facts are neutral, while values are not. Might it be because citizens can more easily agree on a body of facts than on a set of values or virtues to be taught to all children? Perhaps this argument was soundly prudential when Mill made it, but its premise is surely very shaky today. The political controversies that have raged in recent years over the biases of testing and the claims of creationism against evolution amply demonstrate how controversial the reaching and testing of facts can be. This is no more or less controversial, however, than the teaching (or not teaching) of civic virtue. If it is political controversy that we wish the state above all else to avoid, our only alternative is to advocate repression, in its most thoroughgoing and insidious form.

Neither Discrimination Nor Repression

There is no defensible political understanding of education that is not tied to some conception of a good society, and there is no conception that is not controversial. Which conception should we therefore defend? Judge Hull hinted at a conception of liberal neutrality: Secular texts must not be imposed on fundamentalist children because they are not neutral among all competing conceptions of the good life. The Holt, Rinehart readers surely are not neutral between fundamentalist Christianity and secular humanism. Nor, as Judge Hull recognized, could any readers be neutral between deference to God's will as literally revealed in the Bible or authoritatively interpreted by a fundamentalist church, and critical inquiry or mutual respect among persons. Liberal individualists think of themselves as committed only to the latter set of virtues—critical inquiry and mutual respect—but the logic of liberal neutrality does not support their commitment in politics, except as a morally lame expression of personal opinion. This expression is insufficient to justify any form of public schooling. The content of public schooling cannot be neutral among competing conceptions of the good life, and if it could, we would not and should not care to support it.

It is not for us to deny fundamentalist parents the right to draw the wrong line for their children in their homes and churches. Parental freedom entails this limited right.[10] It *is* for us to say that parents do not have a right to veto a line drawn by public schools unless that line is repressive or discriminatory. If parents, judges, or philosopher-kings are allowed to veto lines drawn by public schools when those lines are neither repressive nor discriminatory, then democratic institutions are denied their legitimate role in shaping the character of citizens.

Is democracy not also repressive if it denies the teaching of Christian fundamentalist convictions within public schools, or, what amounts to the same thing, if it requires the teaching of views inimical to fundamentalist convictions? This challenge to democratic education rests on a serious misunderstanding: that a policy is repressive simply because it requires publicly funded or subsidized schools to teach views that are inimical to the sincerely held beliefs of some parents. Nonrepression requires the prevention of repressive practices, that is, practices that stifle rational understanding and inquiry. It is a reductio ad absurdum to claim that preventing such prevention itself constitutes repression.

To defend public schools against the charge of repression by fundamentalist parents does not, however, entail defending the status quo in American public education—far from it. We must criticize schools that fall short of the democratic ideal by, for example, being overly centralized and bureaucratized, and therefore unconducive to the exercise of both democratic deliberation by citizens and democratic professionalism by teachers. (Simply summarized, democratic professionalism authorizes teachers, at the same time that it obligates them, to uphold the principle of nonrepression, for example, by cultivating in future citizens the capacity for critical reflection on their culture. The ideal of democratic professionalism also obligates public officials to create the working conditions that make possible the exercise of democratic professionalism.) These comments can only begin to touch on the problems that plague our schools, judged from the perspective of a democratic ideal of education.

A democratic society cedes to citizens, parents, teachers, and public officials authority over education, but that authority is limited by the very democratic ideal that supports it. Not even an overwhelming majority has the authority to maintain separate schools for blacks, to ban sex education from schools, to teach creationism as science, or to ban politically unpopular books from school libraries. The first two practices are discriminatory, the second two are repressive. The defense of these judgments concerning our educational practices requires interpretation and application of the democratic standards of nonrepression and nondiscrimination. Because the standards are not merely formal, there is no way of mechanically applying them to cases. We cannot, for example, simply ask whether teaching evolution (or creationism) conflicts with some parents' convictions and if it does, conclude that the practice is repressive. The test of nonrepression and nondiscrimination is not popularity among citizens, parents, teachers, or public officials. Repression entails restriction of rational inquiry, not conflict with personal beliefs, however deeply held those beliefs. For every educational practice or institution, we must therefore ask whether the practice or institution in its actual context restricts (or impedes) rational inquiry and therefore is repressive, or whether it excludes some children from educational goods for reasons unrelated to the legitimate social purposes of those goods and therefore is discriminatory.

Some judgments will be relatively easy: Forcing teachers to teach creationism instead of evolution restricts rational inquiry for the sake of furthering sectarian religion and therefore is repressive. Other judgments require more extended argument: Is it repressive to teach evolution but to require equal time for creationism? If equal time for creationism entails teaching that it is as reasonable to believe that the world with all its creatures was created in seven days as it is to believe that it took *much* longer, then the demand for equal time is indirectly repressive: It undermines the secular standards of reasoning that make democratic education possible in this country. If public schools are permitted to teach the reasonableness of creationism, then the same principle will allow them to teach the reasonableness of divine punishment for the sins of non-Christians or any other minority that happens not to control the school curriculum. On the other hand, if teachers may subject creationist ideas to the same standards of reasoning to which other views presented in their classrooms are subjected, then the demand for equal time may be benign—or even conducive to democratic education. Of course, this is not the interpretation of equal time that proponents of creationism have in mind.

Education and Politics

Democratic standards often do not yield either simple or single answers to questions—such as how much money schools should allocate for educating the handicapped, the gifted, and the average student. That democratic standards do not yield simple answers is a necessity, given the complexity of our collective life; that they do not yield single answers is a virtue, which underscores the democratic critique of "the one best system." Democracy is valuable for far more than its capacity to achieve correct outcomes. It is also valuable for enabling societies to govern themselves, rather than to be governed by an intelligence unrelated to their nature. If democratic societies are to be self-governing, they must remain free to make mistakes in educating children, so long as those mistakes do not discriminate against some children or prevent others from governing themselves freely in the future. The promise of a democratic education is to support self-government without sanctioning majority tyranny or sacrificing future self-government.

It is not for me to say whether my theoretical understanding of democratic education fulfills this promise, but I am sure that the practical promise of any decent theory of democratic education is far from fulfilled in the United States today. I believe that the burden of a democratic theory of education is to show how, with the proper will, we could restructure American society to approach the democratic ideal, even if we never realize it entirely. As a democrat, the most I can consistently offer is criticism of our dominant educational ideas and institutions, and constructive suggestions for democratic directions of change. The possibility of constructive change depends on the will of those who wield political and economic power in this country. In a better society, that will would be more democratic.

These are therefore difficult times for democratic education not only because we are difficult people who must find a principled way of accommodating both individual freedom and civic virtue, but also (and as importantly) because our political and economic institutions are so far from being democratic that they discriminate against the very people who would benefit most directly from a more democratic education and therefore would be most likely to support it. Democratic education is unlikely to succeed if these institutions remain significantly undemocratic. We cannot conclude from this that political or economic reform must precede educational reform. Our choices are not so stark, nor so easy. To improve significantly the working conditions, the political opportunities, or the schooling of poor Americans requires political pressure from the poor themselves, yet they are the citizens most likely to have been educated in highly authoritarian schools (and families) and least likely to participate in politics (or to be effective when they do).

To realize democratic education in this country, political and economic institutions must become more democratic. For these institutions to become more democratic, education must be democratized. It would be foolish to focus solely on a single sphere, whether politics, economics, or education: first, because the prospects of success in any sphere are limited, and second, because the spheres are interdependent. Small but significant changes in one often bring small but significant changes in the others.

Democratic education does not simplify our outlook on education, but it reorients it away from conventional goals (such as educating every child for the appropriate occupation or for choice among the widest range of occupations) toward a more political understanding of educational ends. The cultivation of the virtues, knowledge, and skills necessary for democratic deliberation should have primacy over other ends of public education in a democratic society because such political education prepares citizens to share as equals in *consciously* reproducing (not replicating) their own society, rather than being subject to external forces of reproduction beyond their collective control. Conscious social reproduction is the ideal not only of democratic education but of democratic politics as well.

At the level of primary schooling, the primacy of political education supplies a principled argument against tracking, sexist education, racial segregation, and narrowly vocational education. Even when these practices improve the academic achievement of students, they neglect the virtues of citizenship, cultivated by a common education characterized by respect for racial, religious, intellectual, and sexual differences among students. The moral primacy of political education also supports a presumption in favor of more participatory and deliberative over more disciplinary methods of teaching. Even when student participation threatens to produce some degree of disorder within schools, it may be defended on democratic grounds for cultivating political skills and social commitments. Conversely, even when a principal succeeds in bringing order to an unruly student body, as has Joe Clark of Eastside High School in Paterson, New Jersey, he may be criticized on democratic grounds for intimidating students rather than reasoning with them, for not tolerating peaceful dissent among teachers, and for expelling problem students in unprecedented numbers (over a three-year period, more than 1,900 students dropped out of Eastside High, many of them expelled by Clark).

Democratic education aims at the empowerment of free and equal citizens, people who are willing and able to share together in shaping their own society. Democratic education therefore constrains public policies by the principles of nonrepression and nondiscrimination for the sake of securing democratic self-government. Within these constraints, democratic education makes a virtue out of the disagreements that inevitably flow from ethnic, religious, sexual, and intellectual diversity.

Above all, democratic education accepts the fact that we are difficult people. Whereas the Platonic family state denies this fact by subsuming individual freedom into civic virtue and the state of individuals denies it by elevating freedom above virtue, democratic education empowers citizens to make their own decisions on how to combine freedom with virtue. Democratic education thereby authorizes people to direct their individual and collective destinies. Fully recognizing that the aims of democratic education may never be fully realized, difficult people should demand no more of our political and educational institutions, and should settle for no less.

NOTES

1. Allan Bloom, *The Closing of the American Mind* (New York: Simon & Schuster, 1987), p. 238.

2. Socrates, *Republic of Plato,* trans. Allan Bloom (New York: Basic Books, 1968), p. 273 (590D).

3. Ibid., p. 220 (541A).

4. Ibid., p. 274 (592A).

5. Bruce Ackerman, *Social Justice in the Liberal State* (New Haven: Yale University Press, 1980), p. 148.

6. Ibid., p. 139.

7. Immanuel Kant, *Kant on Education,* trans. Annette Churton (Boston: D.C. Heath, 1900), p. 17.

8. *Bob Mozert et al. v. Hawkins County Public Schools et al.,* U.S. District Court for the Eastern District of Tennessee, Northeastern Division, No. CIV-2-83-401 (October 24, 1986), p. 12. The United States Court of Appeals (Sixth Circuit) reversed the decision of the district court and remanded with directions to dismiss the complaint (827 F. 2d. 1058 [6th Cir. 1987]).

9. John Stuart Mill, "On Liberty," in *Utilitarianism, On Liberty, Essays on Bentham* (New York: New American Library, 1962), p. 241 (chap. 5, paragraph 14).

10. The right is limited not by virtue of being weak, but by virtue of leaving room for other educational authorities.

WHAT IS EDUCATION FOR?

David W. Orr

IF TODAY IS A TYPICAL DAY ON PLANET EARTH, we will lose 116 square miles of rain forest, or about an acre a second. We will lose another 72 square miles to encroaching deserts, the results of human mismanagement and overpopulation. We will lose 40 to 250 species, and no one knows whether the number is 40 or 250. Today the human population will increase by 250,000. And today we will add 2,700 tons of chlorofluorocarbons and 15 million tons of carbon dioxide to the atmosphere. Tonight the earth will be a little hotter, its waters more acidic, and the fabric of life more threadbare. By year's end the numbers are staggering: The total loss of rain forest will equal an area the size of the state of Washington; expanding deserts will equal an area the size of the state of West Virginia; and the global population will have risen by more than 90,000,000. By the year 2000 perhaps as much as 20% of the life forms extant on the planet in the year 1900 will be extinct.

The truth is that many things on which our future health and prosperity depend are in dire jeopardy: climate stability, the resilience and productivity of natural systems, the beauty of the natural world, and biological diversity.

It is worth noting that this is not the work of ignorant people. Rather, it is largely the results of work by people with BAs, BSs, LLBs, MBAs, and PhDs. Elie Wiesel once made the same point, noting that the designers and perpetrators of Auschwitz, Dachau, and Buchenwald—the Holocaust— were the heirs of Kant and Goethe, widely thought to be the best educated people on earth. But their education did not serve as an adequate barrier to barbarity. What was wrong with their education? In Wiesel's words,

> It emphasized theories instead of values, concepts rather than human beings, abstraction rather than consciousness, answers instead of questions, ideology and efficiency rather than conscience.[1]

I believe that the same could be said of our education. Toward the natural world it too emphasizes theories, not values; abstraction rather than consciousness; neat answers instead of questions; and technical efficiency over conscience. It is a matter of no small consequence that the only people who have lived sustainably on the planet for any length of time could not read, or like the Amish do not make a fetish of reading. My point is simply that education is no guarantee of decency, prudence, or wisdom. More of the same kind of education will only compound our problems. This is not an argument for ignorance but rather a statement that the worth of education must now be measured against the standards of decency and human survival—the issues now looming so large before us in the twenty-first century. It is not education, but education of a certain kind, that will save us.

Myth

What went wrong with contemporary culture and education? We can find insight in literature, including Christopher Marlowe's portrayal of Faust who trades his soul for knowledge and power, Mary Shelley's Dr. Frankenstein who refuses to take responsibility for his creation, and Herman Melville's Captain Ahab who says "All my means are sane, my motive and my object mad." In these characters we encounter the essence of the modern drive to dominate nature.

Historically, Francis Bacon's proposed union between knowledge and power foreshadowed the contemporary alliance between government, business, and knowledge that has wrought so much mischief. Galileo's separation of the intellect foreshadowed the dominance of the analytical mind over that part given to creativity, humor, and wholeness. And in Descartes's epistemology, one finds the roots of the radical separation of self and object. Together these three laid the foundations for modern education, foundations that now are enshrined in myths that we have come to accept without question. Let me suggest six.

First, there is the myth that ignorance is a solvable problem. Ignorance is not a solvable problem; it is rather an inescapable part of the human condition. We cannot comprehend the world in its entirety. The advance of knowledge always carried with it the advance of some form of ignorance. For example, in 1929 the knowledge of what a substance like chlorofluorocarbons (CFCs) would do to the stratospheric ozone and climate stability was a piece of trivial ignorance as the compound had not yet been invented. But in 1930 after Thomas Midgely, Jr., discovered CFCs, what had been a piece of trivial ignorance became a critical life-threatening gap in human understanding of the biosphere. Not until the early 1970s did anyone think to ask "What does this substance do to what?" In 1986 we discovered that CFCs had created a hole in the ozone over the South Pole the size of the lower 48 U.S. states; by the early 1990s, CFCs had created a worldwide reduction of ozone. With the discovery of CFCs, knowledge increased, but like the circumference of an expanding circle, ignorance grew as well.

A second myth is that with enough knowledge and technology, we can, in the words of *Scientific American,* "manage planet earth."[2] Higher education has largely been shaped by the drive to extend human domination to its fullest. In this mission, human intelligence may have taken the wrong road. Nonetheless, managing the planet has a nice ring to it. It appeals to our fascination with digital readouts, computers, buttons, and dials. But the complexity of earth and its life systems can never be safely managed. The ecology of the top inch of topsoil is still largely unknown as is its relationship to the larger systems of the biosphere. What might be managed, however, is us: human desires, economies, politics, and communities. But our attention is caught by those things that avoid the hard choices implied by politics, morality, ethics, and common sense. It makes far better sense to reshape ourselves to fit a finite planet than to attempt to reshape the planet to fit our infinite wants.

A third myth is that knowledge, and by implication human goodness, is increasing. An information explosion, by which I mean a rapid increase of data, words, and paper[,] is taking place. But this explosion should not be mistaken for an increase in knowledge and wisdom, which cannot be measured so easily. What can be said truthfully is that some knowledge is increasing while other kinds of knowledge are being lost. For example, David Ehrenfeld has pointed out that biology departments no longer hire faculty in such areas as systematics, taxonomy, or ornithology (personal communication). In other words, important knowledge is being lost because of the recent overemphasis on molecular biology and genetic engineering, which are more lucrative but not more important areas of inquiry. Despite all of our advances in some areas, we still do not have anything like the science of land health that Aldo Leopold called for a half-century ago.

It is not just knowledge in certain areas that we are losing but also vernacular knowledge, by which I mean the knowledge that people have of their places. According to Barry Lopez,

> it is the chilling nature of modern society to find an ignorance of geography, local or national, as excusable as an ignorance of hand tools; and to find the commitment of people to their home places only momentarily entertaining, and finally naive.
>
> [I am] forced to the realization that something strange, if not dangerous, is afoot. Year by year the number of people with firsthand experience in the land dwindles. Rural populations continue to shift to the cities. . . . In the wake of this loss of personal and local knowledge, the knowledge from which a real geography is derived, the knowledge on which a country must ultimately stand, has come something hard to define but I think sinister and unsettling.[3]

The modern university does not consider this kind of knowledge worth knowing except to record it as an oddity "folk culture." Instead, it conceives its mission as that of adding to what is called "the fund of human knowledge" through research. What can be said of research? Historian Page Smith has offered one answer:

> The vast majority of so-called research turned out in the modern university is essentially worthless. It does not result in any measurable benefit to anything or anybody. It does not push back those omnipresent "frontiers of knowledge" so confidently evoked; it does not *in the main* result in greater health or happiness among the general populace or any particular segment of it. It is busywork on a vast, almost incomprehensible scale. It is dispiriting; it depresses the whole scholarly enterprise; and most important of all, it deprives the student of what he or she deserves—the thoughtful and considerate attention of a teacher deeply and unequivocally committed to teaching.[4]

In the confusion of data with knowledge is a deeper mistake that learning will make us better people. But learning, as Loren Eiseley once said, is endless and "in itself . . . will never make us ethical men."[5] Ultimately, it may be the knowledge of the good that is most threatened by all of our other advances. All things considered, it is possible that we are becoming more ignorant of the things we must know to live well and sustainably on the earth.

In thinking about the kinds of knowledge and the kinds of research that we will need to build a sustainable society, a distinction needs to be made between intelligence and cleverness. True intelligence is long range and aims toward wholeness. Cleverness is mostly short range and tends to break reality into bits and pieces. Cleverness is personified by the functionally rational technician armed with know-how and methods but without a clue about the higher ends technique should serve. The goal of education should be to connect intelligence with an emphasis on whole systems and the long range with cleverness, which involves being smart about details.

A fourth myth of higher education is that we can adequately restore that which we have dismantled. I am referring to the modern curriculum. We have fragmented the world into bits and pieces called disciplines and subdisciplines, hermetically sealed from other such disciplines. As a result, after 12 or 16 or 20 years of education, most students graduate without any broad, integrated sense of the unity of things. The consequences for their personhood and for the planet are large. For example, we routinely produce economists who lack the most rudimentary understanding of ecology or thermodynamics. This explains why our national accounting systems do not subtract the costs of biotic impoverishment, soil erosion, poisons in our air and water, and resource depletion from gross national product. We add the price of the sale of a bushel of wheat to the gross national product while forgetting to subtract the three bushels of topsoil lost to grow it. As a result of incomplete education, we have fooled ourselves into thinking that we are much richer than we are. The same point could be made about other disciplines and subdisciplines that have become hermetically sealed from life itself.

Fifth, there is a myth that the purpose of education is to give students the means for upward mobility and success. Thomas Merton once identified this as the "mass production of people literally unfit for anything except to take part in an elaborate and completely artificial charade."[6] When asked to write about his own success, Merton responded by saying that "if it so happened that I had once written a best seller, this was a pure accident, due to inattention and naiveté, and I would take very good care never to do the same again."[7] His advice to students was to "be anything you like, be madmen, drunks, and bastards of every shape and form, but at all costs avoid one thing: success."[8] The plain fact is that the planet does not need more successful people. But it does desperately need more peacemakers, healers, restorers, storytellers, and lovers of every kind. It needs people who live well in their places. It needs people of moral courage willing to join the fight to make the world habitable and humane. And these qualities have little to do with success as our culture has defined it.

Finally, there is a myth that our culture represents the pinnacle of human achievement. This, of course, represents cultural arrogance of the worst sort and a gross misreading of history and anthropology. Recently, this view has taken the form that we won the Cold War. Communism failed because it produced too little at too high a cost. But capitalism has also failed because it produces too much, shares too little, also at too high a cost to our children and grandchildren. Communism failed as an ascetic morality. Capitalism has failed because it destroys morality altogether. This is not the happy world that any number of feckless advertisers and politicians describe. We have built a world of sybaritic wealth for a few and Calcuttan poverty for a growing underclass. At its worst, it is a world of crack on the streets, insensate violence, anomie, and the most desperate kind of poverty. The fact is that we live in a disintegrating culture. Ron Miller stated it this way:

> Our culture does not nourish that which is best or noblest in the human spirit. It does not cultivate vision, imagination, or aesthetic or spiritual sensitivity. It does not encourage gentleness, generosity, caring, or compassion. Increasingly in the late twentieth century, the economic-technocratic-statist worldview has become a monstrous destroyer of what is loving and life-affirming in the human soul.[9]

Rethinking Education

Measured against the agenda of human survival, how might we rethink education? Let me suggest six principles.

First, all education is environmental education. By what is included or excluded, students are taught that they are part of or apart from the natural world. To teach economics, for example, without reference to the laws of thermodynamics or ecology is to teach a fundamentally important ecological lesson: that physics and ecology have nothing to do with the economy. It just happens to be dead wrong. The same is true throughout the curriculum.

A second principle comes from the Greek concept of Paideia. The goal of education is not mastery of subject matter but mastery of one's person. Subject matter is simply the tool. Much as one would use a hammer and a chisel to carve a block of marble, one uses ideas and knowledge to forge one's own personhood. For the most part we labor under a confusion of ends and means, thinking that the goal of education is to stuff all kinds of facts, techniques, methods, and information into the student's mind, regardless of how and with what effect it will be used. The Greeks knew better.

Third, I propose that knowledge carries with it the responsibility to see that it is well used in the world. The results of a great deal of contemporary research bear resemblance to those foreshadowed by Mary Shelley: monsters of technology and its byproducts for which no one takes responsibility or is even expected to take responsibility. Whose responsibility is Love Canal? Chernobyl? Ozone depletion? The *Exxon Valdez* oil spill? Each of these tragedies was possible because of knowledge created for which no one was ultimately responsible. This may finally come to be seen for what I think it is: a problem of scale. Knowledge of how to do vast and risky things has far outrun our ability to use it responsibly. Some of this knowledge cannot be used responsibly, safely, and to consistently good purposes.

Fourth, we cannot say that we know something until we understand the effects of this knowledge on real people and their communities. I grew up near Youngstown, Ohio, which was largely destroyed by corporate decisions to "disinvest" in the economy of the region. In this case MBA graduates, educated in the tools of leveraged buyouts, tax breaks, and capital mobility, have done what no invading army could do: They destroyed an American city with total impunity and did so on behalf of an ideology called the "bottom line." But the bottom line for society includes other costs: those of unemployment, crime, higher divorce rates, alcoholism, child abuse, lost savings, and wrecked lives. In this instance what was taught in the business schools and economics departments did not include the value of good communities or the human costs of a narrow destructive economic rationality that valued efficiency and economic abstractions above people and community.[10]

My fifth principle follows and is drawn from William Blake. It has to do with the importance of "minute particulars" and the power of examples over words. Students hear about global responsibility while being educated in institutions that often spend their budgets and invest their endowments in the most irresponsible things. The lessons being taught are those of hypocrisy and ultimately despair. Students learn, without anyone ever telling them, that they are helpless to overcome the frightening gap between ideals and reality. What is desperately needed are (a) faculty and administrators who provide role models of integrity, care, and thoughtfulness and (b) institutions capable of embodying ideals wholly and completely in all of their operations.

Finally, I propose that the way in which learning occurs is as important as the content of particular courses. Process is important for learning. Courses taught as lecture courses tend to induce passivity. Indoor classes create the illusion that learning only occurs inside four walls, isolated from what students call, without apparent irony, the "real world." Dissecting frogs in biology classes teaches lessons about nature that no one in polite company would verbally profess. Campus architecture is crystallized pedagogy that often reinforces passivity, monologue, domination, and artificiality. My point is simply that students are being taught in various and subtle ways beyond the overt content of courses.

Reconstruction

What can be done? Lots of things, beginning with the goal that no student should graduate from any educational institution without a basic comprehension of things like the following:

- the laws of thermodynamics,
- the basic principles of ecology,
- carrying capacity,
- energetics,
- least-cost, end-use analysis,
- limits of technology,
- appropriate scale,
- sustainable agriculture and forestry,
- steady-state economics, and
- environmental ethics.

I would add to this list of analytical and academic things, practical things necessary to the art of living well in a place: growing food; building shelter; using solar energy; and a knowledge of local soils, flora, fauna, and the local watershed. Collectively, these are the foundation for the capacity to distinguish between health and disease, development and growth, sufficient and efficient, optimum and maximum, and "should do" from "can do."

In Aldo Leopold's words, does the graduate know that "he is only a cog in an ecological mechanism? That if he will work with that mechanism his mental wealth and his material wealth can expand indefinitely? But that if he refuses to work with it, it will ultimately grind him to dust"? And Leopold asked, "If education does not teach us these things, then what is education for?"[11]

NOTES

1. Elie Wiesel, remarks before the Global Forum, Moscow, 1990.

2. "Managing Planet Earth," *Scientific American*, 261 (September 1989): 3.

3. Barry Lopez, "American Geographies," *Orion* (September 1989): 55.

4. Page Smith, *Killing the Spirit* (New York: Viking, 1990), p. 7.

5. Loren Eiseley, *The Star Thrower* (New York: Harcourt Brace Jovanovich, 1979), p. 284.

6. Thomas Merton, *Love and Living* (New York: Harcourt Brace Jovanovich, 1985), p. 11.

7. Ibid.

8. Ibid.

9. Ron Miller, Editorial, *Holistic Education Review* (Spring 1989): 2.

10. Staughton Lynd, *The Fight Against Shutdowns* (San Pedro, CA: Singlejack Books, 1982).

11. Aldo Leopold, *A Sand County Almanac* (1949; New York: Ballantine, 1966), p. 210.

PART SEVEN

HUMAN POTENTIAL AND DEMOCRACY'S FUTURE

THIS SECTION contains two readings that present a glimpse of the possible as well as the necessary.

By examining the lives and work of Barry Commoner and Hazel Henderson, Mihaly Csikszentmihalyi, professor and former chair of the Department of Psychology at the University of Chicago, presents a look at human potential (Chapter Eighteen). The lives and ambitions of these two people illustrate how certain kinds of thinking can lead to creative solutions to difficult, even daunting, problems. They demonstrate that it is possible to break free of our inherent shortsightedness and see the larger implications of the choices we make. They also make clear the need for us to think beyond the often-restrictive rules of isolated domains—rules that usually require us to look at the world in a fragmented, piecemeal fashion—and to broaden our perspectives and our thinking. The chapter is appropriately entitled "The Domain of the Future."

Of course, not all of us can be Barry Commoner or Hazel Henderson. Humanity is nothing if not diverse. Commoner and Henderson represent only two points on a vast spectrum of possibilities. True, the problems we face are immense, and yes, the temptation to fall into the trap of fatalism and resignation is at times great. But there are alternative approaches.

This book began with an essay by Neil Postman entitled, simply, "Democracy." In that essay, Postman writes of democracy that "our conception of the word's meaning is, itself, a myth, a kind of fantasy about what ought to be. But such fantasies, when shared by all, connect individuals to each other, providing a common language, a set of ideals, and a program for the future." Whether we want to think in terms of myths, of fantasies, of dreams, of desires, or simply of a thing called hope and a handful of ideals worth striving toward, we must prepare—all of us, as best we can—for an unknowable future.

British moral philosopher Mary Midgley brings this part of the conversation to a close in Chapter Nineteen—a chapter that resonates strongly with Postman's words. She reminds us of the necessity of nourishing what she calls "effective idealism." Cautioning us against becoming paralyzed by the game of realist versus idealist, she draws our attention instead to the vital role that healthy imaginations can play in developing "special ways of thinking" that enable us to confront dilemmas that otherwise seem "too big to even conceive of properly." In "Practical Utopianism," Midgley asks, "Are there effective dreams?" The answer, as Midgley, Postman, and others affirm, is a resounding yes.

THE DOMAIN OF THE FUTURE

Mihaly Csikszentmihalyi

CREATIVITY GENERALLY REFERS to the act of changing some aspect of a domain—to a painting that reveals new ways of seeing, to an idea that explains how stars move and why. But of course there was a time when domains did not exist. The first astronomers, the first chemists, the first composers were not changing a domain but actually bringing one into being. So, in a sense, the most momentous creative events are those in which entire new symbolic systems are created.

To do so, of course, is not easy. The rate of attrition for creativity within domains is very high, and that for new domains must be at least as large. Many people have grandiose ideas about inventing new paradigms, new perspectives, new disciplines. Exceedingly few of them succeed in convincing enough others to form a new field. The . . . people in this [discussion] exemplify these hazardous attempts at bringing about a new set of symbolic rules.

Each was successful within an existing scientific domain before trying to establish a new one. None started out on a new course in order to achieve personal advancement, power, or money. A deep concern for the well-being of the world informs their lives. In each case, they addressed a central social problem in an effort to achieve a voluntary reorganization of the human community. Because they could not see how to address these issues adequately from within existing domains, [both] struggled to develop new symbolic representations and new social institutions dedicated to the solution of global problems. These are important similarities; but as we shall see, the differences are just as impressive.

The Science of Survival

The name Barry Commoner has become synonymous with the ecological struggle. He was among the first scientists to realize, in the 1960s, that some of the fruits of technology—from nuclear fallout to pesticides, from oil consumption to solid waste—posed dangers for human health. Trained as a biochemist and biophysicist, Commoner found himself increasingly frustrated by the abstraction and fragmentation of academic science. He tried to influence public awareness through a number of books, and in 1980 through an unsuccessful campaign for the presidency of the United States. For many years now he has directed the Center for the Biology of Natural Systems, now associated with the City University of New York, where he continues to explore the problems posed by runaway technology and their possible solutions.

At War with the Planet

Commoner did not start his career with any specific sense of mission. He had been a fairly good student in high school, and his father, an immigrant tailor, pressured him to become a radio repairman. But then an intellectual uncle pushed him to enroll at Columbia University—not an easy step for a Jewish boy in those days. At the end of his college career, when it had become clear that Commoner had a knack for science and should continue his graduate education, a biology teacher called him in and told him he was going to Harvard. "What do you mean?" Commoner remembers asking. "'I've arranged for you to become a graduate student at Harvard.' I hadn't applied, nothing. 'As a Jew from Columbia, you'll have a very hard time getting a job; I'm sending you to Harvard.'" And so Commoner moved to Harvard, where he received an interdisciplinary education in chemistry, biology, and physics.

After he started his academic career, Commoner was confronted with a number of ominous developments. One was the threat of a nuclear holocaust, which after World War II cast a pall on an entire generation. Two other defining events he describes in the first chapters of his book *Science and Survival.* The first was an electric blackout that shut down power on a 1965 November night across a huge area of the Northeast and Canada. What struck Commoner about this failure was that it was caused by the elaborate computerized controls built into the electric grid, which overcompensated for a surge in demand by closing down the system entirely (a process not dissimilar to what happened more than twenty years later when the computerized programs for buying and selling stocks circumvented human controls and went into a selling frenzy that brokers were unable to stop, thereby causing a market crash).

The second event Commoner describes in his book was the discovery that fallout from nuclear testing in Nevada produced iodine-131 isotopes that were carried by winds to pastures in Utah, where they contaminated the grass cows foraged on. The iodine passed into the cows' milk, and when children drank it, it deposited itself into the cells of their thyroid glands. There the radiation from the iodine occasionally produced goiters and tumors.

Both the blackout and the iodine-131-produced diseases were typical examples of the kind of unintended chain reactions that occasionally occur when technology escapes from human control. Most people chalk up such events as the necessary price to pay for progress and do not worry too much. But Commoner, either because his interdisciplinary training made him think in terms of systemic patterns rather than linear processes, or because of a long personal history as an outsider who has been forced to take a critical perspective, felt that these events were not just side effects but part of the main history of our time.

The main story, according to Commoner, is that we have unintentionally declared war against the planet on which our lives depend. Science started out as a powerful tool for increasing human well-being. But when knowledge within separate domains is pursued without understanding how its applications affect the whole, it unleashes forces that can be enormously destructive. The sorcerer's apprentice, who sets in motion a magic spell that he cannot stop when it begins to get out of hand, is a metaphor that recurs in Commoner's writing.

Of course, he was not alone in this realization. In fact, several groups founded in the sixties helped hone Commoner's ecological consciousness, such as the Committee on Science in the Promotion of Human Welfare of the American Association for the Advancement of Science, and the Committee for Nuclear Information. But with time Commoner developed a personal approach to the problem of helping the environment, one that made it possible for him to envision solutions that were feasible given who he was and what he could do.

Science and Politics

What Commoner realized was that the solution could not come from science alone. To keep runaway technology under control, science and public policy had to work together. When it comes to applying technology, science predictably sells out to the highest bidder. The military ends up controlling the awesome power of radiation; pharmaceutical companies profit from the fruits of chemistry; agribusiness uses biology for its own aims. None of these entrenched interests has any responsibility to preserve the fabric of life on the planet, although each one owns the means for destroying it. So we must step in and regain control in the name of the common interests of continued life on Earth.

Unlike many others who also have perceived the threats of technology, Commoner has kept his faith in science. He realizes that even though science may have gotten us into this mess, we are unlikely to get out of it without its help. So he continues to use the scientific method both to diagnose the problems and to find solutions for them. In doing so, he works with the dedicated humility of a true scholar. For many years now, the efforts of his institute have been focused primarily on solving problems of solid waste disposal. Garbage is not a fashionable topic, but its exponential growth presents real threats that few want to think about. And what is more, it is a problem that can be solved and thus might serve as an example of how to tackle more complex issues. Like all creative individuals we studied, Commoner tends not to waste energy on problems that cannot be solved; he has a knack for recognizing what is feasible and what is not.

Commoner felt that it was not enough just to demonstrate that when you burn trash in incinerators you create dioxin, which is a dangerous pollutant, or that by using too much fertilizer we poison our water supply with nitrates. This was important knowledge, but it would not make any difference as long as special interests benefited from incineration or fertilization. So he concluded that the first priority was to inform the public about these environmental crises and their origins. To do this he used different means: He wrote books and pamphlets, talked to leaders and opinion-makers, gave press conferences, got money from foundations for environmental causes, and developed networks of like-minded people.

In the process he had to break out of the standard scientific domains and from the academic fields that preserve their boundaries. This meant leaving the safe shelter of the universities, a step that few people trained in them have the courage to take:

> I was brought up before World War II, when a number of my professors believed in a duty that the academic has to society generally. But as the generation represented by the World War II scientists began to get older, the academic world became very isolated from the real world. Academic work was discipline-dictated and discipline-oriented, which is really pretty dull, I think. And so the work that we've done

has become more and more alienated from the current general direction of academic work, because most people in the university work for the admiration of their peers. The work we do is for the sake of people outside the university.

Only by crossing disciplinary boundaries is it possible to think holistically, which is necessary if we are to "close the circle" and preserve the organic balance of planetary life forms.

> The prevailing philosophy in academic life is reductionism, which is exactly the reverse of my approach to things. I use the word *holism* in connection with biology and environmental issues. But the academic world has changed a great deal since I was a graduate student. It has become progressively self-involved and reductionistic. And I find that's dull and I'm not interested in doing it.

Instead of letting specialized academic fields dictate how he should approach problems and attempt solutions, Commoner lets "real-world" events dictate where he should turn his attention, and what means he should use to try to control recalcitrant technology. Specific threats, such as the proliferation of toxic waste or the pollution of drinking water by nitrogen isotopes, are what mobilize his energies:

> The center has always been directed toward the solution of real-world problems in the environment and energy. Not academic problems. Not problems defined by a discipline. Problems defined by the real world. Particularly people in the community who are confronted by a problem. Our approach to this problem then is to solve it, not to write a paper that will fit into a particular discipline or even a combination of disciplines. That's why I say we are adisciplinary, not interdisciplinary.

This quote has a facile, anti-intellectual ring to it. But Commoner is using science in its most basic, truest sense. What he objects to is not systematic, careful observation, only the irresponsible uses of it. What he objects to is the ritualized worship of domain knowledge for its own sake, instead of the integrated knowledge we actually need to avoid becoming history.

Struggling with Reality

Commoner calls himself "a child of the Depression" who always had to struggle to achieve his goals. This, plus the constant awareness of his marginal status as a Brooklyn Jew in what used to be WASP ivory towers, is probably why he maintained his unorthodox views all his life. Those who are not properly socialized by a field are prime material for the skeptical, divergent thinking approach that often leads to creativity.

Like so many of our respondents, Commoner insists on the importance of maintaining two usually contradictory attitudes toward his work: to keep an emotional link to what he does and at the same time a rigorously objective perspective. There is no doubt that he cares deeply about his topic—the entire pattern of his life is evidence of it. And it is equally clear that he takes the rigor seriously: Among his associates he is famous for writing draft upon draft for each speech or press release, until it is free of ambiguities and weaknesses.

It is not easy to be a maverick and to keep to the narrow path of self-chosen excellence in a nonexisting domain. Commoner ran into various difficulties with university administrators who didn't understand what he was trying to accomplish, with fellow scholars who felt he was trespassing on their turf, with the authorities who wanted to silence his opposition to nuclear weapons and the Vietnam War. His stubborn faith in the necessity of his task kept him from giving up. But he also had to find strategies to keep his mind focused and prevent distractions. As with most other creative individuals, a sort of ascetic discipline orders his attention:

> Well, also, I reject an awful lot. I don't answer letters. I don't do things people ask me to do for the sake of helping them. We help a lot of people in areas where we want to help. But, you know, people call up and say, "I've got this invention." Anything that's commercial, I never touch. I have a whole series of rules like that, to just get rid of things. You have to concentrate on one thing at a time, I think. But, you know, I can do two or three things in one day.

Splicing the Cultural DNA

Hazel Henderson's life theme dovetails almost perfectly with Commoner's. She also is struggling to develop a new interdisciplinary—or adisciplinary—domain to deal with the problems of technology. She also has dedicated her life to keeping our species from destroying the habitat in which it lives. But because she was trained in economics instead of biology, her concern is more with how patterns of consumption affect our uses of resources than with the biochemical consequences of our lifestyles.

Henderson was born and grew up in the United Kingdom, in a loving, traditional family in which gender roles were strictly respected. It is impossible to say why, but Henderson seems to have fallen in love with the world quite early in life:

> When I was five—you know, like where you just open your eyes and
> you look around and say, "Wow, what an incredible trip this is! What
> the hell is going on? What am I supposed to be doing here?" I've had
> that question in me all my life. And I love it! It makes every day very
> fresh. If you can keep that question fresh and remember what that was
> like when you were a child and you looked around and you looked at,
> say, trees, and you forgot that you knew the word *tree*—you've never
> seen anything like that before. And you haven't named anything. And
> you haven't routinized your perceptions at all. And then every morning
> you wake up and it's like the dawn of creation.

This a good example of Henderson's spirited and open approach to life.
It is reminiscent of the American philosopher C. S. Peirce's distinction
between what he called "perception" and "recognition"; it is also very
similar to the Yaqui sorcerer Don Juan's practice of "stopping the world."
But derivative or not, this freshness of perception is entirely consistent
with her being.

After high school Henderson made two resolutions: to travel around
the world to see how everyone else lived and not to do anything she did
not enjoy. For a starter, she wrote to a number of resorts in Bermuda,
proposing that she run their hotels in exchange for lodging, good meals,
and afternoon lessons with the tennis and golf pros. Her offer was eagerly
accepted, and she chose the most glittery resort. This experience greatly
improved her tennis game. But what's more important, it showed her the
possibility of stepping out of the money economy and of organizing small-
scale, mutually beneficial exchange systems. She continued to draw on this
experience for the rest of her self-made career. And lack of formal education turned out to be a blessing in disguise. It kept her mind open and
allowed her to see freshly the economic system on a global scale.

The Blindness of Nations

The problem Hazel Henderson eventually identified as the issue she was
going to invest her life trying to resolve is one that many people feel
strongly about: the ruthless exploitation of natural resources and the
growing inequalities between the rich and the poor countries. Although
we are all aware that there is something dangerously wrong with our way
of using energy, the very size and intractability of the problem prevents us
even from trying to do anything about it. The most natural reaction is to
ignore it, otherwise it would hover in the back of our minds, poisoning
each moment with its presence.

What makes Henderson's reaction creative is that she found a way to formulate what is wrong so that she—and others—can do something about it. Like all such conceptual moves, her formulation consists in focusing first on one limited aspect of the problem rather than on the whole intractable mess. Henderson decided to focus on how the seven most industrialized countries—the G-7—measure their progress and wealth. She concluded that these societies, which represent only about 13 percent of the world's population but use up most of its natural resources, have blinded themselves to reality by measuring their Gross National Product (GNP) without taking into account the social and environmental costs of their so-called progress. As long as this shortsighted accounting continues, she feels, the real economy of the planet will go from bad to worse.

Behind this one problem, Henderson feels, stands another one: the epistemological bias of the last few centuries of Western thought, which has progressed by abstracting bits of reality from their context and then treating each bit as if it existed in isolation from the rest. As long as we keep thinking of progress in this way, we will never see the real implications of our choices.

> It's basically linear thinking. Its underlying paradigm is that we're all marching along a time line from the past to the present to the future, and that somewhere along there's lots of assumptions about what progress is, which is normally measured in terms of material abundance, technological virtuosity, and economic growth.
>
> The policy that industrial countries pursue is "OK, top on the agenda is to do this, and second on the agenda is to do that." There's the whole assumption that problems are attacked in that way and solved in that way. I don't think problems are like that. The kind of policy issues that industrial countries are dealing with, maybe you actually have to do ten things at the same time because you're dealing with systems that are all interacting. And if you push the system right there and say, "That's the thing we ought to push on today," all you do is to create six hundred other effects somewhere else in the system that you hadn't noticed. And then you call them, quote, side effects. Whereas there's actually no main effect without, quote, side effects.

The Real Wealth

Having formulated the problem of what is wrong with our dealings with the environment this way, Henderson is able to do something about it. As is usually the case, the formulation of the problem implies its own solution. Formulating the problem is conceptually the most difficult part of the entire process, even though it may seem effortless. In this case, Henderson had two goals: to make people understand the long-term costs of progress and to promote a systemic, instead of a linear, mode of thinking about environmental policies. In terms of the first issue, her position is:

> People are the wealth of nations, you see. The real wealth of nations are ecosystem resources and intelligent, problem-solving, creative people. That's the wealth of nations. Not money, it doesn't have anything to do with money. Money is worthless; everybody knows money is worthless. I do seminars on money. And I start off by burning a dollar bill, saying, "This is good to light a fire but you know it's not wealth. It's a tracking system, to help us track transactions."

And instead of linear thinking:

> My view of the world is systemic and interactive. Unless you have a systemic model of the problem that models all of the interfaces and all of the dynamism—and it probably has to be planetary, within an ecosystem framework—you don't know where to push. When you have a good sense, a good map, of how all of those systems are interacting, maybe the policy will need to be pursued in five places at once in order to have feedback effects, or else your one policy will either dissipate and not change the system, or it will have some bad effect somewhere else, or you may amplify the problem in some other system.

In the most general way, Henderson believes, the problem is to redesign the "cultural DNA," or the set of instructions that keep people motivated—the values and rules of action that direct human energy. The basic question is:

> How do you take natural language and compress it so tightly that it begins to act almost like a mathematical formula? What I'm interested in is the DNA code of societies and of organizations. That is, the program of rules derived from their values. Every culture is really a high-quality program of software, derived from a value system and a set of goals. And every corporate culture and every institution is like that. And so what I like to do is to write the DNA codes for new organizations.

Midwife of Change

Having identified a general approach to the solution of the problem, one now has to devise a method that will do the job. How does one rewrite the DNA of any organization, let alone the entire planet? It is at this point that the really hard work begins. It would be tempting just to bask in the glory of having found a conceptual model for beginning to solve some of the world's worst problems and let others implement it, if they can. But Henderson's creativity is not primarily at the conceptual level; what makes her work stand out from that of many armchair environmentalists is that she actually tries to carry out her ideas.

How does she do that? Her methods are varied and diverse. She writes articles and op-ed pieces. She writes books about alternative economies. She lectures all around the world. She spends time in potentially sympathetic countries like China or Venezuela, networking with government officials and environmental groups. She tries to influence the G-15 countries to adopt new methods of keeping track of their GNP, methods that take into account the hidden social and environmental costs of technological progress. But the main weapon in her arsenal is the ability to create organizations that will implement parts of her vision. These groups may focus on recycling, or alternative economies, or developing an "alternative GNP" such as her Country Futures Indicators, or questioning the environmental appropriateness of consumerism. This involves finding:

> The first people and the first resources to bring in around that DNA code, which will be what you might call the business plan for the organization. And to find these people who really understand what that code is, and then find an initial foundation grant or something. My temptation over the years was, I would hang around too long, because I'd want to make sure that that wonderful little DNA code got etched into the stone tablets of the methodology of that organization so that then I could get back onto the board of directors and generally not worry about it because it was all locked in and everybody agreed on what this organization was. So that it wouldn't be something that had been designed to be a mouse and turn into a hippopotamus.

But with time she discovered that to "hang around too long" was a mistake, because the volunteers who joined her out of idealism would get stifled and dependent on her. Plus her ego would become too tightly bound up with the success of the enterprise. So now she passes on the leadership of the young organization as soon as possible and doesn't worry too much whether her initial design will be followed to the letter.

> I learned through the school of hard knocks, actually. I was more ego-driven when I was younger, and I found that I started a lot of social change organizations, through the sixties and seventies, and I learned

that if you want social change organizations where there's no money involved, there's no motivation of money, it's just a job to be done in terms of an idealized vision of how the society could be in the future, you'd better not be so ego-driven as to want to take credit yourself for having thought of the idea or founded the organization. Because you're trying to recruit idealistic, wonderful people and you're in a position of having to tell them, "Look, the salary's going to be lousy, or there may be even no salary at first." And so all you have really to offer them is identity and identification with an exciting new organization where they can put their whole energy into it. What I found is that the more I stepped back out of the way, and the quicker I did that, the better the organization took off and the more satisfaction the people whom I brought in to run it had. And I found over a period of years that I learned to jump clear faster and faster. I mean, first I'd be worried, "Oh, is my little baby going to be taken care of properly?"

Making High Mischief

How was Henderson able to implement these methods? It is not easy to pull off the kind of guerrilla warfare she has been waging for three decades against planetary economic mismanagement. Certainly having a high goal helps—there are few projects one can devote one's life to with more self-evident justification. But there are a number of more mundane procedures she had to adopt in order to continue with her work without distraction. One thing she had to resign herself to was doing without a normal family life, and eventually her dedication to the solution of the problem she chose led to an amicable divorce. Another thing she had to give up was the financial security of a good job. But then, as she ruefully admits: "I have always known I was unemployable. Because, you know, I would be fired off any job in the first day for insubordination. Because I'd either tell them how to do it better, or whatever. And so I have always realized that I would have to invent my own job."

And finally, by moving to a small community in north Florida she was able to protect her privacy, to express in her location the maverick values she espoused, and by keeping a low profile, to disarm her political opponents. . . . This is what Henderson says about her choice of a place to live:

> It gives me great delight to be able to interact with a big system like the United States and live in a place that's a backwater, where people would say, "What on earth do you live in the wilds of north Florida

for?" To me there's a great delight in that. Because one can be considered by the dominant culture as sort of beneath contempt, you know. I mean, "She's just sort of messing around on the fringes of things." The less people know about your effect on various subsystems, the better.

Being hidden away in north Florida does not mean that Henderson is isolated. Whenever she feels it is worth her time, she travels all around the world. And people who are really concerned with helping solve the problems she cares about come and find her—her house is always full of visitors trying to implement the same "high-level mischief" that characterizes her own enterprises. Her best ideas come either when she is involved in a solitary activity like biking, walking, gardening, or washing dishes, or when talking with interesting visitors. Without the constant dialogue with like-minded people Henderson could not even begin accomplishing her aims.

Henderson's unique career has not been smooth sailing all along the way. Like most creative persons, she had her share of difficulties. At a certain point, twenty years ago, she went through a burnout phase. She had been too involved, too busy, too anxious. The constant traveling and stress were giving her neck pains. She was coming close to a breaking point. So she realized she'd better "make her own mode of sustainable operation." This is when she decided to move to Florida and change her lifestyle. But above all else, she reevaluated her priorities and decided that it wasn't important to get credit for what she had been doing, it wasn't important for her to get anywhere. What mattered was to do the best she could and enjoy it while it lasted, without getting all ego-involved with success. This decision has given her so much peace of mind that now she is busier than before without feeling any stress or pain.

What sustains her instead of the desire for fame is a fundamental feeling for the order and beauty of nature, a calling for creating orderly and beautiful environments around her. In colorful hyperbole she says:

> On one level I feel like an extraterrestrial. I'm here visiting for a while. And I'm also in human form. I'm very emotionally attached to the species. And so I have incarnated myself at this time. But I also have an infinite aspect to myself. It all kind of hangs together quite easily for me. It sounds flippant, but the thing is that this is a spiritual practice for me.

Not many people confess to feeling like extraterrestrials, but one must be able to look at oneself from a certain distance in order to get an objective view of the human condition. And in order to invent new ways of living that are not compromised by past traditions, one must strive to attain such objectivity. Yet at the same time, one must also maintain one's "emotional attachment to the species." This dialectic between rational calculation and passionate involvement [is] one of the traits of creative individuals in general. It is perhaps even more essential for those whose creativity lies outside of traditional domains. This is how Henderson expresses it:

> There's a very harmonious continuum of what Zen Buddhists call attachment-detachment. And you should always be in the state where you're both. There's a yin/yang continuum, which we can't understand in Western logic because we have this either/or. But it's "both/and" logic, and it says that there's a constant dance and continuum between attachment and detachment, between the long view, the infinite view, and the incarnated view where we have to learn about limitedness, and finitude, and action.

. . .

The Domain of Global Responsibility

What [these two people] have in common is that they have realized the systemic interconnection among the events that happen on the planet, and they are struggling to act on this realization. One way of saying what they are trying to do is that they are attempting to develop a domain of global responsibility and a field to implement it. Commoner emphasizes our uses of energy and resources; Henderson [emphasizes] our lifestyles and consumption patterns. . . . The focus of attention is different in each case, but the causal network they consider is interconnected. Any change in the pattern of energy use, of consumption, of peaceful spirituality, of personal fulfillment affects the others. The central message is that every action has a consequence, that in many important respects the planet is a closed system with fragile boundary conditions, and that unless we take informed action, these conditions may easily be violated.

In a sense, this emerging realization is not so novel. Many simple cultures have developed a systemic view of their cosmos. It is implicit in many of the great world religions. In Judeo-Christian faiths, it is expressed obliquely in the belief of an omniscient God who sees and evaluates even the most minuscule event, such as the fall of a sparrow from a tree branch. It is implicit in the Eastern beliefs in karma, in the endless consequences of each action rippling down the ages toward infinity. According to the ancient Zoroastrian creed, each person was expected to pray forgiveness of the water for having polluted it, of the earth for having disturbed it, of the air for having filled it with smoke. But with the glorious advance of science in the last few centuries, these intuitions of a network of causes and effects binding on individuals were discredited as superstition. The human species was seen as all-powerful, its actions above the laws of nature.

What people like [these] are doing is rediscovering, within the domains of different sciences, the grounds for taking these intuitions seriously. [They have arrived at] the same conclusion: It is dangerous to proceed within the rules of an isolated domain without taking account of broader consequences. . . .

But how to formulate these isolated bits of knowledge into a coherent symbolic domain? Scientists in the West started to study systems only recently; we still have no way to represent the kind of problems these . . . creative people are struggling with in any manageable way. To a large extent, we are still at the prescientific, metaphorical stage. The myth of Gaia, which describes the planet as a living, self-correcting organism, is one of them. The anthropic principle, which claims that our thoughts and actions actually make the existence of the universe possible, is another. [Commoner and Henderson both] appear to be poised at the threshold between metaphor and natural law; ready to move from poetic insight to systematic understanding.

They share some common traits appropriate to intellectual pioneers. They [both] felt marginal as they grew up[:] Commoner because he was Jewish, Henderson because her loyalties were split between a loving mother and a powerful father. . . . This feeling of marginality caused them never to take orthodox ideas for granted. It helped them break away from domain-bound constraints on their thinking when real-life experience conflicted with them.

[Both] mentioned repeatedly their constant shifting from action to reflection, from passion to objectivity. In each case, this alternation allowed them to keep learning, to keep adjusting to new situations. Their creativity unfolded organically from idea to action, then through the evaluation of the outcomes of action back to ideas—a cycle that repeated itself again and again.

[Neither] of them seems to be motivated by money and fame. Instead, they are driven by a feeling of responsibility for the common good, a feeling that sometimes borders on traditional religious values but more often seems to depend on a spiritual sense for the order and beauty of natural phenomena that transcends any particular creed. It is a contemporary formulation of that most ancient awe that prompted our ancestors to develop images of the supernatural in the first place. But they wear this feeling of responsibility lightly, as a privilege rather than a duty. Although they work hard to help improve our lives, they claim that they never did anything they didn't want to do. . . .

PRACTICAL UTOPIANISM

Mary Midgley

Comprehending the Incomprehensible

... THOUGHT AND ACTION, philosophy and life, are less alien, more closely connected, than we tend to suppose. How does this work out in politics? The main question here is rather a strange one. It is: how can we think effectively about dilemmas which are manifestly too big for us to handle?

We today aren't actually the first people who have faced this problem, though we often feel as if we were. The people who lived in earlier ages often found their world every bit as confusing and dangerous as we do. It may be true that our world actually is worse than theirs. But that made very little difference for the people involved. You can lose hope and drown just as well in seven feet of water as in seventy.

In the West, for instance, the future seemed utterly hopeless to many people during the break-up of the Roman Empire and again during the Thirty Years War. In many ways, too, things looked very black during the early years of the Industrial Revolution. The reformers who then set about the discouraging business of abolishing the slave trade, or attacking the state of factories in the 1840s, or rewriting political theory after the failed revolutions of 1848 (as Marx did), needed a remarkable degree of confidence to keep up their hope.

But people did do these apparently irrational things. And, though their contemporaries told them that it would be much more sensible to collapse into fatalistic inertia, most of us probably think now that they were right to neglect that advice.

This leads us back to my rather strange question. How is it psychologically possible for anyone to confront dilemmas which are—as those other dilemmas were to the people of their day—manifestly too big even to conceive of properly, let alone to handle? If we're to do anything at all in these situations, we need special ways of thinking. We have, as it were, to make our way through a desperately confused and dangerous landscape. We need light on the crucial features of that landscape, and we need good maps.

Those maps don't have to be fully detailed. In fact they must be limited and simplified, or we shan't make out the features that we need to see. Yet they do have to be detailed enough to make those features recognizable. They must be truthful enough to warn us about the difficulties, but not so alarming that we get utterly discouraged. All this is very hard, and it may sound as if these maps must be misleading. Yet they are not; they are just selective.

The people who have managed to retrieve desperate situations in the past have done so by somehow making maps of this kind. They have formed conceptual schemes, sets of ideas which somehow lit up the problems of the moment, problems that were proving impenetrable to traditional thinking. Those maps—those new conceptual schemes—must leave out, for the time, everything irrelevant, including endless further problems which can't be dealt with yet. They must bring forward the central issues, making them look clear and limited enough to tackle. They must also envisage distant possibilities which haven't yet been considered. Till that clarification is done, confusion reigns and people seem to face a gorgon which turns them to stone. They are paralysed by the mere tangle of conflicting considerations.

Handy Defences Against Thought

In these crises, people often conclude that the most practical thing is to stop thinking altogether. This, rather surprisingly, is a mistake. During drastic change, new ideas are not a luxury but a necessity. We need them, both as a tool for action and as a help to preserving our sanity—both in order to help us envisage our problems effectively and so as to avoid psychic disaster. But since it's very hard to produce these more suitable ideas, we often use instead other defence mechanisms which are much less satisfactory.

The simplest of these defences is, of course, just to forget about large-scale troubles altogether and we all do have to do this some of the time. But if we do it too much we may have to pay a heavy cost in psychic numbing and narrowing, even sometimes in actual depression and despair. Cutting ourselves off from the world blocks the springs of our life, because it shuts us off from reality. Even for our own inner health, we need sometimes to turn our minds to these monstrous topics.

You will notice that this is essentially a psychological discussion. It deals with our own responses, with the ways in which we can face these vast dilemmas or not face them, rather than directly with the dilemmas themselves. Of course this psychological problem is incomparably smaller than the outside dilemmas but it is still a weighty one because it concerns us so immediately. If we don't get started on it, we may find it hard to get any further. So it does seem to deserve some attention first.

Crusades and Jihads

To resume, then—our next simplest defence (after just avoiding these issues) is to polarize them into a black-and-white ritual combat between good and evil. The impulse to do this is very strong; we surely don't fully understand it. Tribal loyalty does, almost necessarily, form a part of our political efforts. But when we see other people disputing, we can usually see how much harm confrontation does. Yet it is surprisingly hard to apply that knowledge when we are involved ourselves.

If, however, we get disillusioned with the various available crusades, we may drop into an even odder polarization, abandoning thought altogether in favour of non-thought. We may become anti-intellectual Realists, rejecting all theory as simply irrelevant to practice. The whole mass of idealistic thoughts and intentions then looks like a gearwheel with no teeth, turning uselessly in the mechanism of the world. From that position, words like *Idealism* and *Utopianism* themselves become simply terms of abuse. Or, of course, we may go the other way and sign up as idealists who are too pure to dirty ourselves with action at all.

This game of Realist v. Idealist is paralysing because it divides the two sides of our own nature which need to work together for action. It divides these two sides even if (as can happen) it's combined with the crusading habit rather than replacing it. Thus, people who are officially conducting a crusade may still choose to play the role of victims, Idealists who are helpless because they are misunderstood by the Realists. They then naturally lose interest in the criticisms that might bring these sides together. In this mood we refuse to think about practical difficulties, so that we can't act or choose any positive policy for action. That can happen even to people who are officially clamouring for immediate change. It is, in fact, one of the commonest of the paralysing factors that waste the goodwill available for reform.

If, on the other hand, we choose to play as a Realist who knows the facts but is too clever to go in for ideals, we may know what the possibilities are all right but, since we have decided that the *status quo* can't be changed, we shall never find any reason to use this knowledge. (That, of course, is the Civil Servant's Syndrome.)

Divisions of Labour

It is surprising how hard it is to bring these two sides of our nature together. One very common way in which people do do it, is to take these roles in succession, starting life as an Idealist and moving to the Realist role as one gets older. This stereotype is immensely old. Or one can reverse it, acting in youth as a realistic rebel who has seen through the fuddy-duddy moral nonsense offered by one's parents.

This dramatic pattern is especially attractive in an age of rapid change. Plato displayed it shrewdly in the *Gorgias* where Socrates meets a sharp young politician named Callicles, an immoralist who gives a striking impression of having just read Nietzsche, Machiavelli and the latest postmodern treatments of ethics . . . [1] As it turns out, Callicles hasn't actually been reading anybody. As he explains, he radically despises all theoretical discussion. Thought and argument, he says, are occupations for boys, games to limber up little minds for the real world, amusements to be dropped when you get there. Adult life is a game too, but it's a violent and final one, a power game to be played as hard as possible for one's own hand. Anyone who lets himself be distracted from it by considerations of truth or consistency, let alone of other people's interests, is simply a fool.

Callicles, of course, is still with us today. In him, the division between Realist and Idealist, between thought and action, is unusually drastic. Callicles claims to throw ideals overboard entirely (though it is noticeable that he is often gripped by fantasies and indeed by conventions). Most people probably take a less extreme position than his, accepting that both aspects of life are necessary but dividing the labour. They commission one set of people to supply the ideals and another, different set to carry them out.

This drama can be played either between the generations or between the sexes. Women may be commissioned to have the ideals while the men do the real acting. Or, in a democracy, the voters may be supposed to have ideals and to shout their horror at current iniquities, thus forcing the

administrators—who themselves have no views about morals—to make
the practical changes. The politicians then form a sort of gear-mechanism,
loosely connecting the two sides and linking the ideals with reality.

Up to a point these divisions of labour do work. But they are awkward,
they waste a fearful amount of energy in friction and, as we know, there is
something very uneasy about them. Two parties who see each other as
(respectively) fools and knaves, humbugs and scoundrels, can't easily
work in harmony together. This isn't a satisfactory principle for any division of labour.

Ideals Are Not Inert

Ought we then perhaps to suspect that the game was wrongly set up in
the first place? Is it possible that the two sides of our nature should not
have got separated as they have? Perhaps, in fact, Realism and Idealism
are *not* alternatives but two inseparable aspects of any true practical attitude. Our tendency to divide them is, however, remarkably strong. It is
shown, rather comically, when people say (as they so often do) that some
proposal is "all right in theory but no good in practice." A proposal that
really is no good in practice has surely got something wrong with it in theory too. And a theory that doesn't fit the facts is a faulty theory. It needs
changing.

This whole question is important to that rather large number of us today, including students, who spend our time doing intellectual work, some
of us being actually paid to do it. Is our occupation with theoretical questions really just a self-contained humbug-factory, a web of idle dreams,
fantasies and wish-fulfilments? Or are there also dreams which are not
idle? *Are there effective dreams?*

On glancing round, it seems pretty plain that there are. The world is
changing very fast, and certain dreams—some of them very bad dreams—
evidently play a large part in directing that change. Some of those bad
dreams formed the noxious part of Marxism. Another set of them has
been active in the monstrous production of weaponry over the past century. Another—more noticeable at present—fuels the monetarist dream
which promises us universal prosperity through "trickle-down" from the
uncontrolled working of the markets. These dreams have not just grown
up spontaneously on their own, like weeds. They have all been deliberately produced by relatively recent thinking.

The seed of the monetarist project was sown by Social Darwinist
dreamers in the last century. It arose, not just from factual beliefs current
in their day, but also from a one-sided, unbalanced obsession with the

ideal of freedom. This attachment was in its own way an idealistic vision and much of its strength has derived from that idealism. The trouble with it is simply that it *is* so one-sided. More generally, even the most cynical and disastrous doctrines usually do owe some of their strength to this kind of one-sided idealism.

Anyone, then, who habitually dismisses idealistic talk as mere idle vapouring, "all right in theory but ineffective in practice," is not living in today's world. It is only in the most stagnant times that practices can be treated as fixed rocks on which the waves of theory will break without making any impression. Today, practices as well as theories fall constantly into the melting-pot.

Things, in fact, do change. And among the factors which change them, the accepted ideals of the day play a central part. The changing imaginative visions that figure in books, films and television programmes aren't just froth on the surface or pieces in a game. They have their effect; they can mean life or death, salvation or destruction. Yet the kind of reality that they have is strangely hard to grasp. Mostly, we oscillate between taking these ideas seriously and ignoring them as mere dreams or shadows.

When we see them as shadows, we easily drift into a kind of fatalism, into believing that the practical world is indeed immutable, armoured against anything we can think or do. That fatalism itself is, however, surely just one more rather ineffective emotional defence, a way of avoiding the notion that there still is something that we might do. It's a defence which splits off the practical from the reflective side of our nature, separating them as chemists separate substances that may explode if they get together. We leave these two parts of ourselves chronically at odds and let them take turns at influencing action. Thus, most of us respond sometimes to other people's cynical fatalism with idealistic protests and sometimes to other people's ideals with fatalistic ones.

Dialectical Tactics

Might all this opposition perhaps be just a useful dialectic, producing a synthesis in the end? Some philosophers have said so, but then, philosophers do tend to be argumentative people. They sometimes exaggerate the usefulness of conflict. Most often, debating only makes the gap between the disputants wider, which is why debating societies, especially for adults, have only a limited use. Each opponent tends to become more divided internally, practising the two roles separately without bringing them together. And when this internal debate is unacknowledged, there can't be any useful dialectic at all.

It is this inner division, not the outside difficulties, which can finally paralyse us, making us give up thought altogether. Even if the paralysis isn't complete, it can still poison our responses. The side that we officially oppose still gives trouble within us until it has been properly dealt with. There is then still cognitive dissonance—unresolved confusion in our thought and ambivalence in our feeling. This can badly distort the way in which we carry on controversies, making us violently unfair to our opponents, who stand for the rejected element. And it fixes the idea of a deep warfare between thought and feeling at the heart of our thinking.

The Unseen Campaigners

What are we to do about all this? I have been suggesting that the idea of thought as being impotent is just one more myth among others, a myth that we devise chiefly to defend ourselves against the exhausting business of confronting reality. This myth is remarkably selective. It draws a contrast between thought and action which lines up, in the oddest manner, with the division between virtue and vice. It suits the immoralist Callicles, who lurks in a corner inside most of us. The myth says that, while virtue is totally ineffective, iniquity actually is effective in the world, even though iniquity works through human consciousness just as much as virtue does.

There is, of course, a grim half-truth here—a half-truth so painful and so much suppressed that no wonder it looks like realism. A great deal of human behaviour is indeed so appalling that we try hard to forget about it. There is indeed a terrible lot of effective iniquity about. But when we have said this, realism calls on our bewildered imaginations to look further. The other half of this truth is the huge and quite effective effort that people are constantly making to fight against these iniquities and produce at least a drawn battle. As the Book of Ecclesiasticus puts it:

> Let us now praise famous men, and our fathers that begat us . . . All these were honoured in their generations, and were the glory of their times. But some there be which have no memorial, which are perished as though they had never been . . . And these were merciful men, whose righteousness hath not been forgotten. Their bodies are buried in peace, but their name liveth for evermore.[2]

We take all this effort for granted. But when those struggling people happen to relax their efforts, we quickly see how much worse things could easily be.

It is not just an idle cliché that "things could be a lot worse." It is a vital part of the truth. Human history, bad though it is, is still the product of constant conflict, a continuing struggle between the worse and the better. If you look at it from the devil's end (as C. S. Lewis does in *The Screwtape Letters*) you see that vice doesn't actually have things all its own way. The reason why we overlook this modest fact is, of course, our bitter disappointment that virtue hasn't achieved more than it has. This recognition is something that realism does demand of us. We are right to be disappointed, right, in a way, to be horrified, by the world. But our disappointment and horror don't license fatalism and resignation.

The balance is really difficult here. There is a fierce tension between ideals and reality, especially, of course, for people who are trying to do something to bridge the gap. This, too, is nothing new. Two thousand years ago Cicero, who was desperately attempting reform but depended on very corrupt allies, cried out that "the trouble is that we have to work, not in Plato's *Republic* but in Romulus's pigsty." When one is in that mood, it is natural to write off all expressions of ideals, including books like the *Republic,* as simply fantasies, dreams irrelevant to reality. But this very natural response surely misses the point. I would like to end by saying a word about the function of these books—these imaginary worlds, these so-called Utopias and dystopias. I think a glance at this topic may help us to see both why we need art as well as why we need philosophy. These books grow in an area where art and philosophy overlap.

The Role of Utopias

In recent times, theorists have denounced Utopias and erected defences against attending seriously to them. This attack began during the Second World War, when several high-minded thinkers (notably Karl Popper and Richard Crossman) decided that Plato was a Fascist. Modern libertarians, however, have widened the charge in a way that accuses all such sweeping visions of narrowness and totalitarianism. Taken seriously, their objection damns William Morris and Ursula LeGuin as much as Plato. It applies, too, to the so-called dystopias—visions of evil like *Brave New World* and *Animal Farm* and *Player Piano*—because those visions too are propagandist and single-minded. They direct us as firmly from behind as the Utopias do from in front.

Robert Nozick, in his book *Anarchy, State and Utopia,* puts the libertarian accusation like this:

> Given the enormous complexity of man, his many desires, aspirations, impulses, talents, mistakes, loves, sillinesses, given the *thickness* of his intertwined and interrelated levels, facets, relationships . . . and given

the complexity of interpersonal institutions and relationships . . . it is
enormously unlikely that, even if there were one ideal pattern for society, it could be arrived at in this *a priori* fashion.[3]

Of course Nozick is right to warn us against seizing on a single one of
these visions exclusively and forcing its pattern on society. But he means to
do more than that. He wants to dissuade us from using any such vast and
remote views of ideals at all. He calls on us to take up a standpoint which
is wholly empirical, realistic and dream-free.

This is a quite impossible project. Every view of the world is selective
and expresses some dream. Anyone who claims to show us only the complexity of the facts is a fraud. To return to the image we began with, any
usable account must simplify the world. We have to represent large problems to ourselves on some kind of map, and we have to make these maps
from some particular standpoint. That is the only way to get these matters within human comprehension.

Nozick himself is using such a selective map as much as anyone else.
It's a map that is easily overlooked because it is so familiar. It is the Social
Darwinist map, shaped by Herbert Spencer's travesty of evolutionary theory. It concentrates exclusively on one ideal—liberty, seen as a beneficent
free-for-all leading infallibly to progress through the survival of the fittest.

In a way, this picture is itself just one more Utopia—one more vision
of an ideal path for the human race. It looks more different than it is from
the earlier ones because it is dynamic while they are static. Like Marxism,
it concentrates much more on a series of means than on any eventual goal.
But since both Spencerism and Marxism exalt and idealize the means they
recommend quite as exclusively as other doctrines have exalted their
goals, this difference is not necessarily very important.

How Imagination Works

Let us look again at the way in which Utopias actually work. Two opposite sorts of charge have been brought against them. They are accused
both of being unrealistically hopeful—of describing impossible reforms—
and also of being totalitarian, describing over-organized places where no
sensible person would want to live. But both charges seem to miss the
nature of our imagination, the way in which it feeds on strange visions.

Writings like this aren't meant as literal blueprints for what ought to
be built or as exact itineraries for our journey. Instead, they act as imaginative pictures of possible houses to be built or as searchlights, plunging

their beams deep into the surrounding landscape at a single point to light up our journey. At times these searchlights show us distant mountains towards which we are travelling. These are landmarks which will serve to direct us even though we don't actually need to reach them, like signposts that say simply "To the North." At other times, they show us appalling precipices over which we might fall. They indicate possible long-term goals and dangers. They light up general directions. And they have to suggest these things in a way that is very far from literal, a way that must often be startling and paradoxical, because paradox can give our imagination the shock that it needs to start it working.

In this way, Utopias are no different from dystopias, though dystopias seem to work better today. Neither genre is realistic. The point is to make it possible for us to envisage a drastic general change, not just as a casual fantasy, but as really possible. This can be done equally by describing a much better world or by describing a worse one which would follow from certain existing trends, as dystopias do. Literal truth is beside the point in both cases, even though the incredible things proposed in Utopias do sometimes happen. For instance, Thomas More suggested a guaranteed nine-hour working day . . . [4] When these things do happen, they are naturally taken as matters of course. So they can then seem to lend force to the second objection, namely, that this is a thin and over-organized way of life.

But of course these books aren't holiday brochures, describing places where we would like to live. Like science fiction, they have to emphasize a few large-scale institutional points at the expense of detail. And because they have to take us to a world that is really far from where we now are they naturally tend to sound rather alarming. If this distant view is never seen—if a society simply never takes the trouble to notice how far it is from fulfilling its supposed ideals—then there is nothing to stop it becoming complacent about its present state.

Utopias then, like science fiction, can't afford to give life to their institutions by developing characters and humanizing the scene. They have to concentrate instead on some particular range of large changes, and they must exaggerate these so as to make them clear. This does inevitably make them one-sided. So of course the critics are quite right to point out that we shouldn't take any one of these stories literally as a blueprint for reform. And since, in real life, this sort of one-sided simplification could only be imposed by force, attempts at it would be bound to lead to totalitarianism. That is why James Lovelock gets accused of ecofascism. And it has, of course, been the central trouble with Marxism.

Pluralism Is Not Nihilism

But—and this is my central point—*we do still need these more distant, simplified visions*. If we try to work with a world-view which shows us only the complexity of existing facts, we lose our bearings and forget where we are going. And of course these supposedly realistic views aren't truly realistic either. Every account enshrines some particular ideals rather than others and expresses some dream. Our imagination needs, then, to be stimulated, not from one but from a hundred points on this spectrum. It needs to be stirred constantly from different angles by different aspects of the truth, if it is to keep its power of responding to what goes on.

Recently, certain "postmodern" theorists have travestied this need for plurality of angles by recommending a mere lack of conviction, a kind of all-purpose "irony" which is so sophisticated that it never commits itself to any position. This attitude is, of course, a relatively labour-saving response to the jubilant Social Darwinist free-for-all. It is a less exhausting option than the continuous fighting recommended by evolutionary prophets. All the same, it doesn't really make sense.

The reason why we have to be open to many kinds of message[s] is not because none of them is ever true or false or—what comes to the same thing—because they are all equally so. Instead, it is because the whole truth is complicated and needs many of them. So far, Nozick and Mill are right. The world really is too complex to be explained by any single formula. That, however, does not make it sensible to talk as if all suggestions about it are equally valuable or valid. We cannot talk like this because we live here. We are not just detached spectators on another planet, writing doctoral theses about this one. We don't have the option of elegant, impartial scepticism. Although our information always is inadequate, we have to come off the fence and form opinions we can act on. We have to make choices.

That is where we need the full scope of our imagination, and it is where our imagination needs both art and philosophy. Most of art does not, of course, deal as directly with our practical dilemmas as Utopias and dystopias do. But all art embodies visions, and our visions express the ideals that move us. If we are to avoid collapsing in fatalistic resignation, we need constantly to drink at this spring. We need to find good visions because, if we don't, we will unavoidably be enslaved by bad ones. Good visions are the necessary nourishment of effective idealism.

NOTES

1. Plato, *Gorgias,* 411b–end.
2. Ecclesiasticus 44: 1, 7, 9, 10, 14.
3. Robert Nozick, *Anarchy, State and Utopia* (Oxford: Basil Blackwell, 1974), p. 313.
4. See Thomas More, *Utopia,* book 2, section "Of Sciences, Crafts and Occupations." More gives them a good long lunch-break too.

INDEX